Also by David Carroll

The Complete Book of Natural Medicines

THE
COMPLETE BOOK
of
NATURAL FOODS

David Carroll

SUMMIT BOOKS   NEW YORK

Acknowledgments are made to Carroll/McBride
Catering Service in New York City for the
contribution of several of their most delicious recipes.

Published by SUMMIT BOOKS
A Division of Simon & Schuster, Inc.
Simon & Schuster Building
1230 Avenue of the Americas
New York, New York 10020
SUMMIT BOOKS and colophon are trademarks of Simon & Schuster, Inc.
Designed by Eve Kirch
Manufactured in the United States of America

10 9 8 7 6 5 4 3 2 1

Library of Congress Cataloging in Publication Data
Carroll, David.
  The complete book of natural foods.
  Includes bibliographies and index.
  1. Food, Natural.   2. Cookery (Natural foods)   I. Title.
TX741.C37 1985   641.3'02   85-10021
ISBN: 0-671-47517-7

CONTENTS

CHAPTER ONE

Introduction to Natural Eating

First, a Brief Experiment

Before you read this book, try an experiment.

Starting tomorrow and continuing for, let's say, seven days, eliminate the following foods from your diet:

1. Sugar
2. Coffee and tea
3. White bread (substitute whole grains)
4. Obvious junk foods like pizza, fried chicken, soda, etc.
5. Beef, pork, any especially fatty variety of meat (chicken and fish are fine in moderation)

Other foods might be added to the list, but we'll start here for now.

Follow the program for a week. Two weeks would get you more for your money and a month would be even better, but seven days is enough to produce tangible results.

During this time you may find yourself with cravings, especially for the more addictive substances like sugar and coffee (if you have a headache the first day don't worry, it's caffeine withdrawal, not malnutrition). Hang on anyway and don't give in. Following the diet faithfully and experiencing the results firsthand will be your best introduction to natural eating.

Now, a week later—notice how you feel when you get up in the morning, say, or around four o'clock in the afternoon, the big slump time. Your energy level should be higher. Certainly it won't be any lower, though you've avoided the so-called high-energy foods like sugar, heavy meats, and coffee. Do you feel more clear-minded? Less heavy-footed? The process is subtle, of course, and won't produce instant miracles. You probably *will* notice a difference though, even after a week. Imagine if you felt this way all the time. And so far all you've done is omit the wrong foods. It gets even better when you start adding the right ones. This is the basis for natural eating.

Food Is More Important Than You Think

As a regulator of your health and as a tonic to your mood, food is enormously underrated. This is so for many reasons. Ignorance and neglect, to start with, plus failure to learn proper nutritional habits in childhood. To this add a nationwide addiction to the synthetic indigestibles that make up foods such as candy, soft drinks, alcohol, caffeine, hot dogs, etc., coupled with an almost religious commitment to denying the scientific evidence that shows how harmful these substances really are. Also, include our culture's emphasis on curing disease rather than preventing it (right eating is one of the best ways to avoid sickness, and one of the most neglected), plus the marketing pressures applied by giant food companies that profit so mightily from sales of processed foods. It all adds up to a world where practically every influence surrounding the food consumer lulls him or her into a false sense of security concerning nutrition.

In the United States today there are fifteen hundred to two thousand chemicals added to the food we eat and the liquids we drink. It is estimated that almost a quarter of these chemicals are *known* to deform, sicken, and even alter the genetic integrity of laboratory animals, that 90 percent of the meat that graces the American table is laced with an array of toxins that run the gamut from tranquilizers to arsenic, and that despite prolonged and intensive lobbying by various consumer groups, the number of dangerous additives being put into our food today is increasing, not decreasing.

Almost two-thirds of the modern American diet is processed in one way or another. As a rule, it takes about seven years to prove or disprove the harmlessness of a chemical additive in the laboratory. With the slew of new chemical offerings coming onto the market every day, an uncomfortably large number of these products is put in use before each is completely tested. Many of these chemicals have been found to be carcinogenic—cancer-causing—and many others have been proved to have adverse effects on humans. And yet they remain on the market; no one is quite sure why.

The result of such a barrage of adulterated foods on our palate is that the sanctity of food has come to be forgotten. At one time, eating was valued as a kind of sacred event, a moment when people gathered from their various tasks to break bread together and to discuss the day's happenings. It was the time for sharing, for humor, for appreciation of life's bounty and heaven's mercies. Now frozen foods and TV dinners take the place of the all-day stew lovingly prepared over an open fire; hydrogenated commercial oils replace those squeezed out on a backyard press; corn preserved in a can replaces the August harvest.

Speed has become the essential factor in food, both in preparing it and then in bolting it down in record time, as if to get finished with a disagreeable chore. The round-the-table family dinner has been replaced with the television table; junk foods, fast foods, packaged foods and instant foods have replaced the bounty from the garden. The idea of food as something to nurture the spirit has been replaced by the view of food as something to fill the belly. In short, the process of buying food, preparing it, appreciating it and showing thanks has been transformed as much as the foods themselves.

No doubt the voices of the hysteric and the paranoid can be heard among those that decry the foods we eat and the way we eat them. And surely it is always easy to blame such likely enemies as unseen poisons and monolithic corporations for all our woes. But while the large food companies and the chemical manufacturers shout their denials and hire divisions of scientists to prove—in *their* labs—that these accusations are false, the cancer rate in our nation rises yearly, the number of identified toxic and carcinogenic substances discovered in our food and drink increases day after day, and the United States continues to slip in the life-expectancy ratings decade after decade. The evidence is there. It is thoroughly documented. There can be little doubt that much of what we have come to call the normal American diet causes long-term risks to our health, and ultimately to our lives.

And yet—and yet—Americans plod stolidly on, acquiescing to the putrid air, the ravaged landscape, the pulverized diet. Even while the ecology movement has been in full swing since the 1960s and even while the dangers in our food and drink have been so thoroughly chronicled by so many intelligent spokesmen, the lessons seem as voices in the wilderness: All of us—you, I, they, all of us—continue to take our daily dose of poison with the morning papers and our deadly nightcap with the evening news.

Still, the fact remains: At any time you *can* change your diet. It is one of the most direct ways in which you can improve your health, and the feedback is quite immediate. Despite our unwillingness to come to terms with our poor eating habits, and despite the trouble we have in changing them, the truth is that eating the right kinds of foods in the right proportions will make us happier, saner, more active and longer-lived. A proper diet is a kind of preventive medicine, some think the most important kind. That's what this book is all about.

Warning: The Foods on Your Plate May Be Hazardous to Your Health

This heading may sound like a bit of alarmist jargon. Yet every day evidence mounts to support the idea that a person's diet can sustain him or, well, yes, kill him. Depending on what it consists of and how it is prepared.

Part of the problem, of course, is that we're all so accustomed to the foods we eat that whatever may be dangerous in them is hidden by familiarity. Today in the West, and especially in America, our diet consists largely of meats, fats, sugars and refined carbohydrates. We take this fare as the norm, and we assume most other folks in the world eat this way too. But they don't.

In fact, far less fats, animal food, refined carbohydrates and sugars are consumed in other countries, especially in many of the poorer third-world nations. And interestingly, a majority of the diseases we take for granted in our nation are practically unknown in these environments.

What's more, when a nation like Taiwan or Japan abandons the diet that the collective wisdom of its culture has developed over the centuries —a diet designed to blend harmoniously with the country's particular climate, topography, soil conditions and adaptable crops—when that country suddenly "goes modern," popping down sweets, coffee, fried chips, hot dogs, and so on, the rates of cancer, heart disease, diabetes, hypertension, obesity and many other diseases invariably take a wild leap forward.

A century ago people in the United States and Western Europe lived on a diet vastly different from the one we are accustomed to in the modern world. Grains and cereals made up a greater percent of the general dietary intake. Sweets were an occasional treat. Chocolate was a luxury for the city gentry. Raw milk, fresh fruits, garden-picked vegetables, unrefined grains and unpolished rice were the typical fare. If meat was eaten at all it was once a week or once a month, whenever the hog was slaughtered or the cow brought to market. Fresh meat was rarely available at the corner grocery, and then not for long unless Grocer Jones happened to own one of those newfangled oak boxes with the place for the big ice block that went on top.

Annual fat consumption in America made up 15 to 20 percent of the average diet in 1880. Today that amount has increased by 100 percent. Our sugar intake has gone up dramatically too, and we eat many times the amount that we did a century ago. This controversial substance is now added almost automatically to supermarket items like ketchup, pickles, bread, mustard, meat, canned fruits and vegetables, often without warning on the label. At least a quarter of the 125 pounds of sugar we Americans average each year is hidden in foods other than sweets.

As our dental bills and blood-sugar levels increase, we also eat less than half the amount of starches and fresh vegetables that our forebears consumed in the 1800s. Today, processed foods make up almost two-thirds of the average daily diet. Cereals and grains, the traditional staff of life for centuries, are on the casualty list. When they are eaten at all it is mostly in the form of commercial white bread and sugary cereals, some of which have literally zero nutritional value. Hyperacidity, stomach cancer, intestinal cancer, diabetes, hypertension, acne, obesity and atherosclerosis were relatively rare a hundred years ago. Today they are our legacy.

In the past, of course, people had little scientific knowledge of nutrition. At the same time, they knew the land, understood the crops, and possessed a cherished body of folk wisdom concerning food and its preparation. Today, although there is an enormous amount of information available on the subject of nutrition, many of us are content to believe the claims written on the cereal box and leave it at that.

The Denaturalization of Food

For many years man ate his food as it came to him directly from the earth. It was sufficient, and he thrived.

Then over the last century or so a new way of life developed. It became the fashion to leave the farmstead and move to the big town, in search of higher wages and a more easeful life. The countryside emptied and the cities filled. America, rather quickly, went from an agrarian nation to an industrial one.

The hordes that poured into the urban world could not, of course, grow their own food any longer. So they quickly became dependent on a middleman, a grocer. Markets appeared everywhere throughout the big cities and ultimately the age of the supermarket began. A person now had little choice but to let someone else do all the growing and harvesting, for his own backyard was mostly concrete; and anyway, life had become so complex in the modern age that people had neither the time nor the skills to bother.

Before long even country people came to depend on the produce supplied by the larger farms. By the middle of this century almost everybody purchased at least a part of his daily menu from the food store, and a majority of people purchased all of it there.

It takes a good deal of effort to grow and harvest food for the millions, and help was needed as the population burgeoned. So people turned to science. And science was indeed Johnny-on-the-spot. It rapidly provided farmers with a multitude of remarkable new improvements: synthetic fertilizers capable of doubling, tripling, quadrupling food yields; powerful farm machinery that could plow and harvest the crop in a fraction of the time it took a horse-drawn team; special feeds and additives that improved the health of barnyard animals, made them grow larger, stronger, faster, fatter; new ways of testing and evaluating the soil; new methods of irrigating fields, draining swamps, clearing forests, razing mountains, of planting, hybridizing, harvesting, cultivating, preserving.

Then came World War II and the most remarkable of all the agricultural advances: insecticides. These wonders were capable of eliminating the terrible hordes of insects that had plundered man's harvest since prehistoric days. Early forms of DDT could pick leaves clean of a hundred insect species and leave a perfect crop in its wake. Tons more food could be brought into market every year, millions more people could be fed, millions more dollars could be earned. It looked as if the epoch of famine and starvation, perhaps even poverty, had come to an end.

Then several uncomfortable discoveries were made. First, since there was so much abundance now on the earth, fewer people starved to death. Which meant there were many more mouths to feed than before. Which meant that no matter how hard farmers tried, modern farming methods simply could not keep up with overpopulation. Which meant that people continued to go hungry, now perhaps more than ever because there were so many more of them to go without food—a vicious circle.

Second, it was learned that many of these new miracle products, the sprays and insecticides and other elixirs used in the cultivation of food, were poisonous to mankind and to the earth itself. After just a few years people began to realize that these substances were showing up in locations where they hadn't been placed, and where they shouldn't be: in the

drinking water, in the rainfall, in lakes, rivers, clouds, at the North Pole—
and in the food itself.

Some of these compounds percolated slowly through the human
system, collecting in fatty tissue and causing gradual cell degeneration
over a period of years. Others worked with surprising swiftness, going
directly to specific parts of the body and causing acute ailments. Washing
fruits or vegetables before eating them was of little value either, it was
discovered, for the toxins had been absorbed into the heart of the plants
and could not be removed by soap, love or tears.

Moreover, since the insect world mutates rapidly, many species
promptly developed immunities to the sprays. This meant newer, more
powerful chemicals had to be developed continually just to keep up with
natural selection. The more immune the insects became the more poisonous the sprays became, And so, the more harm they did to man, and to
the land.

The new insecticides, what's more, while neatly eliminating the harmful insects from the countryside, had a way of killing the *good* ones too,
the bees, the butterflies, the ladybugs, the mantis, further throwing off the
balance of nature and, ironically, eliminating the very pollen-bearing insects that were of most importance in the human food chain.

The new technology began to pervade the distribution of produce as
well as its cultivation. Fresh foods were no longer fresh. They were
trucked now over great distances and stored for weeks, sometimes even
months, in giant warehouses until the demand arose for them or until the
produce had ripened from its premature harvesting. Foods were put up
in cans, in jars, in plastic wraps, in freezer boxes. Synthetic materials were
substituted for real on the grounds that they gave the product a longer
"shelf life." Chemical preservatives were added even when they were
unnecessary, and a number of destructive refining processes were made
standard. Money was spent in increasing amounts for advertising and
packaging while the quality of the food itself steadily plummeted.

As all this became evident, of course, many people complained. But
the government has been slow to act. It has outlawed dangerous substance here, an unnecessary processing procedure there, yes, but more
often than not it has simply allowed the manufacturers of these products
to replace them with equally questionable goods and services.

Many people despaired of the authorities *ever* curbing the guilty parties. Some of these dissenters eventually decided that they would return
to the kind of farming and food handling that was practiced before the
reign of modern food manufacture. Thus, sometime in the middle of this
century the natural food movement began in earnest.

What Are Natural Foods? What Are Organic Foods?

While natural foods are spoken of by everyone with casual familiarity, an exact definition is not so easy to come by. With the growth of the natural food movement, words like "natural" and "organic" have been abused in direct proportion to their growing attractiveness to consumers.

Cosmetic manufacturers, for instance, advertise shampoos as "organic" because they contain herbs and spices. Look more closely at the label though and you'll see a long list of toxic chemicals accompanying the herbs that might put the makers of pesticides to shame. Breakfast-food companies regale us with claims about their "natural" cereal. What makes it natural? Why, the fact that no preservatives have been added to the grain. But what of the fact that preservatives have been put into the box it comes in, a common trick among cereal manufacturers. And that the grain itself has been both processed and refined. And that sweeteners have been added. Just how natural is this cereal anyway?

It is necessary first to distinguish between natural foods and organic foods. Natural food is simply fresh, nutritious food that has not been adulterated, refined or processed. It is food as it comes out of the ground, food as it was once eaten by the human race before the chemical age, food that has not yet been "improved" by industry.

Organic foods, on the other hand, are foods that are not only unprocessed but which are grown without the use of synthetic fertilizers or inorganic chemical aids of any kind. They are fertilized with natural fertilizers—manure, compost and mulch mostly—sprayed with natural sprays, such as pyrethrum or rotenone, and otherwise left alone.

Natural foods, therefore, are not necessarily organic—they may have been sprayed or synthetically treated during cultivation—though they may be, and usually they are so labeled in the store when they are. Strictly speaking though, the term "organic" describes the manner in which food is raised. "Natural" pertains to what happens to it—or does not happen to it—after it is harvested. The distinction is an important one, though it is not always made.

The next question is whether organic foods are really any better than natural foods.

Clearly, organic foods are a good deal more expensive than ordinary foods. Markups at health food stores are sometimes as much as 100 percent, and one is occasionally hard put to taste the difference between organic produce and the supermarket brands. Organic foods rarely look attractive, moreover, and they often seem disfigured, or colorless, or small when compared with the commercial competition.

So the question again: Are organic foods really better? And the answer: In truth, no one knows for certain. That artificial fertilizers, pesticides and synthetic additives are harmful to the people who are exposed to them, of this there is little question. How harmful, how deleterious they are to human health, how destructive they are to the planet, are questions that simply cannot be answered with mathematical certainty.

Taking what *is* known and understood about the subject though, and adding a bit of common sense, it seems fair to say that eating inorganic sprayed foods can scarcely be as healthy for the human body as not eating them. Many of the sprays are, after all, known poisons. The FDA and the Department of Agriculture claim that in small doses they do no harm. But are we so sure of that? Small dose after small dose, year in and year out, can build up to a big dose. And if we know nothing else concerning the way our biology deals with foreign substances we know that even microscopic amounts of certain compounds can put the body into a tailspin.

Given the multitude of poisons our bodies are already exposed to at any given time, a microdose of certain questionable substances may act as the last straw, pushing us out of the zone of wellness into disease. Dioxin, a poisonous chemical much in the news of late, has been found to be harmful even in doses as small as one part in a trillion.

Limited research, moreover, has been carried out on the effects of *combining* various chemical additives and the ways in which these new combinations may affect the human organism. Indeed, research on the harmful effects of food additives has been limited in general. This includes studies of such an inexplicable and disturbing phenomenon as the fact that some additives are more poisonous in smaller doses than in larger ones. For example, diethylstilbestrol, a highly carcinogenic chemical regularly fed to beef cattle, has been found to cause death more frequently in laboratory animals when given in one-tenth of a milligram doses than when administered in doses of five milligrams a day.*

Much depends, of course, on just how much spraying and conditioning have been done to a crop. Also important is what kind of spray has been used—some are decidedly more lethal than others. Each person reacts to particular chemicals in different ways, as each of us seems to have a different tolerance level for different toxins. What makes one person sick is scarcely noticed by another, and this must be kept in mind.

In general, then, if you can get hold of organic foods, if you can afford them, or if you can grow them, by all means do so. All signs indicate that they are better for you, perhaps a lot better, than foods treated with modern methods and means.

* William Longwood, *The Poisons in Your Food* (New York: Simon and Schuster, 1968), p. 135.

If you find it too difficult to make a regular practice out of organic eating, however, do not be dismayed. Most of us from the DDT generation are still alive to tell the tale, and the body is indeed a marvelous mechanism, capable of neutralizing many harmful substances. All is far from lost. Moreover, *avoiding* certain nonorganic foods can often be as useful as eating organic ones. By this we mean that when a food is heavily sprayed, if a piece of meat screams processing and assembly-line tampering, whatever—then pass it by. That's all. Eat something in its place that seems more wholesome.

What you *can* do, if organic eating is not practical or if the means are not available, is to focus on other aspects of the natural-eating process. If you buy fresh foods and foods that have not been overprocessed, prepare them in a proper way, and eat them in intelligent balance, much of the harm that comes from nonorganic foods will be offset. The sections in this book that follow on carbohydrates, fats, proteins, and developing your own natural-eating plan are designed to help you do just that.

Basic Lessons in Nutrition

Give the man or woman on the street a food quiz sometime. For starters, ask them about carbohydrates. Fattening! they'll tell you, almost by reflex. How about sugar? Rots the teeth, stay away from it (if you can). Starch? Heavy and unnourishing. Makes one think of potato chips and chocolate cake. What about protein? Oh, now you're talking! Body can't get enough of it. Quick energy. The perfect food. Beefsteak and a glass of milk.

And so on. There's some truth to all this, of course, but it's only half the story. Carbohydrates *can* be fattening. They can also help you lose weight. It depends on which kinds of carbohydrates we're talking about and what variety of foods they come in. Protein is a body builder, yes, but it's not the food to eat if you want quick energy; and moreover, it can be a poison as well as a tonic—too much of it will put you in the hospital. Some sugars are bad, certainly. But sugar is also our fundamental source of energy. Without it our brains stop working. When deprived of it completely, we die, and quickly. After an operation or a serious accident it's not beefsteak or vitamin C that people are given in the hospital ward. It's glucose, straight into the bloodstream.

Thus when we speak of proteins, fats, or carbohydrates we should beware of making a value judgment where none is warranted. A protein or a fat or a starch or a vitamin is not particularly "good" or "bad" by itself, any more than carbon, hydrogen or helium is good or bad. They are simply the different components that make up food. Each has a function in the nutritional chain which it should perform; each has functions it *should not* perform. To really understand all this, it's time to define our terms.

Carbohydrates, Fats, Proteins: What Are They, Really?

Everybody knows what a carbohydrate is, right? And a protein? And a fat? Right? No, not right. Quite wrong.

While it's true that terms like "carbohydrate diet," "polyunsaturated fats," "protein supplements," and others have become part of our daily language, most people have no idea why these mysterious substances are so good for them or so bad for them. Or what they really are in the first place.

Quite simply, carbohydrates, fats and proteins are organic chemical compounds that we call "nutrients." Along with vitamins, minerals and water, they comprise the full range of substances that nourish and sustain us. Just about every liquid and solid we consume comes from one of these nutrient families; just about every function our bodies perform is dependent on a steady input of all of them.

Known as the "large nutrients" (as opposed to vitamins and minerals, which are called the "small nutrients"), carbohydrates, fats and proteins are broken down in the stomach and gut, absorbed through the intestinal wall, and passed into the bloodstream. Eventually they are transported by the blood to trillions of hungry cells throughout the body, where they may be used to form new tissue, stored for future use, metabolized for energy, or used to provide fuel for any number of regulatory systems.

Most of our foods contain all of the large nutrients—with the exception of meat, which is pure protein and fat—and a combination of all three large nutrients is vitally necessary for the maintenance of health. In fact, there is not, and never has been, any argument among nutritionists that all three are necessary in a well-balanced diet. No one but a lunatic would suggest that you eliminate *all* fats from your menu, or eat *nothing* but protein. The real questions are: How many carbohydrates, proteins and fats are necessary each day? What kind? And in what proportion?

A Few Hints Before Beginning

This book is divided into five chapters. This introduction is Chapter One. In Chapters Two, Three and Four we investigate natural foods from a number of different vantage points, framed by the perspective of the three major nutrient types: carbohydrates, fats and proteins. In Chapter Five we put all this information together and discuss how you can devise your own personal eating plan. Before we go on, here are a few practical hints that will help you get the most out of your natural-eating plan.

1. Don't Try to Do It All

A good deal of guilt surrounds the field of natural foods; people feel they are somehow never quite matching up to some undefined ideal. No matter how pure the meals they eat, no matter how wholesomely they may feed their families, there is always some special food or some critical vitamin they are missing, some drastic mistake they are making in the kitchen, some new poison they don't know about lurking in the bread and cheese.

Don't fall into the "it's never natural enough" trap. Do what you can, enjoy what you do, and forget about the rest. It would be nice to dine on organic meats each night, but that's not always possible for a number of reasons. It would be nice to take the most complete multiple vitamin in the world, the one selling for sixty dollars a bottle (when you can find it). But there are less expensive varieties that will do the trick too, and besides, there is no final proof that megadoses of vitamins are necessarily best for everyone.

Concentrate on what you can reasonably do and have; it will probably be more than adequate, and it will certainly be far better than the average American diet.

2. Don't Be Too Influenced by Fads

If the truth be known, there are very few things we know about nutrition that can be touted as absolute truth. Indeed, much of our so-called knowledge changes at the mercy of fashion. Several decades ago milk and dairy products were only a step or two removed from the Divine. Today there are many nutritionists who blame milk for just about every ailment you can think of, from headaches to cancer.

So it is with other foods too. Even such sacred cows as yogurt and honey have had their turn on the firing line, and in the end, when all the smoke has cleared, one comes to feel that the only safe things left to eat in the world are raw turnip strips and carrot-seed tea.

Ugh! Better to avoid the faddish schools of natural foods and the food extremists who assure us that the payment for good health must be made in the coin of all our favorite tastes. Better to go with what seems right for your own state of well-being. Meat may be one man's poison, but it can also be another man's meat—we are all different, and we all have a different physiological bias. True, there are bottom lines. Junk food is junk. Period. Overprocessed and adulterated foods are bad for you. Period. White sugar is inimical to human health. Period. But beyond the fundamental givens there are many gray areas, and the approach to them must be navigated on an individual basis.

3. Don't Think That Natural Eating Must Be a Chore or an Effort

No so very long ago natural eating was sarcastically equated with untasty eating by just about everyone. People laughed about sprouts and raw turnips, then passed the pizza and ice cream. Health food diets were equated with the kind of eating one must do on a weight-loss diet— stringent, boring, tasteless. Natural eating got a bum rap.

Today much has changed, even if some people have not yet heard the good news. There are dozens of books on the market filled with delicious recipes for a cavalcade of good natural eating, and these works include recipes for desserts and snacks as well as for good main meals.

Occasionally in this book we will provide recipes. While the book is not intended to be a cookbook, and while the emphasis is on the health side of natural eating rather than on cooking per se, some of our favorite recipes have nonetheless been sprinkled here and there, and each comes guaranteed to shatter the illusions of anyone who still believes that natural foods naturally cooked don't taste good.

4. Decide for Yourself

So read, try, experiment, consider. See which natural foods make you feel good, which ones don't. Give them all a chance, try out the various suggestions and recipes offered here, and stick with it for a while. Then go ahead and decide what suits you, as an individual, best. You'll find that other than the basic assumption that natural foods are better than processed, this book offers no final solutions. It presents the evidence, then lets you make the choices. *Bon appétit!*

CHAPTER TWO

Carbohydrates: The Unsung Heroes

Say the word "potato" and what comes to mind? Dirt farmers? A down-and-out family picking at boiled spuds? Say "rice." And see the teeming Oriental masses. The peasants gleaning in the fields. Think of an eccentric, or someone stone broke. Then say "vegetarian." It is no accident that carbohydrates are called "the poor man's food."

There is some truth to this saying—vegetarians do, in fact, pay less for their grocery bills than meat eaters. But contrary to popular opinion, carbohydrates offer just as much nutrition as protein, pound for pound. They provide *faster* energy than either protein or fat, and they are digested far more easily. They're less expensive, more abundant, easier to produce and easier to preserve. And if the right kinds of carbohydrates are eaten, they are less fattening than either protein or fats.

If you don't believe this last claim check it on any calorie counter. Turn to hot dogs for a case in point. Two hot dogs without buns and hold the mustard will still give you about a 500-calorie lunch. Now look up the calorie facts on those carbohydrates with particularly fattening reputations, and compare. Try the much maligned potato. Cooked in the skin and eaten plain, it will give you 93 calories, 400 calories less than the hot dogs. Surprise! With butter it still tallies only 188. Next, take that dieter's perennial favorite, the steak. A half-pound piece will fill you with 900 calories. Compare this to a plate of spaghetti with tomato sauce and cheese sprinkled all over it, a shameless example, perhaps, but still guilty of only 260 calories per average-sized serving. More? A leg of chicken fried to a golden-tan has 1,065 calories. Two pieces of good whole-grain bread without butter have 110. How about a can of tuna fish packed in oil? Make a salad out of it and you've filled up on 853 calories, not counting the greens. Contrast that to a double teaspoonful of natural peanut butter spread on two pieces of fresh-baked whole-wheat bread: 250 calories. You can add a teaspoonful of jelly to the concoction and still have only 55 more calories.

It's the same right down the line. Caloriewise, carbohydrates are a bargain.

All You Need to Know About Carbohydrates

Despite increased consumption of fats and proteins in the West, carbohydrates—fruits, vegetables, grains and dairy products—still make up the majority of most people's diet. Typical eaters in America and Europe take in two hundred pounds of carbohydrates for every twenty pounds of proteins, and this is as it should be, for tissue building and energy production are both dependent on carbohydrates, as is the proper functioning of nerve cells. Without them the brain would malfunction and the nervous system would rebel. In laboratory tests, subjects fed strictly noncarbohydrate diets quickly experience hallucinations, confusion, lethargy; ultimately they collapse. In young people long-term deprivation of carbohydrates causes permanent neurological damage. Children deprived of natural carbohydrate sources, fresh fruit, grains and vegetables especially, often display lower than normal intelligence, and in many ghetto areas in the United States where diet consists mainly of junk carbohydrates like white bread and sweets, the rate of birth defects, malnutrition and retardation among children is disproportionately high.

One might then ask why carbohydrates have been the target of such a powerful smear campaign through the years. And why has the very word "carbohydrate" become synonymous with fattening foods and junk foods?

The problem is due to a mix-up in terms. There are, you see, two kinds of carbohydrates, the *natural* variety and the *processed,* and the two are often confused.

Natural carbohydrates are carbohydrates as nature makes them. Fresh fruits, like pears, apples, guavas, bananas, berries, pineapples, plums. Fresh vegetables like tomatoes, lettuce, beans, peas, squash, beets, turnips, cucumbers. Whole grains like wheat, corn, oats, rye, barley, millet, rice. And dairy products (we will consider these separately in the chapters on fats and proteins).

Processed carbohydrates, on the other hand, are carbohydrates taken out of their natural state: refined, strained, stripped, cooked, extracted, heated and otherwise disfigured, then marketed alone or added back to other foods. Most commercial cakes, pies and confections fall into this category. Alcoholic beverages do too. And refined flours, polished rice, canned fruits and vegetables, processed cheese, and any fruit, vegetable, grain or dairy product altered from its natural state.

Processed carbohydrates are largely responsible for the many-calorie-little-nutrition syndrome that afflicts the modern diet. A piece of dark chocolate cake made from refined bleached flour provides literally *no* nutrition. None. Zip. Unless the manufacturer has added the nutrients back, and even then how could it be the same? Processed carbohydrates are eatables; often tasty eatables; but they are not much in the way of food.

Carbohydrates come almost exclusively from plants. The one exception is milk, which though often ranked as a protein actually contains more carbohydrates, primarily because of its high lactose-sugar content. All other major carbohydrates are composed of plant material, which the plant itself manufactures through the process of photosynthesis, taking the light from the sun and synthesizing it into green plant matter, using carbon dioxide in the atmosphere and water in the earth to complete this dazzling alchemy. All life on earth derives its energy from the sun. Seen from this standpoint, carbohydrates are simply solidified solar energy. Our major foodstuff, a poet might remark, consists of congealed sunlight!

Chemically speaking, carbohydrates are simple compounds made up of carbon, hydrogen and oxygen atoms. All contain either simple-sugar molecules or substances that can be reduced to simple sugars by digestion. The way in which these molecules of sugar or sugar-reducible matter are chemically arranged is what creates the different carbohydrates that end up on your table. Of these there are three varieties: *simple sugars, double sugars,* and *starch and fiber.*

1. Simple Sugars (Monosaccharides)

Simple sugars, or monosaccharides, appear in nature as discrete molecular particles that, chemically speaking, cannot be broken down into smaller molecular units. Because of their structural simplicity they dissolve easily in the digestive system, and with a minimum of transformation they are quickly released into the bloodstream.

There are four simple sugars in this family. The first is *fructose,* sweetest of the sugars, too sweet in fact for many. More than a few drops in a cup of tea would likely provoke complaints from any but the true sugar addict. It is found in many fruits, especially very ripe fruits, and is sometimes referred to as fruit sugar. It is also one of the sugars manufactured by bees from nectar and is what imparts the strong and sometimes cloying sweetness to honey.

Two other members of the simple-sugar family, *galactose* and *mannose,* play secondary nutritional roles (galactose results from the digestion of milk; mannose, combined with protein, is found in both meat and vegetables). The fourth variety, however, *glucose,* is the most important of all sugars. Sometimes called dextrose, corn sugar or grape sugar, glucose is what gives especially sugary fruits like grapes and peaches their zest and what endows fresh-picked garden corn with its almost candylike sweetness.

From the standpoint of human nutrition, glucose is among the most important of all bodily materials. All other carbohydrates, simple or complex, are ultimately broken down to this substance, which serves as the primary source of energy for both the nervous and the muscular systems. Most of the crushing, dissolving and refining that the digestive system puts carbohydrates through is dedicated to the production of glucose, and to its release into vital tissue. Clearly, glucose is the basic energy food of the human organism.

2. Double Sugars (Disaccharides)

There are three members of this family: *maltose, lactose* and *sucrose.* Maltose is formed in the starchy part of certain plants, especially cereals. (It's what gives beer its peculiarly acrid sweetness and whole-grain cereals their mildly sugary quality.) Lactose, or milk sugar as it is often called, is produced exclusively in the milk of mammals and is an essential ingredient in human mother's milk. Most common by far though is sucrose, or common white table sugar. Mainly derived from sugar cane, it can also be extracted from a selection of fruits and vegetables as well as from maple sugar, sorghum cane and molasses—indeed, whenever a fruit or vegetable tastes sweet, sucrose is likely in there somewhere. Half the solid matter in a carrot or in a ripe pineapple is composed of it.

3. Starch and Fiber (Polysaccharides)

Starch—Starches are not crystalline like commercial sugar, not sweet like sucrose, not dissolvable in coffee, tea, lemonade or any other dinner-sipping liquids, and not digested with anywhere near the ease of simple or double sugars. Yet they represent the main source of carbohydrate energy. They are found in a number of plant foods, including grains, seeds, tubers, green bananas; also, in foods derived from these substances, such as breads, cereals, noodles, cakes and pastas.

Since they are composed of many branching molecular chains, as opposed to the more compact molecular structure of single and double sugars, starches are referred to as *complex carbohydrates.* This distinction in molecular structure is more than academic, for while the simply constructed single and double sugars digest easily and release energy into the bloodstream with something approaching instant speed, their action is short-lived. The energy quickly depletes itself as the blood-sugar level shoots up and then falls just as rapidly, with the eater's appetite returning relatively soon.

Complex carbohydrates, on the other hand, are absorbed slowly, bit by bit, over a matter of hours, first in the mouth, where they are partly dissolved by the saliva, then by the gastric juices and pancreatic enzymes. Portions of the partially broken-down substance are then dispatched to the liver in the form of glucose, which will be turned into glycogen and stored. As required, the glycogen is then released into the muscle cells and nerve tissue, where it is converted back into glucose, but in a slow, intermittent way, like water dripping from a spigot.

The result of this slow breakdown of starch is that the blood-sugar level is elevated evenly over a period of time and remains high as long as the starch continues to be absorbed. When blood sugar is high, a person feels filled; when it drops, hunger begins. For this reason the slow digestion of complex carbohydrates keeps the appetite at bay far longer than simple sugars. Next time you breakfast on pancakes and syrup notice how quickly the energy dissipates. Most people will be hungry—and listless—by midmorning. Compare this to the sustaining power of hot oatmeal with bananas on top, which will last you till lunch.

Thus, while starch is spoken of as fattening food, nothing could be farther from the truth. Assuming that you eat the right kinds of starch—whole grains, fresh potatoes, legumes, bananas—and not the overprocessed varieties, nutritional gains are inevitable.

Even more important is the way that starches work to reduce fat. At the University of Oregon Medical Center, scientists have shown that diets high in starchy foods reduce the amount of fat in the bloodstream of diabetics and keep the insulin-processing mechanisms in better working order. Other studies have demonstrated that people who eat many complex carbohydrates tend to have fewer blood-sugar problems and better health records in general. For these reasons those who suffer from atherosclerosis are often put on complex-carbohydrate diets, for diets rich in starch have been demonstrated time and again to be of help in reducing the blood lipids (fats) that contribute to hardening of the arteries. High starch content in the diet is even believed by many to be one of the major reasons why people in underdeveloped countries suffer far lower rates of heart disease and diabetes. The Quechua Indians, for instance, inhabitants of the high country in the Andes Mountains of Peru, survive predominantly on a diet of potatoes and grains. Yet they are among the longest-lived people on earth.

Fiber—The second member of the polysaccharide family is composed of a group of plant substances with names like cellulose, pectin, hemicellulose and lignin. Collectively they are known as fiber. Biologically, they are the indigestible residues of the plant.

Fiber is found in the bran of grain products and in the skins and flesh of fruits and vegetables. Think of the little filaments that get caught in your teeth after eating a tough string bean or a ripe orange and you'll get some notion of what certain kinds of fiber look like.

Cows, sheep, horses and other grass-eating mammals have the digestive apparatus to break cellulose fiber down to glucose; the human stomach though is missing the enzymes necessary for this feat, and so fiber passes through the bowels undigested and ends up in the excreta. Not, however, before it performs several useful chores including moving the stools swiftly through the intestines and hence promoting regularity. Long considered dross, nutritionally speaking, and something to be scorned, fiber's value has recently been rediscovered. We'll have plenty more to say on the subject a little farther on.

The Many Perils of Carbohydrate Deficiency

Dietary fats can be packed away throughout the body for long periods of time. But when carbohydrates are stored, mostly in the liver in the form of glycogen, they remain there only for a brief time before being turned into glucose and consumed by energy-hungry tissue. The more physically active a person is the greater is the turnover.

When this supply is burned out, more is required, and so on hour after hour through the day. If the fires are not immediately replenished, blood-sugar level drops and fatigue and hunger set in. The average person needs an absolute minimum of 400 to 600 carbohydrate-produced calories every day to maintain his or her body in good working order.

What takes place if the fires are not stoked at all? That is, what will happen if natural carbohydrates—especially complex carbohydrates— are severely lacking in the daily diet? When this occurs the body plays a rather mean trick on itself. In desperate need of energy, the body turns to another power source for its nourishment: stored fats and proteins.

The catch is that without carbohydrates to help burn these substances their consumption becomes not only inefficient but, over the long run, destructive as well, leaving dangerous residues of acetone in the blood as leftovers from this inefficient oxidation process. Collectively these leftovers are known as *ketones*. The condition itself is called *acidosis*.

Ketones are the hidden ambush lying in wait for anyone foolish enough to maintain a prolonged high-protein, low-carbohydrate diet. Such diets include not only the weight-loss varieties but the sundry "high energy" eating plans practiced by athletes in the mistaken notion that eating only meat, dairy products and high-protein, high-fat foods makes for health, wealth and a strong backhand.

In reality, when your body is deprived of natural carbohydrates, the ketones slowly build up in the bloodstream day after day until they reach a saturation level. At this point an extra demand is placed on the kidneys, forcing them to work double time extracting ketones from the blood and dispelling them through the urine. If the kidneys are already stressed, or if kidney disease is present, the additional burden can severely tax the kidney mechanism.

Carbohydrate deprivation can also cause dehydration. In fact, much of the sudden and dramatic weight decrease that characterizes typical high-protein diets does not happen because fat is being dropped. It's simply water that's been eliminated, expelled through frequent eliminations. After a week or two of normal eating this weight is returned, hopefully without too much damage having been done to the body's electrolyte balance when all this artificial drying out was taking place. Watch as well for signs of calcium deficiency in a low-carbohydrate diet with its accompanying symptomatology: defective muscular coordination and premature fatigue.

And that's not all. The nervous system, if deprived of the glucose that carbohydrates normally bring it, turns in panic to the adrenal glands for support, robbing them of cortisone to help convert protein into sugar. This desperate reflex proves a temporary remedy at best. Damage to the adrenals often results, and the keenly sensitive balance of the body's endocrine system is thrown dangerously out of whack.

Pregnant women should be especially careful to avoid carbohydrate deprivation, as babies in utero are especially dependent on the nutrients they provide. If an expectant mother does not take in sufficient carbohydrates, development of her child's nervous system may be impaired, causing motor problems and even retardation, while she herself may feel logy and apathetic. The carbohydrate-starved expectant mother may even pass her pregnancy with a stubborn and seemingly inexplicable case of the blues—all quite remediable with a regular dose of salad, some baked potatoes, or a loaf of good whole-wheat bread. Pregnancy is no time for weight-loss diets of any kind, it might be added, especially of the high-protein, low-carbohydrate species.

Carbohydrates, it should be clear by now, are important not just for general nutrition but for your fundamental state of health. They play a critical role both in metabolism and in cell construction. They are the body's main source of fast energy, they are easy to digest, they are inexpensive to purchase and they produce no toxic side effects. Without them sickness comes to the starved organism as predictably as the plow follows the ox. Carbohydrates should comprise at least—at least—40 to 50 percent of your diet, and ideally far more.

A Few Questions and Answers About Carbohydrates

Is It Possible to Eat Too Many Carbohydrates?

A diet consisting literally of 100 percent carbohydrates is impossible. Many carbohydrates, most perhaps, include small amounts of protein and fat as part of their chemical constitution. Or they contain nutrients that are automatically transformed into these substances during digestion. Cooked lima beans, for instance, are about 35 percent carbohydrate. But they also contain 15 percent protein and 1 percent fat. Mashed potatoes, besides their 25 percent carbohydrate rating, are approximately 4 percent protein and 9 percent fat. This wide distribution of all three basic nutritional building blocks in most carbohydrate foods is one reason why a person can live on a strictly vegetarian diet and still remain healthy.

How Much of the Diet Then Should Include Carbohydrates?

What the precise amount of carbohydrate should be in the diet is still a subject of much debate. Vegetarians will tell you a diet 80 to 90 percent carbohydrate is not out of line. Champions of meat suggest far less. So do apologists for fats.

In 1977 Congress appropriated funds for a definitive study of nutrition in America chaired by Senator George McGovern. After exhaustive research, and perhaps the highest budget ever granted for a single nutritional study, the McGovern Committee reached its conclusions. Besides calling for Americans to eat less fats, less processed carbohydrates, and more complex carbohydrates, it recommended a specific regime for the

daily intake of carbohydrates, fats and proteins. According to the Mc-
Govern Committee, the following guideline should be followed:

COMMITTEE RECOMMENDATIONS

1. Carbohydrates:
- 48 percent of the diet should include complex carbohydrates, single and double sugars
- 10 percent of the diet should include processed carbohydrates and refined sugars

2. Fats:
- 10 percent of the diet should include saturated fats
- 10 percent should include monounsaturated fats
- 10 percent should include polyunsaturated fats

3. Protein:
- 12 percent of the diet should include protein

Isn't This Carbohydrate Rating a Very Conservative Estimate from the Standpoint of Natural Eating?

Yes. Most nutritionists sympathetic to natural foods would disagree
with these percentages. Many would, for instance, suggest that carbohydrate intake include a good deal more than the 58 percent mentioned
here, and that fat intake be lower than 30 percent. Or that intake of
refined sugar be drastically reduced, to zero percent if possible.

What About the Medical Findings in the 1960s Which Showed That Carbohydrates Increase Cholesterol Levels in the Blood?

Early studies on cholesterol and heart disease did indeed indicate that
individuals placed on high-carbohydrate diets showed both raised triglyceride (fat) levels in the blood and increased cholesterol counts. The panic
button was pushed, and for a decade or more the word "carbohydrate"
became an authorized profanity.

But further studies demonstrated that blood fats increased only tem-
porarily with a high-carbohydrate diet, then dropped back to normal. The
sudden rise was due, researchers theorized, not to the carbohydrates but
to the sudden change in the diet itself. Further studies showed that triglyceride and blood-cholesterol levels not only returned to normal after a
certain period of time but in some cases even *decreased*.

Unfortunately by the time the new findings were released the damage had been done, and the bad press lingered on. Today most people recall the early tests but are unaware that many nutritionists and doctors now consider the carbohydrate scare to have been based on false assumptions and carbohydrates themselves to have been cleared of all charges.

One Often Hears Liquor and Beer Spoken of as a Dietary Carbohydrate. Is This Accurate?

Although dieters often talk of beer and spirits as carbohydrates, this represents wishful thinking rather than fact. Most spirits are made from the fermentation of carbohydrates—rum from sugar, beer from hops, wine from grapes, Scotch whiskey from barley. By the time the brewing process is finished, however, the original carbohydrate has been transformed into pure ethyl alcohol. This new material, despite some claims, has almost no nutritional value (while beer is often spoken of as a source of protein, you would have to drink approximately fifty cans a day to meet the minimum daily protein requirement).

Athletes Sometimes Follow a Special High-Carbohydrate Diet Before an Important Sporting Event. What Exactly Is the Purpose of This? How Does It Work?

The diet is called "carbohydrate loading." It was developed in Sweden in the late 1960s. First you deplete the body of its regular energy supplies, then you build them back up using a veritable *blitzkrieg* of glycogen stimulation. It's all done through diet and it's quite effective, especially in types of sports that require long-term endurance such as marathon running. Here's how it works.

Approximately a week before a sporting event the athlete exercises to exhaustion, intentionally using up the body's supply of glycogen and reaching the point of total energy depletion. During this period the diet remains normal.

On the sixth, fifth and fourth days before the event the athlete switches to a 90 percent fat and protein diet, working out on the sixth day, resting on the fifth, working out again on the fourth.

Now three days before the event the athlete changes gears again, this time gorging on carbohydrates, staying away entirely from proteins and fats, eating a number of small meals rather than three large ones, and working out strenuously to deplete glycogen reserves.

The last two days before the competition the same high-carbohydrate, low-protein/fat diet is followed, this time with complete rest. On the day of the meet a high-carbohydrate, low-protein/fat breakfast is eaten. During the competition sugar water is taken at various intervals.

Utmost caution must be followed when practicing carbohydrate loading. Since ketones build up during carbohydrate deficiency, eight to ten glasses of water should be taken each day to help eliminate acidic toxins. Studies in dietary physiology show that a sudden shift to a high-carbohydrate diet can provoke elevation of blood fats, with cardiac arrhythmia and chest pains as possible side effects. If dizziness, lethargy, stomach cramps, unusual urination or any other physical symptoms result from carbohydrate loading the diet should be stopped immediately. This diet should not be attempted without the supervision of a doctor or experienced health professional.

A Carbohydrate Sampler: Grains, Sugars, Vegetables, Fruits, Fibers

So much for theory. Now down to a practical look at the various carbohydrate foods: what they do for you, what you can do with them. We'll start the survey with the food that originally turned mankind from a nomadic creature into a domestic one: grains.

GRAINS

Since grains produce considerably more food per acre and per working hour than hunting or fishing, humankind turned to their cultivation many thousands of years ago. They seemed then, as now, an ideal food. Not only do grains deliver abundant carbohydrate energy; they provide a goodly share of protein requirements as well. A cup of whole-wheat flour, for example, has 15 grams of protein along with its 82 grams of carbohydrate. Barley has 18 grams of protein as well as 173 grams of carbohydrate.

Grains are easy to harvest and transport. Many varieties can be grown anywhere, at the equator or in the Arctic Circle, at sea level or at eleven thousand feet. As opposed to other carbohydrates such as soft vegetables and pulpy fruits, they can be stored for long periods of time and will retain much of their nutrients. Being grasses, they germinate quickly. The seedlings are easy to keep alive once sprouted; they do not require elaborate fertilization; and they are as agreeable to man's livestock as they are to man.

Entire civilizations thus sprang up around the cultivation of grains. In most of these there was a deity who ruled over the rites of sowing and reaping—the very word "cereal" is derived from Ceres, the Roman goddess of the wheat harvest and the prototype of Mother Nature. In the Bible, grain is known as corn. In Psalms (65:13) its growth becomes a pastoral ecstasy: "The pastures are clothed with flocks; the valleys also are covered over with corn; they shout for joy, they also sing." Indeed, from a certain standpoint, the history of humanity over the past four thousand years has been the history of the cultivation of grains.

A grain seed contains all the nutrients vital to germination, just as the nucleus of a cell houses its most essential life-producing chemistry. This seed can even, in a sense, be looked upon as a kind of miniature embryo and womb, and as such it contains all the mysterious forces of life that emblazon the universe.

Each of these individual "wombs" is composed of three distinct parts: the *germ,* the *endosperm* and the *bran.*

The *germ* is the nutritional heart of the grain and the part responsible for germination. When the seed is dropped onto the earth it is this portion that produces a sprout and becomes a new plant. For this reason the germ contains most of the seed's vital enzymes and vitamins, especially vitamin E and thiamine. It is also rich in protein and minerals, especially iron, plus a selection of major B vitamins.

The *endosperm* makes up most of the grain's inner bulk and serves to nourish the germ with its own starchy matter in the first days after the germ has sprouted. Nutritionally the endosperm is primarily a source of protein and complex carbohydrate. Its vitamin quotient is meager, however, and as a result it has less food value than the germ. Modern refined flours are made up primarily of the endosperm. The milling process removes both the germ and the bran.

Finally there is the *bran.* This is the "skin" of the grain, a thin, coarse outer membrane that protects the fragile inner seed in the way that the shell protects the nut; foodwise, it provides its cultivators with a solid source of nutrition and roughage.

The bran is arranged in several layers of "sheathing." The inner layer is called the *aleurone layer*—some consider this section to be a fourth and separate part of the grain—and is replete with both phosphorus and protein. The outer veneer of skin, the bran proper, is rich in B vitamins and many minerals, especially iron. Though endowed with so much nourishment, this outer skin is nonetheless rubbed away during the process of commercial refining and discarded, along with the germ from the grain. This vastly reduces the grain's nutritional value and lowers the fiber content to virtually zero.

For most people of the world, grains are the staple diet, and wisely so. Though in the West, cereal foods have a reputation for being fattening and are often avoided—grains constitute only about 30 percent of the American diet—in the East and especially in countries like China and Indochina where grains account for as much as 70 percent of the diet, high grain intake supplies almost all the people's thiamine requirements plus two-thirds of their protein, carbohydrate, niacin and riboflavin needs. In fact, as a food, grains supply humankind with almost every nutrient the body needs, with the notable exceptions of vitamin A, vitamin C and calcium.

WHEAT

At some unrecorded moment in the middle of this century wheat surpassed rice as the most widely cultivated grain in the world. Each year billions of bushels are harvested, enough to fill a freight train that would circle the world one and a half times around.

While far from being the magical manna that certain people have claimed it to be (several decades ago word was out that bread was a total food, and that *by itself* it could keep a person full and fit; but this rumor, it turned out, was simply PR staged by the farm lobby), wheat in the form of whole-grain bread and cereal can go a long way toward filling man's daily dietary requirements.

The reason for its power is that internally *every part of the wheat grain* contains crucial nutrients. Chemically it is about 20 percent protein and is rich in phosphorus, potassium, iron and niacin. The bran is loaded with vitamin B, the germ with vitamin E, and the endosperm, besides containing valuable starches, includes two vital protein substances, *glutenin* and *gliadin*. Together these proteins form a compound known as *gluten*.

Gluten is both a catalyst and a glue. It's what gives dough its springy, elastic quality and what allows the baker to knead the dampened wheat into folds and the folds into bread. Without gluten the world would be without its favorite food. When gluten combines with the magic catalyst yeast, millions of carbon-dioxide bubbles are released within the dough, causing it to stretch and expand—to "rise" in baker's parlance—and when heated, to harden, forming what we know as a baker's loaf.

Dough that is low in gluten is less nourishing than dough with a high gluten count. Yet because flour low in gluten produces a light, delicate product when baked and because it is so pleasing to the palate (especially with sugar added) it is the kind of flour most commonly used for making commercial cakes and pastries.

Wheat comes in two varieties, *winter wheat* and *spring wheat.* Winter wheat is planted in the fall. It germinates, then goes dormant for the cold weather. Next spring it rises phoenixlike and continues to mature through the summer months until harvesttime. A moderate climate is necessary if winter wheat is to survive; due to the extra farming chores required for its cultivation, it is more difficult to grow than spring wheat. As if by compensation, however, it is also more nutritious, containing as much as 5 to 10 percent more protein than spring wheat, depending on where it is grown and in what kind of soil.

When shopping for winter wheats, the most nutritious kinds are the hard wheats, especially *hard red winter wheat.* You'll know this species by its long, narrow kernel.

The second variety, spring wheat, is grown in cold climates where frozen soil prevents winter wheat from surviving. Sown in the spring, it goes through a ninety-day growing season and ripens a few weeks after the winter-wheat crop is brought in. Spring wheat does well in temperate climates, is easily cultivated, but, as mentioned, is somewhat less nutritious than its slower-growing sister. *Hard red spring wheat* is highly prized by bread bakers, because of its high gluten content, and every good health food store should have a stock of it. The kernels of spring wheat are smaller than winter wheat, more stubby and hard.

Other varieties of wheat include: (1) *Soft red winter wheat,* a more starchy, less nutritious seed than either of the hard wheats. Its low gluten content makes it excellent for the preparation of pies, cakes and any pastry products that do not require kneading. (2) *Durum wheat,* a particularly hard grain used mainly for making pasta. Its high gluten content helps spaghetti strands keep their shape, but generally it is unsatisfactory for baking bread. (3) *White wheat,* the least nutritious of all the wheats. It is also the most widely used in commercial bread products, in pastries and in cereals, perhaps because its smooth texture produces such a pretty fluffy appearance and because it is easy to use. If you intend to bake your own bread and get the most nutritional mileage out of it, white wheat should be avoided.

Whole-Wheat Flour Versus White Refined Flour: What You Should Know

As we have seen, the germ and the bran of the wheat kernel are removed in the modern grain-milling process, leaving only residues from the endosperm to make into bread. As a result the most nourishing parts of the wheat are removed, the least nourishing parts are kept. What is the logic here? What purpose does the refining process serve? Who ever dreamed up such a thing?

The refinement of wheat flour, it so happens, arose innocently enough as a method of preservation. Traditionally, farmers harvested wheat seeds whole and pulverized them with a millstone, germ, bran, endosperm and all. The final product was true whole-wheat flour. The problem was that in the pulverization process the germ released various oils that after a certain amount of time caused the rest of the flour spoil.

As far as the typical farmer was concerned this posed no great hitch, providing the time between grinding his wheat and baking it was minimal, which was usually the case in those days, as people milled their wheat and baked their bread on the same day.

Time passed, and one fine year the modern commercial store made its appearance. Here, wonder of wonders, food supplies were sold directly over the counter, and grains and feeds were the specialty items (many of the earliest markets were known as "grain stores"). When stored on the shelves of these establishments wheat had the habit of going rancid due to the oils released from the crushed germ. Before too long some nineteenth-century genius came up with a dandy way of handling the situation: *Remove the germ from the wheat grain entirely,* and thus avoid the whole problem.

Eventually the stone milling wheel became obsolete and was replaced by giant steel roller mills. These ingenious machines flattened rather than pulverized the grains, so when the flour was winnowed, the germ, loosened from its matrix within the seed, fell through a sifting screen and was discarded. The method worked wonderfully well. And there was an added surprise: Not only did degermed flour last longer but rodents and insects wouldn't touch it. Within fifty years true whole-grain bread was almost forgotten.

Meanwhile, since the time of Marie Antoinette, cake lovers had developed a penchant for white flour. The choice was based purely on aesthetics: White flour was prettier and smoother than the darker, natural variety. Whole-wheat bread and cereal and pastry thus became poor man's fare, and the poor man's meal ticket to good health. The wealthy, meanwhile, malnourished themselves with the pure white leftovers. Accommodating them all the way were bakers who outdid one another inventing whitening agents. Some used chalk or ammonium carbonate to lighten the flour; others mixed whitish powdered potatoes or barley meal into the dough. By the time the nineteenth century had dawned, the most ingenious of them were putting the new milling techniques to use as well, this time making sure that in the whitening process both the germ *and* the bran were removed. Gradually white flour became the desired food. Eventually it became the expected food.

Just How Bad Is White Flour?

Worse, probably, than you think. Modern milling machines are amazingly sophisticated. The best can not only skin off the top outer layers of the bran but they can remove the delicate inner skin of the bran too, the aleurone layer, which is the most digestible and nutritious part of the food. According to studies run at the University of California,* about 50 percent of wheat's calcium and potassium are lost in the refining process, along with 65 percent of the copper, almost 100 percent of the manganese, and more than 75 percent of the iron. And vitamins? Thiamine, about 80 percent; niacin, 75 percent; pyridoxine and pantothenic acid, almost 50 percent, as well as measurable reductions in the important B vitamins, including folic acid, choline, biotin and inositol.

True, bread manufacturers put some of the vitamins and minerals back into the bread during the baking. They have to; it's the law; so-called "enriched" bread, it turns out, is enriched at the point of a gun. Aside from the question of whether or not dismantling a living seed and then reconstituting it with synthetic replacements actually does produce an equally nutritious product, it should be pointed out that only *some* of the vitamins and minerals must by law be replaced.

Enriched white bread, for instance, contains less than 25 percent of its original vitamin E supply. Less than 50 percent of the amount of pantothenic acid is put back. Less than 66 percent of the pyridoxine and biotin are replaced. Serious deficiencies of protein amino acids also exist, along with lack of digestible carbohydrate matter and several important B vitamins. Phosphorus, manganese, and potassium are not replaced at all.†

Commercial flours are also adulterated with a wide range of chemical oxidizing agents to give the baked product "body." They are treated with various propionic acids as preservatives, artificial dyes and colorings to get that pretty golden-brown look into the crust, and copious amounts of sugar and salt as seasonings; also emulsifiers, dough conditioners and

* Eleanor Baker and D. S. Lepkovsky, *Bread & the War Food Problem* (Riverside, Calif.: College of Agriculture, University of California, June 1943).

† Henry Schroeder, *The Trace Elements and Man* (Old Greenwich, Conn.: Adair Publishing Co., 1973), pp. 54, 55.

mold inhibitors. Silicones are ordinarily used to grease the dough pans in modern bakeries, and these commonly absorb themselves into the crust of the bread. Eggs, butter, milk and natural flavorings are now routinely replaced by nitric acids, hydrogenated fats, condensed milk solids and an amazing arsenal of imitation flavorings.

Even more unfortunate is the bleaching of the flour, a process that makes use of such violent chemicals as chlorine dioxide in order to keep bread insect-free. Neither the cries of agricultural experts that such bleaching agents are poisonous nor the warnings of nutritionists that bleaching removes whatever vestige of nutrients may be left in the flour have swayed commercial bakers from this insideous practice, so that today the majority of flour used in baked products is indeed 100 percent pure thanks to the bleaches, though exactly pure of what few are saying. All in all, because of the more than eighty additives that may legally be blended into a commercial loaf, it is estimated that flour constitutes only about one-half the weight of commercial bread, the rest of the bulk being taken up by additives, artificial flavorings, sugar, salt and chemical preservatives.* Moral: Buy your bread at the health food store. Or better, bake it yourself.

Yes, You Can Bake Your Own Bread

Through the years a great deal of mythology has sprung up concerning how difficult it is to bake bread. Where this rumor came from is hard to say, especially when you consider that less than a century ago *everyone,* or every mother or wife, at any rate, performed this task with ease, and as a matter of routine.

In reality, making bread is a relatively easy matter. The only tricky part is kneading the dough, and most people get the hang of this pleasant and therapeutic activity within ten or fifteen minutes. With a little luck you'll be producing excellent, savory loaves after one or two tries.

In this section we're going to take you step by step through the bread-making process. We'll start off with a loaf that is simple to make and wonderful to eat. Anyone who tastes it will be a convert. Following the initial how-to recipe we'll provide several variations on the first loaf, all of them equally easy to prepare and just as delicious. Follow these directions closely and you'll soon be an expert. Bread baking is like any food preparation, a series of short, easy steps that ultimately add up to a complex final product. We're willing to wager that even after the first

---

* Beatrice Trum Hunter, *Consumer Beware!* (New York: Simon and Schuster, 1971), pp. 286–300.

attempt you'll agree that not only is the staff of life easy to prepare but that the process of making it is somehow satisfying for the soul. Before we begin though, a few general principles.

First of all, the materials. Probably the only ingredient you won't find in the supermarket is whole-grain flour. While any health food store carries them, be warned that whole-grain flours are *not* all the same.

Some, for example, have been milled with steel plate rollers. These crush the seeds between converging drum rollers that spin at very high speeds. The method is rather violent and tends to rip the grains apart rather than to pulverize them. While the germ and bran are retained in this process, a great deal of heat is generated, burning out both the vitamin and enzyme content of the grain. The natural oils in the germ, moreover, those that contain high vitamin E supplies, do not fare well when exposed to high temperatures, with the result that the germ oil coagulates within the flour and forms greasy little lumps. When the bread is baked these do not dissolve well and tend to give the final product an oily, rancid taste.

The best variety of whole-grain flour tells you on the label that it is *stone-ground.* In New England, people sometimes still keep millstones in front of their homes for good luck, some as large as eight to ten feet in diameter. Here and there you can still see them at work in old-fashioned grain mills, turning day and night, grinding the grain seeds beneath their enormous weight, powered by the force of flowing water.

Stone-ground grain is superior for several reasons. The relatively slow motion of the turning stone generates very little heat, sparing the precious volatile oil in the germ. The wheel neither chops nor mutilates the way steel plates do, but mashes the grain steadily into a dissolvable powder. This means less mangling action that might destroy nutrients. At the same time, the gentle steadiness of the stone's turning motion grinds the wheat evenly and distributes the germ throughout the flour in equal proportions. As is often the case, the slow, rhythmic method works best.

A few years ago the evocative term "stone-ground" was commonly used as a piece of come-on advertising by commercial bread companies. As it turned out, most of this wheat had never been within a hundred miles of a real millstone. The FDA has tightened up on the indiscriminate use of this slogan, and today any product that makes such a claim must live up to its title.

Other things have changed too. While stone-milled flour was once almost impossible to find, the renaissance of natural foods in the 1960s inspired many entrepreneurs to set up their own stone-grinding operations. Though most of these rigs are not as picturesque as the old-fashioned water mill, they still get the job done, and today you should have no difficulty finding stone-ground flour on the shelf of most good health food stores and occasionally even in the supermarket.

As soon as you get the flour home pop it into the refrigerator and keep it there until baking day. Exposure to the heat of the kitchen may cause the fatty oils to go rancid. Even when refrigerated, though, whole-grain flour should be used as soon as possible. Don't count on it lasting longer than a month. Three months is maximum.

If you buy in bulk and keep your raw grains in a pantry be sure that (1) the temperature is well on the cool side; (2) the room is dark; (3) the humidity is as low as possible; and (4) the containers are all tightly sealed. Sacks of perishables should be kept off the floor and fastened securely. Small insects that stalk grain sacks, especially the weevils, can squeeze through remarkably tight seals. You may also find that the eggs of grain moths and weevils are sometimes laid in the grain *before* you buy it, and that if unchecked these unwelcome guests will quickly hatch and infest your pantry. The easy way to nip this problem in the bud is to keep the stores as chilly as possible. Forty degrees is not too cold.

The next ingredient is yeast. Yeast is a living plant. When warmed and wetted in soft flour its cells start to grow, giving off gases that cause the dough to rise. This is why lukewarm water is used when mixing the dough and why the dough should be placed in a slightly warmed oven to help it rise.

Yeast comes in two varieties, dry and compressed (caked). The dry type stores well on the shelf for months at a time. The compressed is more volatile—more alive—and spoils within a week unless kept frozen in a ventilated container. The compressed kind is often said to be better nutritionally because it is fresher, though opinions are divided on this matter.

You'll know when your yeast has gone bad if its normal gray hue turns to a dirty brown. When the yeast fails this color test throw it away, and avoid the disappointment that comes from a dough that sprawls before you sticky, insolent and unrisen in the pan.

Commercial yeast, the kind generally sold in the supermarkets, is often mixed with a substance called BHT (butylated hydroxytoluene) as a defoamer and preservative agent. BHT is a petroleum-based antioxi-dant that has been accused of causing weight loss, liver damage, bald-ness, kidney disease, growth retardation in children and several other pernicious conditions. Examine the labels on the yeast packages before you buy. Health food stores regularly carry yeast untreated by preserva-tives.

What about grinding your own grains? This is certainly the route to go if you want the freshest flour human effort can provide. Be warned, though, that it entails a bit of work and an outlay of money, sometimes as much as three hundred dollars.

First you'll need access to a home food grinder. There are a number of these on the market and more coming all the time. The cheaper kinds are of the hand-crank variety with a handle that you turn yourself, something like an old-fashioned coffee grinder. This is a bit of a workout, and unless you're dealing with a precision instrument the machine's blades may grind unevenly. Electric mills are more costly and as might be expected more rapid and efficient. Some can grind five pounds of flour in five or six minutes. One variety, the Magic Mill II, pressurizes and explodes the grains into tiny specks by a process known as micronization. More commonly, a Carborundum stone is employed to mash the wheat in the traditional crushing fashion.

While all of these machines get the job done, some bakers claim Carborundum wheels leave metallic residues in the wheat (though the substance itself is inert and by official reckoning harmless). Others say that the atomization process that takes place during micronization damages the subtle nutritional virtues of the seeds. Whatever kind you choose be sure your machine does not heat the grain too much. Feel the flour as soon as it comes out of the mill. If it's noticeably hot this means some of the volatile oils and enzymes are being roasted out—the cheaper mills, you'll discover, tend to run on the warm side. (This, by the way, is the problem with using a blender or food processor for grinding wheat.) The best thing is to try out the different machines for yourself and see which suits your fancy. Many health food stores allow you a test batch or two in the store. Suppliers of grain mills are listed in the Appendix.

Now to baking the bread.

To get started on our learning loaf you'll need the following ingredients and materials:

2¼ cups lukewarm water	tablespoons extra to
2 tablespoons dry yeast	grease the pans
3 tablespoons unrefined oil—	5 tablespoons unrefined honey
(soy, corn and safflower oils	5½ cups whole-wheat flour
are all good), plus a few	1¼ teaspoons salt

You'll need a medium-sized bowl and your largest bowl plus a set of measuring spoons, a knife, and a large mixing spoon. Also, either a wooden board, a butcher-block counter, or any wooden surface for kneading the dough. And two 9″ x 5″ loaf pans. Now here's what to do, step by step:

1. Fill the medium-sized bowl with 2¼ cups of lukewarm water. Dis-

solve the yeast in the water. Test to be sure the water temperature is just right, first by measuring the degrees with a thermometer—95 to 115 degrees is perfect—then by dipping your elbow into the water. The water should feel warm but not hot. (After using this elbow trick several times you'll develop a feeling for the proper temperature and no longer require the thermometer.) Now add the oil and the honey.

2. Place the flour and salt into the large bowl. Mix so that the salt is well distributed throughout the flour.

3. Add the yeast, oil and honey to the flour mixture. Mix with large spoon. When the dough becomes thick and sticky, continue mixing it with your hands until all the ingredients are evenly blended.

4. Now cover the dough with a towel and place the bowl in an unlighted oven. The towel protects the dough against drafts and keeps it from drying out. Some people dampen the towel slightly to prevent it from sticking to the dough. The warmth generated by the pilot light will provide enough heat so that the dough will rise. Any warm place will actually do the job, but the controlled temperature of an oven is best. Let the dough rise for 1½ hours. The mixture will expand considerably, usually to within an inch or less of the top of the bowl.

5. Sprinkle a small handful of flour over the entire wooden board. Spread so that it covers the entire surface evenly. Turn the dough mixture onto the board and begin kneading.

6. Kneading: First, sprinkle a little flour on your hands to prevent the dough from sticking. Place the dough lump directly in front of you, then dig your fingers firmly in at the top of the dough pile. Pull and fold the top toward you, simultaneously pressing the heels of your hands forward into the bottom of the dough. Repeat the same push-pull action several times until the dough mass is shaped into an oblong, then turn the dough mass the long way in front of you. Repeat the same folding action until you mold another oblong. The action is a rhythmic back-forth motion. You'll get the hang of it in a few minutes. After a while it becomes automatic. You will know you're doing the kneading correctly if the dough starts to compact into an elastic ball after several minutes and the stickiness disappears. Repeat this same routine for about 5 minutes until the dough is springy and fairly dry. If the dough sticks to the wood as you knead, sprinkle a little flour onto the board or onto the dough to loosen it up.

7. Now cut the dough mass in half with a knife and shape each section into an oblong loaf.

8. Pour approximately a tablespoon of oil into the loaf pans, and with your hands or a paper towel rub the oil around the pans until the inner surfaces are entirely covered. Tuck the loaves into the pans and

place them in an unlighted oven with a towel over both. Allow loaves to rise for approximately an hour, or until their size has doubled.

9. When the loaves have risen, remove them, then preheat your oven to 400 degrees. Place the loaves back in the oven and bake for 10 minutes. Then reduce the temperature to 350 degrees and bake for another 20 minutes. You'll know the bread is ready by the golden-brown look of it. Also, when you tap it you'll hear a hollow sound. If you stick a toothpick into the bread and it comes out clean this is another good indicator.

10. Allow the loaves to cool in the pans for at least an hour before removing. Bread just out of the oven is not at its best. One or two hours' cooling helps the dough congeal and allows the ingredients to settle, locking in the tastes. Bread too hot out of the oven has a gummy consistency and an undefined taste.

11. Removing the loaves from the pans can be tricky, especially if you're new at the game. When removing a loaf, tap the pan smartly several times on a hard surface. If the loaf loosens up, then carefully turn the pan over and shake it, cradling the loaf in your free hand as it slips out. This is the moment of truth. Too much force can cause the loaf to crumble. Not enough and it will remain in the pan. If, after continuous tapping and shaking, the loaf still refuses to come out, take a knife and c-a-r-e-f-u-l-l-y insert it around the edges of the pan, running it around the four sides until the clinging dough particles have been cut. Then remove.

Voilà! Homemade bread. Here are a few more bread recipes that you'll find easy to follow.

HONEY WHOLE-WHEAT BREAD

1 tablespoon dry yeast *or* 2 ounces compressed yeast	3 tablespoons refined oil
	3 tablespoons honey
	1½ teaspoons sea salt
½ cup lukewarm water *or* 2 cups warm milk	5½ cups whole-wheat flour

1. Dissolve yeast in water. Add the oil and the honey and stir until all ingredients are well mixed. Add the water or milk, stir again, and add the salt and half the flour. Stir the whole mixture thoroughly.

2. Continue to add the rest of the flour until the dough stiffens so much it can no longer be stirred with a spoon. Place the mass of dough onto a floured wooden board and knead it for about 10 minutes, or until the dough becomes compact and dry.

3. Put the dough into a lightly oiled bowl, cover it with a slightly dampened towel, and place in an unlighted oven for about an hour, or until the dough mass has doubled in size.

4. Remove the dough, knead it for several minutes until all the air is out, then cut it in half and place each half into a lightly oiled loaf pan.

5. Let the dough rise for another hour, or until it doubles in size again. A few minutes before it's finished rising preheat the oven to 375 degrees.

6. Place the loaves in the oven and bake for 10 minutes. Then turn the heat down to 350 degrees and bake for about 40 more minutes, or until the bread is done. Remove the pans from the oven, and let the loaves sit for an hour or two before eating.

DATE-NUT WHOLE-WHEAT BREAD

1½ cups whole-wheat flour	1 egg
1 teaspoon sea salt	1 cup whole milk
¼ cup honey	1 teaspoon baking soda
1 cup chopped dates	¼ stick soft butter
½ cup chopped prunes	2 teaspoons cooking oil
1 cup chopped nuts	

1. Mix the flour, salt, honey, dates, prunes and nuts together in a mixing bowl. Beat the egg in a separate bowl until frothy, then add to the flour mixture along with the milk, soda and butter.

2. Oil a large bread baking pan, making sure all the sides are evenly covered. Place the dough into the pan and allow it to stand for 30 minutes.

3. Preheat oven to 350 degrees. Place pan in oven and bake for 50 to 60 minutes. Remove pan and allow it to cool for an hour before removing bread. This bread is delicious with cream cheese spread on it or with a hearty vegetable soup.

SOY WHOLE-WHEAT BREAD

1 cup lukewarm water	1½ teaspoons corn oil
1 package yeast	¼ cup nonfat dry milk
3 cups whole milk	6½ cups whole-wheat flour
3 tablespoons honey	¼ cup soy flour
1 tablespoon sea salt	¼ cup wheat germ

1. Pour lukewarm water into a mixing bowl and stir in the yeast. Place bowl in unlighted oven for an hour.

2. Remove bowl from oven. Warm the whole milk, then mix it and honey, salt and oil with the water and yeast. Allow mixture to stand another 10 minutes in unlighted oven.

3. Remove from oven. Mix in dry milk, whole-wheat flour, soy flour and wheat germ. Stir for several minutes, then remove dough from bowl and knead it on floured board for 15 minutes, or until it becomes smooth and elastic.

4. Return dough to lightly oiled bowl, cover with moist towel and place bowl in unlighted oven for an hour, or until the dough doubles in size.

5. Sprinkle flour over wooden board and on your hands. Remove the dough mixture from the oven, turn dough onto board and punch it with your fist until it falls. Knead for another minute or so, then sprinkle dough with a little flour, cover with moist towel, and leave it on the board for 15 minutes.

6. Cut the dough into two equal loaves. Put each loaf into an oiled or buttered loaf pan. Cover with towel and place in unlighted oven for another hour, allowing dough to rise once more.

7. Remove pans. Preheat oven to 375 degrees, then place pans back in oven. After 20 minutes turn heat down to 350 degrees and continue to bake for 30 or 40 minutes, or until bread seems done. Remove loaves from oven and pans and allow them to cool for an hour before eating.

Dealing with Wheat and Yeast Allergies

Many people suffer from wheat allergies, mainly because of the gluten in the wheat. For some people gluten does not digest properly and may cause a variety of gastrointestinal symptoms. For others, perhaps more than we realize, the protein in gluten trips off episodes of mental malaise or depression. When taken off wheat substances these people's symptoms usually improve rapidly.

The same is true for yeast. Being a living fungus, yeast can prove a pesky allergen for some, capable of causing a wide range of allergic symptoms. Children are often especially susceptible.

Both yeast and wheat are often hidden in foods, making them harder to avoid. Besides residing in most baked goods and breakfast cereals, wheat may also be lurking in almost any variety of food, including candy, pastas, soups, stuffing, beer, salad dressings, bologna and coffee substitutes. Yeast is often included in stuffing, soups and alcoholic beverages, especially beer.

The practical treatment for both problems is, of course, avoidance. This does not mean one must forever be deprived of bread and cake, only that special kinds of breads—nongluten breads or nonyeast breads —are in order. The following recipes are especially designed for allergy sufferers. To find further recipes for allergics check the shelves of your library and the book section of most health food stores.

Two Delicious Nonyeast Breads

SPOON BREAD

1 cup cornmeal	**1 teaspoon salt**
2 cups warm milk	**2 tablespoons soft butter**
3 eggs	

1. Combine cornmeal and milk in a saucepan. Place pan on medium heat and stir thoroughly until the mixture boils.

2. Remove pan from heat and set the mixture aside for 20 minutes, allowing to cool. Separate the eggs and whip the yolks, then add the yolks to the mixture along with salt and butter. Mix for 5 minutes until all ingredients are blended.

3. Beat the egg whites until they are fluffy, then fold into batter. Preheat the oven to 350 degrees and bake in oiled loaf pan for 5 to 15 minutes, or until the bread seems done. You'll have to test the dough continually during this time. When it's baked properly the bread should be moist and springy, yet firm.

INDIAN CHAPATI

2½ cups unrefined whole-grain	**1 cup water**
flour	**2 teaspoons butter**
1 teaspoon sea salt	

1. Sift the flour into a bowl, add salt, and while mixing the ingredients, slowly add the water, Knead the dough on a floured board for 5 or 10 minutes until it becomes light and smooth.

2. Set the dough aside in a bowl for one hour, then knead again, adding a little water if the dough becomes too thick.

3. Place the dough onto the wooden board or counter. Sprinkle a little flour on your hands and on the counter to prevent the dough from sticking. Tear off a small handful from the dough mass, form it into a ball, and flatten it into a pancake about 5 or 6 inches across. You can use your hands or a rolling pin.

4. Grease a frying pan or griddle with a little butter (or ghee, see page

163) and heat it well. Keeping the burner at medium heat, bake the chapati until one side is browned, occasionally flattening it in the pan with a spatula. When done on one side, turn and cook on the other, allowing the bread to rise. This it will do quite quickly, ballooning to twice its size with surprising speed. Make sure the bread is baked on both sides, then remove and repeat with the rest of the dough until you have a pile of chapatis. Serve hot with butter.

Three Delicious Nonwheat Breads

MILLET FLAT BREAD

4 cups millet flour (obtainable   1½ cups water
   at any health food store)   1½ tablespoons butter
1½ teaspoons salt

1. Sift the flour into a mixing bowl. Mix in the salt. Separate out a small handful of the mixture and knead it into a stiff dough, adding just enough water so that the batter remains elastic.

2. Form the dough into a pancake 5 or 6 inches in diameter by pressing down on the dough or rolling it out. Heat a buttered pan and place the pancake on the hottest part. Cook slowly on both sides, continuing to flatten the bread with a spatula or any handy flattening instrument as it cooks.

3. Remove from pan when lightly browned and spread a pat of butter over the bread, allowing it to absorb while still hot. Repeat the same procedure with the remainder of the dough until you have a pile of delicious flat breads.

BARLEY WALNUT BREAD

¼ cup water   2 tablespoons oil
⅓ cup honey   2 cups chopped walnuts
1 package yeast   ½ teaspoon sea salt
2 cups milk   6 cups barley flour

1. Heat the water until it is lukewarm, then add the honey and yeast. Mix thoroughly and allow mixture to stand several minutes.

2. Scald the milk in a separate pan. Add the oil, nuts and salt. Allow to cool.

3. Add the milk mixture and flour to the honey and yeast mixture. Mix steadily for at least 5 minutes until the batter is well blended.

4. Knead the dough on a floured board for 5 minutes. Then slice it into two even loaves, place both loaves on a cookie sheet, cover with a damp cloth and place cookie sheet in an unlighted oven for an hour. (Since there is no gluten in the batter to combine with the yeast the dough will rise only a little.)

5. Preheat the oven to 350 degrees. Cook the loaves for 10 minutes, then reduce heat to 325 degrees and continue baking for another 50 to 60 minutes, or until the bread seems done.

OATMEAL BREAD

3 cups oatmeal	1 cup water
4 tablespoons honey	1½ cakes yeast
3 tablespoons soft butter	6 cups rye flour
2 tablespoons sea salt	

1. Boil three cups of oatmeal until it is of breakfast-cereal consistency. Place it in a mixing bowl and add the honey, butter and salt.

2. Warm the water and allow the yeast to dissolve in it for several minutes. Add the yeast water to the oatmeal, then the rye flour, stirring the dough until it is thoroughly blended and no longer sticky.

3. Knead dough on floured bowl for 15 to 20 minutes. Cover bowl with a moist cloth and allow dough to rise for an hour. Then remove dough and punch it down with your fist and knead it again for another 5 minutes.

4. Slice the dough into three equal loaves. Preheat oven to 350 degrees. Bake loaves for an hour.

A Short Dictionary of Wheat Terms

Bulgar—Cracked wheat (see below) that has been thoroughly cooked and parched before the cracking. While bulgar is a popular grain in Middle Europe and Russia, it is still little known in the United States. Most health food stores have a stock of it, though it can be made at home by boiling a cup of wheat berries (see below) for about an hour in two cups of water, then straining off the water and baking the kernels in a low oven for another 45 minutes to an hour, or until all the moisture has been removed. Allow the grain to cool thoroughly, then grind it to a coarse consistency in a food processor or blender. That's it. Bulgar makes a hearty accompaniment to meat dishes and is excellent in a salad. The following Middle Eastern recipe for tabooley salad makes one of the most satisfying and unusual lunches around.

TABOOLEY SALAD

¾ cup bulgar
1 cup boiling water
3 chopped tomatoes
1½ cups chopped fresh parsley
1 clove garlic, chopped
½ cup fresh mint, finely
    chopped

½ teaspoon pepper
1 teaspoon salt
½ cup lemon juice
½ cup olive oil

Soak the bulgar in the hot water for an hour. Mix in the chopped ingredients, then add the pepper, salt, lemon juice and olive oil. Mix thoroughly and serve with slices of feta cheese, lettuce leaves and whole-wheat bread.

Couscous—The grain of North African cuisine. It is a granular semolina (see below), rich in gluten and protein. It is often served in stews or as a side dish with meat. Not as sweet as bulgar nor as pleasantly nutty as cracked wheat, couscous is for some the manna of life and for others an acquired taste.

Cracked wheat—Consists of wheat berries that have been chopped up to allow their soft, starchy insides to be exposed. The exposure helps them cook more quickly.

Enriched white bread—White bread that has had the nutrients removed from it along with the germ and bran, then has had some of these nutrients artificially replaced at the time of preparation.

Self-rising flour—Refined white flour that has had a leavening agent and salt added to it. The leavening agent in these products is often weak and has a short shelf life when stored. The only advantage to it is that it saves you the thirty seconds or so it would take you to add these ingredients yourself.

Semolina—Coarse-milled durum wheat consisting mostly of the endosperm part of the wheat. It is used mainly as an ingredient in pasta.

Wheat berries—The seeds or grains of the wheat before the wheat is milled. They have a chewy texture when cooked and are sometimes added to rice to provide extra protein. Try cooking a cup of whole-wheat berries in two cups of water for several hours, adding sea salt as it simmers, and serving as a vitamin-packed breakfast cereal. Or next time you cook rice add a handful of wheat berries to the boiling mixture. They will add a chewy, nutlike taste to whatever rice dish you happen to be serving.

RICE

Rice serves as a staple for half the population of the world, especially for inhabitants of the Asian countries where approximately 95 percent of the annual rice crop is grown. Indeed, anyone who has jetted over the Far East has been struck by the fact that one can travel ten, twelve hours and see nothing out the window as the time passes but rice fields. Field after field after field. Tons uncountable. There are approximately a billion people in China today. Estimates have it that each of them eats a pound of rice a day.

While brown rice has an ancient heritage, its adulteration began thousands of years ago, according to legend, when an unnamed Chinese emperor decreed that the whiter the kernel the purer the rice. To oblige him the court cooks and agronomists quickly devised a method of stripping the grain of its brown outer skin, creating the fluffy but less nutritious stuff that falls off our chopsticks so easily at Chinese restaurants today. Rice first came to the United States in the 1600s when a damaged ship from Madagascar took refuge in the Charleston, South Carolina, harbor. In gratitude for help received, the story is told, the ship's captain presented Charleston's governor with a single sack of grain. Inside it were rice seeds.

Rice is a member of the cereal family, closely related to wheat, oats and barley. After it is harvested the stalks are bundled in sheaves and dried. The kernel is then removed by pounding and percussion. The favorite threshing technique in the Orient is to rattle the stalks against special mesh screens until the grains are loosened and they fall through the small openings in the screen. The separated grains, still encased in a loose fibrous hull, are then further pounded until this outer husk is removed. What remains is rice still fused to its inner skin, or bran coat. This is known as brown rice.

If the milling process then continues, the rice kernels are rubbed against revolving bands of leather or felt until the bran coat and some of the kernel starch is removed. This process is called polishing. The result is a whiter, lighter product known as white rice.

As in the case of wheat, the less the rice is refined the more nutrients remain. Witness: The section removed in the polishing, the bran coat, contains 10 percent of the rice's protein, 75 percent of its minerals, a majority of its niacin and riboflavin, and practically all its thiamine. Since brown rice is an excellent source of thiamine, without which people develop beriberi, among other diseases, this alone should be enough to discourage polishing.

Choline, another crucial vitamin substance, is lavishly laced throughout the unpolished rice grain. Along with the many benefits it brings to the constitution, choline acts as a fat and cholesterol emulsifier, literally eating up excess fats in the bloodstream, and holding the blood-cholesterol level in check as a result. Another effect of this cleansing process is that fatty deposits that build up in the liver are also kept under control. (Choline supplements, for this reason, are frequently given to people with an alcohol problem, both to prevent and later to control cirrhosis of the liver.) Since most of the other foods that choline naturally comes in, foods like liver, yeast, turnip and spinach greens, soybeans and organ meat, are all regulars on most people's food hate list, unpolished brown rice remains one of the most agreeable foods in which this important nutrient is available.

Is cosmetic appearance the only reason rice is polished? Not entirely. Fortunately there is at least a touch of method in the madness. As Dr. Rudolph Ballentine points out in his classic work, *Diet and Nutrition,** it is difficult to believe that billions of people throughout the world, including many of the poor and starving, would bother to hand-pound their meager rice supplies each day for hours at a time simply to improve the looks of the rice. According to Dr. Ballentine, research has shown that despite nutrient loss in polishing, certain vital substances, protein in particular, are somehow increased. This extra nutrition is especially important in countries such as India where meat is not widely eaten and where rice is the primary protein.

Dr. Ballentine goes on to say that in India, where lightly polished rice is a staple, folk wisdom has circumvented the problem of nutrient loss in an ingenious way. The traditional Indian method is to steam or boil the rice first, *then* to husk it. Besides loosening the husk so that it can easily be stripped from the kernel, this technique drives the important nutrients deep into the central flesh of the grain. Here the nutrients remain safe from the polishing process, which removes only the grain's outer skin.

This system is known as parboiling, and it seems to work. According to Dr. Ballentine, beriberi is practically unknown on the Indian subcontinent even though polished rice is the norm there. The only documented cases of the disease in India have been found in sections of Madras, and these areas, it turns out, are the only parts of India where the people do *not* parboil their rice before polishing it.

* Rudolph Ballentine, M.D., *Diet and Nutrition, a Holistic Approach* (Honesdale, Pa: The Himalayan International Institute, 1982), p. 78.

Rice: A Food for All Seasons

Like the Eskimos who make use of every conceivable part of the whale, Easterners consider rice *the* all-purpose item. Besides serving as an excellent starch at mealtime, it can be pounded into flakes, then packed into a knapsack and eaten along the trail. In Nepal, when traders go on long journeys, they fill their packs with this crushed rice, which they call *chura*. Crossing some of the world's most difficult terrain, they live on a diet of *chura* supplemented only by mangoes and a few dried vegetables. You can make your own *chura* if you like. Start with a half cupful of cooked brown rice. Spread the rice evenly on a cookie sheet and place it in a 200 degree oven for about thirty minutes, or until the grains are thoroughly dried. Then remove and with any handy pounding device—a mortar and pestle is best—mash the rice until all the grains are flaked. That's all there is to it. The mashing loosens the rice grains so they become easy to chew and digest. They also get lighter in the grinding process and hence more transportable and imperishable. Next time you head overland take a batch of *chura* with you. It's curiously crunchy and filling, and surprisingly sustaining.

Rice can also be fermented into wine—think of *sake*—or congealed into rice cakes or ground into flour. The chaff is excellent feed for animals, and in some regions oils are extracted from the bran and used for cooking or making soap. Starch extracted from rice is used in cosmetics and as a laundry starch. In Japan the rice hulls are burned in winter as a fuel— recently a rural Japanese inventor developed a car that runs on burned rice hulls—and in Korea the rice straw is mixed with mortar to fashion hard adobe bricks. Asians use rice sheaths to make hats, fans, shoes, raincoats, purses, screens. They thatch their roofs with rice sheaths. They make rope out of them. The list goes on.

As important as rice's household and food value is, it also functions as a kind of dietary medicine. Because rice is a starch that breaks down slowly and evenly in the blood, it is an excellent food for hypoglycemics. Measurements have shown that 50 percent less insulin is required to digest a large serving of rice than is needed to digest a small potato. Since it contains less protein than wheat, rice is often included in protein-restricted diets, mainly because its protein includes many essential amino acids, and because it combines so well with other carbohydrates. And, of course, for B-vitamin deficiency diseases such as beriberi and pellagra, rice has the status of a magic cure-all.

For followers of macrobiotics, the Japanese-inspired diet cum spiritual philosophy (see page 216), rice is *the* curative food, an aid for practically every physical problem from schizophrenia to the common cold. Practitioners of macrobiotics have worked out a number of special rice-based diets, each numbered according to its potency and the benefits it bestows. Though often maligned by the Western medical establishment, macrobiotics has nonetheless logged many astonishing—and well documented— medical cures, sometimes healing the most intractable diseases, including cancer. These cures are largely due, its proponents claim quite openly, to the power of grains and specifically to the curative qualities of rice.

Finally, rice can also be made into flour, and in this form it can be used to create new culinary delights. Here are some good examples.

HONEY RICE COOKIES

½ cup butter	½ cup raisins
5 tablespoons honey	2 eggs
¼ teaspoon salt	½ teaspoon vanilla
½ cup chopped pecans	1 cup rice flour

1. Mix the butter and honey. Add the salt, nuts and raisins, and stir thoroughly.
2. Whip the eggs in a bowl and add the vanilla. Continuing to stir add the rice flour, a little at a time. Then combine with butter and honey mixture. Place the batter in the refrigerator until it is thoroughly chilled.
3. Remove and dollop out two dozen cookies onto a cookie sheet. Bake at 350 degrees for 15 minutes, or until the cookies are done.

CARROLL/DE PERSIS RICE FLOUR COFFEE CAKE

2 cups rice flour	1 tablespoon grated lemon rind
½ teaspoon sea salt	2 eggs, well beaten
4 teaspoons baking powder	1 cup whole milk
⅓ cup honey	2 teaspoons vanilla
½ cup raisins	

TOPPING INGREDIENTS:

4 tablespoons butter	1½ teaspoons cinnamon
4 tablespoons honey	1 egg

1. Sift the flour, salt and baking powder into a mixing bowl. Stir in honey, raisins and grated lemon rind.
2. In another bowl mix together eggs, milk and vanilla. Add these to the flour mixture and stir until the batter is smooth.
3. To prepare the topping, melt the butter in a separate pan and add

the honey and cinnamon to it while butter melts. Remove this mixture from the heat and beat in an egg.

4. Pour the batter into a buttered 8″ shallow baking dish. Dribble the honey-butter topping over the batter.

5. Place in oven and bake at 350 degrees for 30 minutes, or until ready.

The Best Way to Boil Rice

Boiling rice is an art. Each country in the Orient has its own special lore concerning which variety tastes best, which must be cooked longer, whether the long-grained variety is superior to the shorter. But despite the hair splitting that does go on among aficionados, there is, nonetheless, something of a consensus on the basic do's and don'ts.

First, make sure the rice has been cleaned several times before cooking. Place it in a sieve or a colander with small holes and hold it under cool running water for a minute or two, then pour the rice into a pot of clear lukewarm water. Let it soak for a few minutes (this softens the rice as well as cleans it), drain the water off, then drain once or twice again until the rinse water no longer turns murky.

Now take a cupful of rice—this will feed two or three people as part of a main dish—and pour it into a medium-sized cooking pot. Cover the rice with approximately two inches of water. Turn the heat up to full and bring the water to a boil, then turn the heat down to a low simmer and cook for about fifty minutes. While simmering, do *not* stir the rice. Stirring will cause the rice to congeal, sacrificing both lightness and flavor. Some people like to add a teaspoonful or two of sea salt or a bouillon cube to the rice while it's boiling, though purists prefer their rice unseasoned.

If the water cooks out of the pot before the rice is ready, add extra water; or, if you prefer, let the grains on the bottom get a little burned. This will add a warm, nutty taste to the flavor of the rice. Whatever your choice, after several tries you'll get a feel for precisely how much water should go into the pot relative to your cooking time and the amount of heat you use. Generally the rice is ready when it is, to steal a phrase from pasta lovers, *al dente,* that is, soft but firm. Again, it's a matter of personal taste. You'll discover what you like best by experience.

Experiment. Try cooking different varieties of rice in different ways. Try parboiling it and pressure-cooking it. Rice cooked in a lot of water at very low temperatures for several hours is especially soft and tender. Rice cooked quickly is stiffer but has its own taste virtues. Talk to other cooks, especially macrobiotic cooks, who are expert on the subject. One thing is certain: No matter how much you may be accustomed to polished white rice right now, if you switch to brown rice and stay with it for a few weeks you'll understand why people make such a fuss over it. You'll never go back to that white stuff again.

A Short Dictionary of Rice Terms

Congee—A short-grained rice used in China for making puddings and desserts.

Mochi—A Japanese rice cake, often used as a staple for diabetics and as a nourishment for new mothers having difficulty with lactation. It is prepared by first cleaning sweet, glutenous brown rice and letting it soak for a day and a night. The rice is steamed for three hours, removed from heat, dried, and pounded flat in a mortar and pestle. It is then shaped into rice balls or a flat cake. It can be toasted, fried, or added to soups.

Precooked rice—Packaged rice that has been cooked before it is polished. Besides cooking rapidly it tends to have a higher protein and mineral content than regular polished white rice. This is due to the fact that in the precooking some of the nutrients are driven into the center of the grain and are not lost in the milling.

Rice cream—Ground, toasted rice that is usually cooked with milk (or water) and salt and is eaten as a cereal or thick broth. Make your own by grinding cooked rice to a coarse consistency in a blender, then roasting it in the oven for a few minutes. Try it for breakfast this way:

RICE CREAM

2 cups milk	**½ cup ground, toasted**
1 teaspoon sea salt	**rice**

1. Bring the milk to a boil and add salt. Turn down heat and slowly add the ground, toasted rice, stirring as you go. Let the mixture simmer for 15 minutes, stirring occasionally.

2. When the mixture has thickened it is ready to eat. You can sprinkle sesame seeds over the top and serve with a little honey and milk,

Rice milk—The cooked, strained waters of slow-boiled rice, often fed to infants who have difficulty tolerating milk. Make it in the following way: Take one cup of rice and seven cups of water. Cook the mixture over very low heat for at least two hours. Then place the cooked rice in a piece of cheesecloth and filter the liquid through the cloth into a pot. Boil the strained liquid over low heat for about an hour. The resulting potion is a healthful drink for convalescents and a tonic for weak stomachs.

Wild rice—A cultivated grass plant that, though it grows in aquatic areas and has a long, ricelike grain, is actually from a different biological family than rice. It grows abundantly in the watery areas near the Great Lakes and has been harvested by Indians for centuries. Wild rice is considered a great delicacy by gourmets, and goes well when cooked with regular brown rice. Both its protein content and iron supply are greater than that of regular brown rice. Here is an excellent natural gourmet recipe. Use it for your most special dining occasions.

WILD RICE SUPREME

1 cup wild rice	15 finely chopped mushrooms
6 cups homemade chicken	1 teaspoon butter
stock or water	½ bunch finely chopped parsley
1 teaspoon sea salt (optional)	Salt and pepper
1 small finely chopped onion	
2 carrots, peeled and chopped	

1. Boil the wild rice in the stock or, if you prefer, vegetarian style, in 6 cups of water with the sea salt added. Cook it for a minimum of 30 minutes and a maximum of 45; the idea is to find the point where the rice becomes its fluffiest and lightest. Generally the longer the grain the better the wild rice and the more cooking time it requires. After cooking, drain the rice and let it stand 10 minutes. It will puff up considerably.

2. Sauté the onion, carrots, and mushrooms in butter until tender, adding the parsley last. Mix into the rice and serve. Add salt and pepper to taste.

3. One of the nice things about this recipe is that you can sauté the vegetables in the afternoon and set them aside in a covered dish till dinner. Then, when the time is right, simply cook the wild rice as per the directions above, and when ready, quickly heat the sautéed vegetables, combine all together, and serve.

CORN

Like wheat and rice, corn is a versatile plant. Its cobs are burned as fuel, its husks are fed to domestic animals, its kernels are used to make liquor, syrup, popcorn, oil, cereals and flour. Every part of the plant is utilized, sometimes in surprising ways. Industrially, its stalk is employed in the manufacture of wallboard and insulation; the cobs are used to make charcoal. And what more American item than the corncob pipe?

Nutritionally corn is less potent than some of its relatives in the grain family, and in parts of the world where people exist upon it as a staple, pellagra, a niacin deficiency disease, is not unknown. In 1947 the Department of Agriculture set standards for enriching many corn-derived products, and the various southern states where cornmeal, grits and hominy are staples followed suit, making it law that iron and B vitamins be added back to refined cornmeal and flour.

Corn on the cob—the more freshly picked the better, of course—does supply fairly good amounts of thiamine, riboflavin, magnesium and some vitamin A. The germ of the inner kernel contains protein plus vitamin E. And since almost a quarter of the sweet corn kernel is sugar, this makes it a fast-energy food. Still, it may be said that the greatest attractions of corn are the ease with which it can be grown and its incomparably sweet flavor, *not* its great nutritive value. Those who live on a diet rich in this grain should be certain to complement their meals with generous portions of salads, legumes and fresh vegetables, to supply the vitamins and minerals not found in corn.

A Cornmeal Sampler

Cornmeal is corn that has been ground and milled. It is a form of flour, if you will. As with wheat and rice, commercial cornmeal is frequently degermed, overheated and stripped of its essential proteins, fiber and vitamins. As most of the corn used to make cornmeal is a variety called "flour corn," which is extremely starchy and rather low in protein to begin with, processing simply adds insult to injury.

Shop for the unprocessed varieties. The package label will tell you how refined or unrefined the contents are. Despite the fact that cornmeal is less nutritious than other grain flours, the whole-grain kind still has enough substance to make your stomach happy, and its uses are almost endless. Try a few of these old standards.

CORNMEAL MUSH

4 cups milk	**1 teaspoon sea salt**
1 cup cornmeal	

1. Scald the milk. Then slowly stir it into the cornmeal, along with the salt, until the batter has a creamy consistency.

2. Cook in a double boiler for 30 minutes, giving an occasional stir. Serve as a breakfast cereal with warm milk or cream over the top. Some people like to add a little honey as well.

POLENTA

1 tablespoon refined oil	Pinch of nutmeg
6 cups water	Pinch of cayenne pepper
1½ cups cornmeal	1½ tablespoons butter (optional)
Pinch of sea salt	½ cup freshly grated Parmesan
1 teaspoon paprika	

1. Grease the inside of a saucepan with oil. Add water and bring to a boil.

2. Add cornmeal, salt, paprika, nutmeg and cayenne to water, stirring until they are well blended.

3. Bring the mixture to a rapid boil for several minutes, stirring constantly, then reduce the heat to a simmer and cook for 30 minutes. Serve with a pat of butter in the center (if desired), and sprinkle liberally with the freshly grated cheese. Polenta, an Italian dish, goes well with meats or stands alone as a cereal.

POLENTA VEGETABLE SOUP

Here is a further use for polenta. Prepare the polenta as above, leaving out the nutmeg, butter and cheese. Then follow the recipe below. This soup makes a particularly robust meal for cold winter nights.

1 teaspoon oil	1 sectioned turnip
6 cups water or homemade	2 chopped carrots
chicken stock	1 stalk celery, chopped
2 chopped scallions	½ cup cooked polenta

1. Place the oil into a saucepan, then add water (or stock), scallions, turnip, carrots and celery, and sauté for 30 minutes, or until vegetables are tender.

2. Prepare polenta as above, without the nutmeg, butter and cheese, then add it to the soup and boil for 10 minutes. Serve with homemade bread.

HASTY PUDDING

1 cup cornmeal	3 cups milk
2 tablespoons yeast	

1. Mix the cornmeal, yeast and one cup of milk together until they reach a creamy consistency.

2. In a double boiler heat the rest of the milk to a boil. Add the cornmeal mixture and stir. Cook in the double boiler until the milk has evaporated and the pudding reaches the desired thickness.

STEAMED CORN BREAD

1 teaspoon baking powder	4 cups cornmeal
½ teaspoon sea salt	¾ cup rice flour
4 tablespoons honey	4 eggs
2½ cups milk	1 tablespoon butter

1. Combine the baking powder, salt, honey and milk in a bowl. Stir until well dissolved. Slowly mix in the cornmeal and the rice flour, stirring until batter comes to an even consistency.

2. Beat one egg for 30 seconds, then add to above mixture, along with the butter. Separate 3 eggs, beat the whites for a minute, then add whites to mixture. Fold in eggs, butter and egg whites until evenly distributed.

3. Preheat the oven to 250 degrees. Place the batter in a pie pan and bake for 20 to 30 minutes, or until the corn bread seems done.

MILLET

You've probably seen more millet in birdseed than on the dinner table. This is due less to any deficiency on the part of the millet grain itself than to recent eating fashions in the West. In many African and Oriental countries millet is a staple, and our food bias to the contrary, it makes a pleasant change of pace as a nutritious bread flour, a hearty breakfast porridge, or as a thickener for soups. Millet does tend to be a little less sweet than the other grains, however, and it may take one or two samplings before its complete range of virtues becomes apparent.

Nutritionally millet is endowed with a protein that contains almost all the essential amino acids. It has good supplies of iron and magnesium plus potassium, enough to put it in the category of a super-nutrient food. It is also low in gluten, making it a perfect wheat substitute.

To prepare basic cooked millet cereal, add one part cracked millet grain (available at natural food stores) to three and a half parts water. Let the mixture stand in a warm room overnight so that the grains fully expand. Next day put the millet and water on the stove and bring the mixture to a boil, then simmer for a half hour, or until the grain is soft. Strain and serve for breakfast with honey and cream. If you find the flavor of the millet too bland you can add a teaspoon of sea salt during the cooking. You'll probably need to experiment a little with preparing this grain as it tends to stick to the pan. Try adding a cup more water while it's boiling to solve this problem.

MILLET CHEESE CASSEROLE

This recipe is easy to prepare and helpful for vegetarians who want to get their complete protein in one dish. It is substantial enough to stand alone as a main dish.

1 cup cracked millet	½ cup finely diced strong
1 egg	Cheddar cheese
Several drops Tamari or soy	Freshly grated Parmesan
sauce	cheese

1. Prepare the millet as described above.
2. Add the egg, Tamari or soy sauce, and cheese. Stir. Place mixture is a preheated 225 degree oven for 5 minutes. Serve with fresh Parmesan cheese grated on top.

MILLET DESSERT

2 cups milk	1 orange
¼ cup honey	2 eggs
¼ cup cracked millet	½ teaspoon vanilla
1 lemon	

1. Warm the milk. Dissolve the honey in the milk, then add the cracked millet. Boil for 30 to 45 minutes, until grain is soft and porridge-like. Stir frequently.
2. Extract juices from the lemon and the orange. Add the beaten eggs to the millet mixture, stirring well, then place mixture on stove and simmer for another several minutes. Remove from heat, add vanilla and extracted juices, and give mixture a final stir. Chill in the refrigerator for several hours before serving.

BARLEY

Millet is a hard-skinned grain and difficult to overmill. Barley is hard-skinned too, but not hard enough to withstand the usual refining process.

As a result, the barley grains you purchase at the supermarket are really barley "pearls," the inner starchy part of the seed with the healthful outer skins removed. This starchy part is full of coupounds that break down into sugar, and not a great deal more. This is where, incidentally, the sugary taste in beer comes from—most of the barley grown in this country is used for brewing. On the whole the unrefined varieties of barley are better tasting and better for you.

Locating unrefined barley is no easy chore, however. You may have to special-order it from your natural food store, and even then not every dealer will know where to find it. It's worth the chase though. Unrefined barley has more protein, more iron, more calcium. If you absolutely cannot find a true unrefined product then look for the *partially refined* varieties. Some natural food stores carry such items, lightly milled barley with a bit of the bran left on. Something is better than nothing. If you really want to get serious about your barley hunt you can write to the mills listed in the Appendix, several of which from time to time lay in stores of unrefined barley grains. If they don't carry the product they will know who does.

Like several other grains, barley has medicinal as well as nutritional value. One of its most effective functions is as a stomach settler, both for children and adults. "Barley water" it's called. Making it is simple. Cook a cupful of barley in approximately a gallon of water for five hours over low heat. Strain off the barley to use as you please, then bottle the water and refrigerate. Keep it on hand for when you get an attack of gastritis, indigestion or a plain old bellyache. It's excellent warmed for children's stomach maladies and for colicky infants. It's also good for relieving that "stone in the stomach" feeling after overeating.

Another good way to use barley is in a stew.

STEW À LA BARLEY

10 cups homemade chicken stock or water	2 chopped scallions
1 cup split peas	2 stalks celery, chopped
½ cup barley	1 small clump parsley, chopped
¼ cup unrefined oil	½ teaspoon sea salt
2 chopped carrots	1 bay leaf
1 clove garlic, minced	2 teaspoons caraway seeds

1. Boil the stock. Then add the peas and barley. Simmer for an hour.

2. In a separate pan warm the oil and sauté the carrots, garlic, scallions and celery, adding the parsley during the last few minutes of cook-

ing. When the vegetables are soft, add them to the barley stock along with the salt and bay leaf. Cook for an hour. Then add the caraway seeds and cook on low heat for another 30 minutes.

RYE

Though rye is not eaten extensively in the United States, it is more familiar than many of the other grains because of its use in rye bread and rye whiskey. The fact is, ironically, that most rye breads actually contain only a small amount of rye flour; rye alone tends to make a rather heavy loaf and is at its best when blended with other grain flours to impart its unique, pleasantly sour taste. Pumpernickel rye is especially filling and delicious. Try a loaf.

PUMPERNICKEL BREAD

1 tablespoon dried yeast
1½ cups warm water
1 tablespoon salt
2½ teaspoons caraway seeds
½ cup molasses

2 tablespoons vegetable oil
2 cups rye flour or meal
4 cups whole-wheat flour
2 tablespoons cornmeal

1. Dissolve the yeast in the warm water. Wait several minutes, then add the salt, caraway seeds, molasses, oil and rye flour. Stir the dough until it reaches an even consistency.

2. Stir in 2 cups of whole-wheat flour. Place the dough on a floured breadboard and knead in the rest of the flour.

3. Cover bread. Let it rise on a bread board until it doubles in size. Knead for 5 minutes, then slice the dough into two loaves. Oil the surface of a baking sheet, dust it with the cornmeal, set the two loaves on it and let them rise for another hour.

4. Bake the loaves for 10 minutes at 450 degrees, then lower to 350 degrees and bake them for another 30 minutes. This pumpernickel goes well with hearty soups and with just about any main meal.

One of the great benefits of rye is its hardiness as a crop. Where other grains perish from cold or lack of fertile soil, the rye seed flourishes, and for this reason it is a staple in Russia and Scandinavia where cold nights outnumber warm days.

Unrefined rye flour comes rich in calcium, iron, magnesium, potassium, riboflavin and thiamine. It gives almost as much protein as whole-wheat flour and contains significant trace-mineral supplies. The cracked rye grains can be made into a breakfast cereal, or for a pleasant change, they will serve as a rice or potato substitute.

To cook rye, purchase the whole-grain groats from your natural food store, then boil a cupful with three cups liquid (either water or milk), giving the mixture at least forty-five minutes cooking time until the grain is soft. (If you let the grains soak in water overnight they will cook more thoroughly and quickly.) When serving as a breakfast cereal, cook the rye with milk rather than water, and drop in a pinch of sea salt during the boiling. Add raisins to the finished product, milk topping to taste, and a little honey.

OATS

Most of our exposure to oats has been at the breakfast table, mainly in the form of instant oatmeal cereal. While it is true that of all grains, oats retain the greatest number of nutrients after being processed, commercial cereal manufacturers nonetheless insist on precooking their oatmeal first, storing it for relatively long periods of time, then adding preservatives and sugar. None of this need be, as untampered-with oatmeal is easily located and simple to prepare.

Start by purchasing a bag of *steel-cut oats* at any natural food store. This is the most natural of all oat varieties. The oats have been hulled, sliced, and otherwise left unmilled and unadulterated.

If you can't find the steel-cut kind, *rolled oats* are a reasonably good substitute, though these have been flattened on high-heat-producing steel rollers that tend to reduce their nutritional content. *Flaked oats,* when you can find them, are not exposed to high heats during the milling and are generally more nutritious than rolled. (Steel-cut oats, it should be noted, are somewhat difficult to digest. People with particularly delicate digestive systems will be better off making their oatmeal with rolled-oat varieties.)

If you want to really make oatmeal taste good, toast the groats—the hulled oat grain—in a 375 degree oven for about ten minutes before boiling them, mixing them occasionally as they bake. You'll lose a few of the vitamins this way but not many. Remove the mixture from the oven and boil a cupful in three cups of water for thirty to forty minutes, or until it reaches that nice porridgelike consistency. Serve with milk, raisins, bananas, or slices of fresh apple.

In the nutrition department, oats, especially the flaked variety, have just about the highest protein content of any of the cereals. They are also endowed with reasonably good amounts of calcium, potassium, phosphorus and niacin. Their hardiness as a crop makes them a promising backyard project for any amateur agrarian, especially those who farm in the colder climates where oats thrive (it is no accident that porridge, oatmeal fritters, oat stew and mealie pudding, all made from oats, were originally developed on the chilly moors of Scotland).

Oatmeal cereal itself produces a mild, natural laxative effect, which, incidentally, is true of whole grains in general. Anyone who ups their daily intake of grains should notice an increase in regularity within a couple of days.

OATMEAL PANCAKES

1 cup rolled, steel-cut or flaked oats	1 teaspoon baking powder
2 cups milk	2 eggs, beaten
1½ cups whole-wheat flour	3 tablespoons butter, melted
½ teaspoon sea salt	2 teaspoons honey

1. If time permits, soak the oats overnight in the milk, keeping the mixture in the refrigerator. Next day mix in the flour, salt, baking powder, milk (if not used overnight), eggs, melted butter and honey.

2. Lightly butter a skillet, set heat at medium, and place pancake-sized scoops of the batter onto the skillet. Flip each pancake as it starts to bubble and brown. Serve with honey or pure maple syrup.

A standard natural breakfast cereal that also features oats is this delicious version of granola (recipe from Carroll-McBride Catering).

GRANOLA

⅓ cup unrefined oil	½ cup sunflower seeds
⅔ cup honey	½ cup freshly shredded coconut
6 cups oat flakes	1 cup raw peanuts
1 cup fresh wheat germ	1 cup sesame seeds, unhulled
Pinch sea salt	1 cup raisins

1. Mix together all the ingredients except the raisins, and spread them out on a baking sheet. Bake in a 300 degree oven for about 30 minutes, stirring mixture every 10 minutes or so.

2. Remove granola and allow to cool. Mix in the raisins. Store in a cool, dark area in a sealed glass jar.

Like other grains, oatmeal has its therapeutic uses. A dab of cooked oatmeal on a bee sting will quickly reduce the pain. The straw from the oat plant can be boiled for a half hour and taken as a tea, reputed to strengthen the heart and circulatory system. Or, you can place the tea or raw oats in bath water as a tonic to sensitive skin.

SUGARS

Sugar gives us life. Sugar kills us. Probably no food on our table is so controversial, so dangerous, so necessary and so unnecessary. It is the fundamental building material of our favorite vegetables, fruits, grains and dairy products. And yet it can be the harbinger of disease, malaise, and yes, even death. Why?

Take the life-giving side first.

As we have seen, all carbohydrates are composed of simple or complex sugar molecules. These include (1) the monosaccharides such as glucose, constructed from a single strand of sugar molecules and incapable of being broken down further during digestion; (2) the disaccharides, or double sugars—table sugar and lactose; and (3) the polysaccharides, starch and fiber, composed of large, more complex sugar chains that are less water soluble, more stable, and slower to break down in the intestines. All of these substances, no matter what their degree of molecular complexity, are *sugar*. All are absolutely necessary for your body's sustenance and welfare. Without them you perish.

Now for the bad news.

The problem begins with semantics. In most people's minds the word "sugar" means white table sugar. For the nutritionist, however, the term connotes multiple meanings: honey, for instance, or galactose and maltose, or the chemical components of starch. The problem with sugar (as with love, it might be said) is that there are so many varieties of it and only one word to describe them all.

So let's be specific. From now on, unless otherwise stated, when we speak of sugar we're referring to one type only: table sugar. The delectable, delicious, delirious, yummy white poison.

What's So Bad About Sugar?

There's no argument, of course, over the fact that it tastes good—although many years ago in Nepal I offered a twelve-year-old boy an

English candy bar, complete with raisins and nuts. The boy had never tasted chocolate before. Taking a large, enthusiastic bite, he spit the candy out with equal dispatch, howling that I was trying to poison him! One wonders how many of our cherished tastes are culturally learned. Be that as it may, sugar does seem to have a fairly universal appeal. But at the same time, it is necessary to weigh the evidence. On one side is sugar's delectability. On the other is a fistful of reasons why it will poison you. You be the judge. Here's the list.

1. Sugar Is Not a Real Food

Question: Exactly what is a food? Answer: Any substance that provides nourishment for the human body. Question: What are the components of nourishment? Answer: The things we've been talking about throughout—protein, fats, vitamins, minerals, and so on.

Now have a look at the vitamins, minerals and so forth present in white sugar (table, page 67). This chart is based on data issued by the United States Department of Agriculture.

Hmmmmm. Doesn't take much figuring to see that the sum total of nutrients in sugar is a good deal less than one milligram per eating ounce. How small is a milligram? Well, one milligram is a thousandth part of a gram. And there are 28.3 grams in an ounce. Figure it from there. Don't be fooled either by the numbers for sodium and potassium. Sodium is nothing but salt (yes, even sugar contains a little salt), and is present in a microscopic dose. Ditto the potassium. As one writer noted, there is more potassium in the paper on this page than in an ounce of sugar.

In other words, when you are eating sugar you are technically eating nothing. This is not, by the way, the fact as far as the digestive apparatus is concerned. To the stomach and the intestines sugar is *very* real, as we shall see, and can cause perverse problems when it comes visiting. But from the standpoint of cellular nourishment sugar simply does not exist. It is a nonfood.

What about sugar cane? it might be asked. Seems we've all heard at one time or another how fresh cane is so good for you, and how sucking the raw stalk is helpful for the digestion and the teeth, and how on plantations the bosses who eat refined sugar get diabetes and the workers who eat the cane don't.

All of these reports are by and large true. But remember, the sugar you buy at the store is *refined* sugar. It is sugar cane that has been denatured—heated, filtered, rubbed, evaporated, clarified, had its color removed, and then adulterated with such mouth-waterers as lime and

Table of Nutrients Present in Sucrose (Table Sugar)
(milligrams per 1 ounce)

Substance	Amount
Protein	0
Fats	0
Vitamin A	0
Vitamin C	0
Vitamin D	0
Vitamin E	0
Niacin	0
Thiamine	0
Riboflavin	0
Calcium	0
Iron	0
Sodium	.24
Potassium	.76
Phosphorus	0

diatomaceous earth. All of the cane's natural nutrients are whisked away in the process and the leftovers are bottled and sold at fancy prices under the name of molasses. In this way the manufacturers double their product *and* their profits.

Let's look at another chart, this one a comparison of the food values found in refined sugar and in the molasses stolen from sugar cane during refinement. The table on page 68 is taken from *Diet for a Small Planet* by Frances Moore Lappé, who adapted it from a government handbook on the composition of foodstuffs.

Here at a glance is where the goodness goes when your cane sugar is refined. The manufacturer, selling the sugar and the molasses, makes it both ways. And you, the consumer, are left with less than half of what was there to start with.

But wait. That's just the beginning.

2. Sugar Robs the Body of Precious Vitamins and Minerals

As if it wasn't bad enough that sugar contributes absolutely no nutrition to the body, it also *steals nutrients that are already there.*

When sugar reaches your digestive tract it uses a certain number of vitamins and minerals in order to be metabolized, plus small amounts of protein and fat. As it burns up these vital materials, however, it fails to

Refined Sugar and Molasses Compared
(milligrams per 3½ ounces)

Vitamins and minerals	In Molasses	In Sugar
Calcium	684	0
Phosphorus	84	0
Iron	16	0
Sodium	96	1
Potassium	2,927	3
Thiamine	.11	0
Riboflavin	.19	0
Niacin	2	0

replace them with equivalent energies. Like a parasite, it takes but gives nothing back.

Especially significant are the supplies of B vitamins that the sugar demon gobbles up as it courses through the body. An hour after taking in a load of sweets your supplies of these vitamins can be lowered by as much as half. B vitamins are partly responsible for the maintenance of the brain and nervous system, and when large amounts are depleted from the body various nervous disorders may result such as irritability, headache and depression, all part of a spectrum of reactions that is sometimes called the "sugar blues."

If this nutritional thievery is allowed to continue too long, moreover, a condition eventually develops that Dr. Rudolph Ballentine terms "nutritional debt." * This means that while a person may technically meet his or her carbohydrate requirements by eating sweets, that person still "owes" himself or herself a corresponding amount of vitamins, minerals, fats and proteins to make up for the amounts stolen by the sugar. The more a person indulges in sugar the larger this debt becomes.

Eventually the deficit becomes so great that rather sizable amounts of vitamins and minerals get removed from the cells and the body begins to weaken. All the excess sugar that pours into the system can no longer be burned away at the same time and is transformed into fatty adipose tissue. Thus, even while a person may be gaining weight, he or she is simultaneously losing the valuable food components that constitute good health. In the end a strange condition occurs. The person becomes obese *and* malnourished. An odd combination one might say, but a common one in Western countries where sugar has become a staple.

* Ballentine, pp. 59–60.

3. Sugar Wreaks Havoc in the Digestive System

While natural sweeteners like honey or rice syrup have been around for ages, white sugar is new to the human biological experience. Just several centuries ago, before the coming of mechanical refining, it took endless hours to separate crystals of sugar from their brown coating. This made white sugar an important status symbol, like white bread and white rice, a luxury for captains and kings. A pound of granulated sucrose in 1600 was as costly as a pound of gold today.

With the invention of refining techniques all this changed. Sugar plantations in the Caribbean sidelined their rum business with the lucrative exportation of white sugar and molasses. By the middle of the nineteenth century a mammoth sugar-refining industry had risen in the United States. By the middle of the twentieth, profits had passed the $6-billion-a-year mark, profits well supported by the power of the American sugar conglomerates whose lobby in Washington made certain that importation of any foreign refined sugar was illegal.

Improvements in refining techniques, aided by massive advertising and an incredibly thorough distribution network, then went to work, inspiring a craving for sweets in this country the likes of which had never been seen on earth. Before long sugar was on every American table, shoulder to shoulder with the salt and pepper, and was included as a matter of course in dozens of foods that for centuries had gotten along quite nicely without it.

But though sugar became an American staple in record time, thanks to the powers of media and manufacturing, internally, in the human gut, hundreds of thousands of evolutionary years had not prepared these organs to deal with this strange new substance.

To understand the full implications of this, let's go inside the body for a moment and follow the journey of a teaspoonful of white sugar through the digestive system.

As we've seen, sugar contains no nutrients. This means there's really nothing in it to absorb or assimilate. At the same time, since the organs of digestion are wired to respond to *any* carbohydrate, nutritious or not, when sugar is received in the digestive tract its "carbohydrateness" immediately sends a chemical message to the pancreas, saying "Big rise in blood-sugar level! Must be a hefty carbohydrate load, probably a serving of starch, a potato or hunk of bread. Better get busy!"

So the pancreas rushes a load of insulin into the blood to keep blood sugar at an even level—this is insulin's job, to stabilize blood-sugar level. But since the sucrose is only a kind of phantom blip on the radar screen, by the time the insulin arrives at the liver ready to go to work on what it thinks will be a major load of glucose, the sugar has already burned itself out and disappeared.

The insulin, nonetheless, is now on an inexorable mission. After removing what remains of the sucrose, it turns to the sugar *already present in the blood* and metabolizes this too, sending it to the liver to be stored as glycogen. In the process the blood-sugar level is quickly, violently and needlessly lowered. Hence, sudden low blood-sugar crash.

Now let's see what happens in the outer world, to the person himself. This hungry soul takes his spoonful of sugar, perhaps in the form of a candy bar or piece of chocolate cake. As his blood-sugar level rises he gets a surge of energy and his appetite is sated. He feels great. Within a few minutes, however, as the insulin gushes into the blood and devours the sugar, his blood-sugar level plummets down, down, down in roller-coaster fashion and he begins to feel listless, out of sorts, even hungry again. The only remedy, he reckons, is more sugar. This will make him feel energized again, for sure. And then, of course, he'll need more sugar after that. And more, and more, and more . . .

So you see, sugar literally tricks the digestive organs into a frenzy of busy work, all of it useless and destructive. Nor does the mischief stop here. There is some evidence that once sugar gets into the system, traces of it remain permanently, causing pyruvic acid to accumulate in nerve tissue, causing destruction of brain cells, and slowing down the process of cellular oxidation. The liver, glutted with so much glycogen from the excess sugar, starts to develop fatty tissue and slowly swells to an abnormal size. Elsewhere, calcium is leached from the bones by sugar deposits. The entire skeletal system is weakened. The digestion is impaired.*

The list goes on. But you get the point.

4. Sugar Is Hidden in More Than Half the Foods You Eat; You Cannot Escape It, Like It or Not

Think this is an exaggeration? Here's a partial list of supermarket items in which sucrose is found:

meat	almost all canned soups
canned fruits and vegetables	beer, wine, liquor
bread	mayonnaise
nondairy creamer	salt
some smoked foods	olives
certain cheeses	artificial sweeteners
hot dogs	peanut butter

* Judy Goeltz, *Natural Food Guide and Cookbook* (Salt Lake City: Hawkes Publishing Co., 1981), pp. 29–30.

baby food
ketchup
bouillon cubes
pickles
most breakfast cereals
all cured foods
jams and jellies
pasta
salad dressing

canned clams
mustard
tomato sauce
pancake mix
almost all frozen entrées and
   TV dinners
cigarettes
vitamin pills

And almost all fast foods—pizza, burgers, fried chicken and the like
—contain hefty portions of sugar too.

This is only a sampling. Check the listings yourself on the side of the
bottle or package.

Don't let the sneaky jargon on the labels fool you. Manufacturers
sometimes substitute the term "corn syrup" for sugar in hopes that you'll
think it's some kind of healthy vegetable derivative. Forget it. The two are
more or less the same thing. Likewise with "beet sugar," "dextrose,"
"kleenraw," "raw sugar," "cane syrup," "invert sugar," "pure cane
sugar," "turbinado sugar," "muscovado sugar." They're all fancy cam-
ouflage for plain old sugar. The fact is that a hefty part of most people's
diet, more, we blush to say, than *a fifth of the daily menu,* is made up of
sugar. Margo Blevin and Geri Ginder in *The Low Blood Sugar Cookbook*
make this point with a vengeance in their chronicle of a typical American's
daily meals:

> For breakfast, begin with an instant fruit drink (sugar), presweetened
> cereal (sugar, starch), with milk, toast (starch, sugar) and jam (sugar),
> and perhaps a cup of cocoa (sugar, chocolate). Then on to lunch: a can
> of soup (sugar, starch), a sandwich of bologna (sugar, corn syrup solids,
> dextrose), two pieces of bread (starch, sugar), and mayonnaise (sugar).
> Milk or soda (sugar, possibly caffeine) just wouldn't taste right unless
> accompanied by cookies (starch, sugar), and possibly canned fruit (in
> thick sugar syrup). Dinner might consist of some frozen fish cakes (starch,
> sugar), tartar sauce (sugar), salad with bottled salad dressing (sugar), and
> canned peas (sugar). Don't even mention dessert: it's about 90 percent
> sugar, whatever it is. Later, there will be TV snacks of popcorn (starch),
> pretzels (starch), and candy, for "energy" or reward.

The world consumes 32 billion pounds of sugar a year. Americans
eat 129 pounds of the stuff per person per annum. The average American
child takes in 15 pounds a year in candy bars alone. He or she washes it
down with about 600 sodas, an average of almost two a day. The white

bread we purchase at the supermarket is approximately 10 percent sugar. Many breakfast cereals, including some of the so-called "health" kinds, are almost 50 percent sugar. Some imitation fruit juices and breakfast drinks are almost 100 percent sugar! Sugar is the number-one additive in American food, used far more frequently than any spice, herb or preservative you can think of. It is ubiquitous. Inescapable. And most of it comes disguised, hidden in the box, in the grain, in the gravy, in the syrup, in the coating, in the paper, in the water, on the tricky label.

Sugar Is Addictive

Sugar's advocates insist there is no scientific evidence to prove that sucrose is physically addictive. They say that a penchant for sweets is natural to all humankind. According to this line of thought sugar's universal appeal is based not on cultural conditioning but on a fundamental biological drive whereby we select from our natural environment the most eatable foods—which are usually the sweet foods such as fruits, grains, vegetables, dairy products—and avoid the poisonous ones, which by and large are bitter (one of the rules followed by wild-food foragers is that if a plant tastes good it is probably safe; if it tastes bitter it is probably poison).

Technically, there is some truth in this. Sugar does have a broad appeal to the human palate. And if we take addiction in its most formal sense, whereby sudden deprivation of a substance causes severe withdrawal symptoms, then no, sugar is not physically addictive.

As most of us understand, however, there are degrees in everything, including addiction. A person can be addicted to a substance without being driven mad by it. Or becoming deathly ill for lack of it.

The fact is that most of us who have been eating sugar since it was introduced to our tender palates by those kindly folks at the baby-food factories find it an *extremely* difficult item to give up. The ultimate case, of course, is the "sugarholic," who may go through a physical mini withdrawal if deprived of his daily quota, complete with shaking and nausea. Even those more temperate in their sugar habit, however, suffer from the lack when deprived. After a dinner that is missing some kind of sugar, one feels unfilled. Without dessert the meal may seem incomplete. Without a soda in the afternoon, the energy level dips. Without sugar to garnish the grapefruit or cereal, breakfast seems stale. Really, for many of us sugarless eating just doesn't seem like eating anymore. In short, most of us are addicted.

For our purposes then, an additive food is any food that (1) causes a dependence; (2) causes a physical and/or mental craving when withdrawn.

And sugar clearly fits the picture. Not like beets or lettuce, for instance, or carrots, olives or cream. While we'd probably miss all of these if they were taken away we might not *crave* them. But we would crave sugar. Sometimes to a surprisingly intense degree.

If you think this is an exaggeration, try it yourself. Drop sugar—*all* sugar—from your diet for two weeks and study your reaction. Start now, today, immediately. Next meal leave the sugar out of your coffee or tea. Forget the sweet dessert. Keep away from any recipe that calls for two heaping cups of maple syrup. Pass up the mints at the restaurant counter. Steer clear of sweet snacks between meals. Don't chew sugared gum. Then see how you feel. If eating just doesn't seem like eating anymore, and if you have an itching drive to say the heck with the whole experiment and race down to the ice-cream store, then you know: You're an addict. But don't worry, you're in good company. Approximately three-quarters of the country is in the same predicament.

Sugar Substitutes: The Real Story

Saccharin

First, the saccharin story. Saccharin is derived from coal tar. This is the same substance used to make bug balms, perfumes and creosote. It was discovered approximately a century ago and was promptly removed from consumption when its obvious harmful properties were recognized.

Then, according to Dr. David Reuben's amusing account,* it was as swiftly returned to the marketplace because Teddy Roosevelt was on a diet. The great man, it seems, was trying to lose some of the extra pounds that had plagued him all his life. Like so many of us today, he had dropped sugar from his menu and was using saccharin instead. Things were going well, reducing-wise, until one day T. R. was rudely informed that his favorite artificial sweetener had been banned from the scene. Immediately he flew into a rage—so the story goes—and called for a committee to look into the matter. The head of this appointed group, it then happened to turn out, was one Ira Remsen, the man who discovered saccharin in the first place. The outcome of the investigation need hardly be questioned. Within a year or so the product was quietly returned to the market, and there it has remained to this day, poisoning more people than the substance it replaces.

Saccharin has long been linked to cancer, so convincingly that it is

---

* David Reuben, M.D., *Everything You Always Wanted to Know About Nutrition* (New York: Avon Books, 1978), p. 190.

banned in a number of countries, including several behind the Iron Curtain. In 1950 tests showed that the bladders of rats exposed to large doses of saccharin quickly become cancerous. Supporters of the artificial-sweetener industry quickly sloughed off the findings. Two decades later several studies produced similar results, while tests in Canada demonstrated that people who eat saccharin are *twice* as likely to develop cancer as those who don't. Many subsequent tests have confirmed these findings.

One thing that is certain about saccharin is that pregnant women and very young children should avoid it entirely; many studies indicate that both the fetus and the newborn are particularly vulnerable to its effects. Also, as a kind of cruel irony to the whole question, there is, according to Jane Brody,* "some evidence that saccharin stimulates the appetite and interferes with blood sugar reduction, suggesting that it may be counterproductive in weight-control and diabetes."

Researchers at the University of Delaware † have found that once the body is accustomed to sweeteners of *any* kind, the insulin response is approximately the same to substitute sucrose as it is to real. This means, if these scientists are correct, that the blood-sugar level will be adversely affected by saccharin as much as by any surrogate sweetener.

Ironically, some saccharin products, especially the powdered sweeteners, contain up to 80 or 90 percent dextrose—sugar—as a base. It has the exact same effect as sucrose.

All things considered, the saccharin story is bleak. In the murky, serpentine world of food testing and regulation, it is true there has not been absolute, total, incontrovertible proof that saccharin causes disease. There rarely is such proof for any carcinogen, not surprising since we don't really understand what cancer is in the first place. Still, the question can be asked: If substantial doubt exists, might it not be better to play it safe and avoid this substance entirely? Especially if it has no nutritive value whatsoever, and no reason for being in the human digestive system in the first place?

Raw Sugar

Raw sugar is cane sugar with some (and only on the rarest occasion all) of its outer nutritious coating left intact. Hence, its supporters argue, it is better for our health.

This would be more or less true if not for the fact that most raw sugar

* Jane Brody, *Jane Brody's Nutrition Book* (New York: Norton & Co., 1981), p. 484.
† "Science News Letter," April 29, 1961.

sold in the United States has been refined almost as much as white table sugar. The fact that it is brown or gray or off-white, moreover, is no guarantee of its rawness. It simply means that a little of the original coating has been left on. Usually a very little. Some manufacturers even color their sugar brown to give it a more "natural" look.

Real raw sugar is made by extracting the water from the cane juice and allowing the remains to solidify. The end product is simply crystallized sugar cane, sometimes known as "rock candy" or "rock sugar."

But the real surprise is that real raw sugar is illegal in the United States. You can't buy it anyway, no matter what the labels tell you. The prosecution claims that unprocessed cane contains dirt particles, insect wings, wax and other impurities. Sounds right. But it is still a relatively simple matter to remove this debris without refining away all the sugar cane's food value in the process.

In reality the reason behind this pseudo altruism is not to protect you, the consumer, but to shelter the sugar-refining industries in this country that have such a large investment in your continued willingness to eat their processed product. If real unrefined sugar was made legal in America, there would be an alternative to the more expensive white sugar, and manufacturers' profits would drop. It's as simple as that.

Be that as it may, the point is that raw sugar sounds like a good idea. And it would be a good idea, or at least a better idea, if you could get the real thing. But unfortunately anything you're likely to buy over the counter under that name—or under other names such as "turbinado sugar," "Yellow-D," "Demara sugar" and so forth—is mostly sucrose with a thin brown overcoat on for good looks.

Brown Sugar

A little better but only a little. Brown sugar is 100 percent sucrose with a smidgen of molasses poured over it. How beneficial it is depends on how much molasses has been added—the nutrition is in the molasses— and how refined the sugar is beneath it. Commercial brown is usually bad news on both counts. A little molasses has been added to a lot of refined sugar, usually about 95 percent. If you are trying to cut down on sucrose, brown sugar is a poor substitute.

Molasses

There are plenty of nutrients here, potassium, some trace minerals and most of the B vitamins, with the exception of thiamine and folic acid, which are destroyed in the heating process. Also, an abundance of iron (which is why molasses is sometimes prescribed for menstruating women) and about as much calcium in three spoonfuls as you might get in eight eggs.

Of all the molasses varieties, blackstrap is the purest. Its taste though is tough to take for many people. A rule of thumb is: The sweeter the molasses, the more palatable, the lighter and clearer it is, the more sucrose it contains and the more it will devil your blood sugar. Still, of all the sugar-cane derivatives, molasses is the most healthful and in some circles is even considered to have marvelous curative properties.* Here is a recipe that shows off its good taste.

SWEET BROWN COOKIES

1 cup whole-wheat flour	½ cup molasses
⅓ cup milk	½ teaspoon powdered ginger
2 eggs	½ teaspoon cinnamon
¼ cup honey	¼ teaspoon sea salt
½ cup fresh wheat germ	Freshly grated orange rind
½ cup powdered milk	1 tablespoon butter
⅓ cup corn oil	

1. Place the flour and liquid milk into a large mixing bowl. Stir, then beat in the eggs separately. Add honey and wheat germ, then the powdered milk, oil, molasses. Mix them all together.

2. Add the spices and salt. Grate the orange rind directly into the mixture. Stir thoroughly.

3. Thoroughly butter a large cookie sheet. Spoon cookie-shaped dollops onto the sheet from the batter, then bake in a 350 degree oven for 10 to 15 minutes.

Honey

Of all the sweeteners not derived from cane sugar, honey is the most popular and most highly touted. Although it has considerable merits, there are a few bugs in the honey jar too. Most of these are overlooked by natural food buffs in their enthusiasm to find the perfect sucrose substitute.

For example, anyone with hypoglycemia is well advised to eat this gooey, golden elixir in moderation, if not to avoid it entirely, for while it

* For information on the curative powers of molasses, see Cyril Scott, *Crude Black Molasses* (Simi Valley, California: Benedict Lust Publications, n.d.).

is absorbed at a slower rate than sucrose, honey can still be disruptive to the blood-sugar level. Chemically honey consists mostly of water and two monosaccharides, glucose and fructose, which in combination make short work of tooth enamel, encouraging dental caries as fast and probably faster than sucrose. (Bears are the only large mammals in nature besides man that forage for honey, and curiously, they are also the only other mammals that suffer heavy tooth decay.) When lengthily boiled, subtle chemical changes take place in honey along with the loss of nutrients. There is some evidence that over-boiled honey may even be harmful for the digestion.

Mark also that while there may indeed be undiscovered "ethereal" nutritive and medicinal properties in honey, as some claim, honey still makes a rather poor showing in the nutrition department when compared to molasses and even to maple sugar. The following chart is adapted from Frances Moore Lappé's book, *Diet for a Small Planet.*

NUTRITIVE QUALITIES OF SUGARS COMPARED (composition per 100 grams or 3½ ounces)				
Minerals	*Brown Sugar*	*Molasses*	*Honey*	*Maple Sugar*
Iron	3.4	16	0.5	1.4
Potassium	344	2,927	51	242
Calcium	85	684	5	143
Phosphorus	19	84	6	11

All these points considered, honey is still an attractive and immensely tasty alternative to table sugar. It comes complete with small quantities of potassium, phosphorus, calcium, iron, B vitamins, and if the pollen has not been filtered out, it even has vitamin C. Dark honeys are usually richer, stronger tasting, and more nutritious than light, and thick honeys generally are more nutritious than thin. Honey is easy to digest. Most of the work has already been done for you in the bee's stomach. It is, as well, a rather low pesticide risk, as bees foraging for nectar usually dive deep into the flower where the pesticide levels are the lowest. (Bees are also particularly vulnerable to sprays and those heavily exposed will die before they have a chance to gather the honey and return with it to the hive.)

Honey comes in a number of flavors, sixty varieties of which are harvested in the United States alone. Alfalfa is the *vin ordinaire* of the lot, the kind you're likely to get at the market. Often this name is just a kind of catchall title meaning that the honey is a mixture of whatever wild flowers happen to grow in the area where the honey was gathered.

Specific varieties of honey, buckwheat, say, or apple blossom, are collected by placing hives in the region where and when the particular plant crop flowers. The bees gather their nectar predominantly from this flower and make it into a honey that is specifically flavored with the essence of that plant. As soon as the honey flow of that particular crop ceases the hive is removed.

High on the good-for-you list is tupelo honey, found in remote swampy regions of the American South; and leatherwood honey, a rare variety imported from the island of Tasmania near Australia. Buckwheat honey is dark and syrupy, and has a peculiar aftertaste that some people relish and others avoid. Sage honey bears the scent and taste of its namesake. It also is something of an acquired taste. Easier to love are the heather honeys, especially the kinds imported from England or the moors of Scotland. Linden, raspberry and borage are all superior too. Also, orange blossom with its indescribably sweet aftertaste; and good old mellow white-clover and red-clover honey, two all-time American favorites.

One other feature of honey also makes it stand out from other sweeteners: its medicinal qualities. No, it won't cure cancer. But if you're in the wilderness and lacerate your hand, honey's germ-inhibiting and water-absorbent properties will keep the wound clean and infection-free until you get aid. A teaspoonful of honey at bedtime is believed by some to help troubled sleepers relax. Note too that because honey inhibits the growth of bacteria, it does not spoil like other foods and never needs to be refrigerated—ever. It is among the most enduring organic substances in nature. Alexander the Great, ancient records tell us, was kept preserved for several hundred years after his death, entombed in a crock of the sweet golden stuff, while the first archaeologists into the tombs of the Egyptian pharaohs sampled the crystallized honey left there by temple priests and found it to be tolerably eatable. (Honey's preservative powers can be put to work on a more mundane level: When used in baking it produces cakes and loaves that keep longer than those made with ordinary sugar.)

Try honey as a gargle next time you have a sore throat. It's also a fair suppressive for coughs from a cold. If you get a small burn, extract the heat from the wound by placing it under cool water, then, when the wound is dry, place a honey poultice on it for quicker healing. During hay-fever season try chewing honeycomb from a local apiary. The pollens that make you sneeze will go directly into your system, and by a kind of homeopathy—like cures like—will help you establish immunity. The same effect is at work when you do what every beekeeper does when he gets stung: put a dab of honey on the wound.

With all its benefits, honey nonetheless cannot outrun the long arm of processor, refiner and preserver. In fact, there are such a large number of caveats to be aware of when shopping for honey that they deserve a list of their own:

1. The laws governing honey advertising are vague. For instance, honey is often labeled "organic." But in order to be organic *all* the plants from which the nectar was taken would have had to be unsprayed. At best, this is difficult to control. Some honey brands also promote their product as "raw" or "natural," both nebulous terms. Same with phrases like "old-fashioned," "untreated" and the most ludicrous of all, "home-made." Such terms have become health food buzz words and are difficult to depend on.

2. Nothing is worse for honey than heat. Keep it away from heat sources, direct light and hot pantries. More to the point, commercial honey cooked at high temperatures, especially over 125 degrees for a prolonged period of time, is depleted of its important enzymes and nutrients, turning it into a useless sugary syrup, no better than the sucrose it is replacing. Most honeys sold at the supermarket have been heated this way. Why? Heated honey does not crystallize and harden in the bottle. Doesn't liquid, watery honey look purer, and doesn't it pour more easily? The irony is that the "purer" this honey looks, the more it has been refined.

Almost all commercial honey is heated to some degree. In certain cases it is "flash heated"—exposed to high temperature and then quickly cooled. This is better than prolonged heating, which is guaranteed to kill every nutrient in sight. Still other honeys are heated but at low temperatures, say 120 degrees, and for short periods of time. A few are not heated at all, and these are the best. Look for honey that crystallizes easily, that is not *too* clear in the bottle, that seems a bit smoky and granular when held up to the light, and that is marked "unheated" on the label. The faster honey crystallizes, the greater your guarantee of getting the untampered, unheated McCoy.

3. Honey is also filtered. The impulse is certainly correct here, to remove the pollen, propolis, wax and so forth that collects in the hive. The problem is overdoing: overstraining with fine mesh strainers until the honey takes on that watery, anemic look of the commercial brands. Honeys are graded on the amount of filtration they undergo. Grade A is filtered the most. Grade B is filtered less, and so on. The lower the grade the better the honey.

4. A word of caution vis-à-vis packaged honeycomb: Just because honey is sold in pretty square little combs this by no means guarantees that the product is direct from the hive. Many suppliers remove the comb from the hive, extract the honey from it, slice the comb into little boxes, then refill it with other honey taken from who knows where. Usually comb honey direct from the hive has a kind of raw, noncosmetic look about it, as if a slab had been cut away at random, packaged with all its jagged edges, and sent off to market. Any beekeeper, and some natural food stores, will have samples of real comb. Once you see the contrast between the real and the fake you'll never mistake the two again.

5. In most states, it is illegal to dilute honey with water. By and large, most suppliers comply with this law, though some like to supplement their honey with the cheaper and more abundant corn syrup, the legality of which is far less clear-cut. The terms "unadulterated" and "undiluted" *should* mean that neither water *nor* sugar syrup has been added. But they don't. They mean simply no water.

6. Your best bet is to purchase honey from local sources, direct from the beekeeper if possible. Beekeepers are, by and large, an upright group and are usually willing to tell you everything they've done and not done to their product. Besides, honey that comes to you from your own neighborhood is, in a sense, the essence of the natural world that immediately surrounds you. It is the distillate of local nature, the essence of the flower that is the quintessence of the plant that is the essence of vegetable nature. While the premise may be unscientific, perhaps, intuition suggests that foods taken from the land upon which one lives, moves and breathes must in some way be better for the body and for the soul than foods trucked in from a thousand miles yonder.

If you are going to use honey as a substitute for sugar, the usual ratio of replacement is around three-quarters of a cup of honey to one full cup of table sugar—you may find you prefer more or less. Also try reducing the amount of other liquids used in the same recipe. This will compensate for the honey's greater moisture until a proper balance is struck.

Be aware that honey doesn't work well in certain recipes. It may cause whatever you're cooking to become a bit heavy or crumbly, especially if you're substituting honey in a recipe that calls specifically for sugar— you'll have to experiment. The following recipes are all tested winners.

BROWN RICE MUFFINS
(from Lundberg Farm, Richvale, California)

1¼ cups sifted flour	1 cup milk
2 teaspoons baking powder	2 beaten eggs
½ teaspoon sea salt	4 tablespoons soft butter
2 tablespoons honey	1 cup cooked brown rice

1. Sift together the flour, baking powder, salt and honey.

2. Mix the milk, eggs, butter, rice, then stir. Combine the two mixtures. Do not overbeat as the muffins will become too heavy.

3. Pour mixture into 12 buttered muffin tins and bake in 425 degree oven for 20 to 25 minutes, or until lightly browned.

EREWHON FRUITCAKE
(from Erewhon Natural Foods Company, Boston, Massachusetts)

Though many people think it is impossible to make good fruitcake without sugar or rum, the following recipe from the famous pioneer health food company Erewhon proves it can be done and done well.

4 cups whole-wheat pastry flour (reserve ½ cup to mix with fruit and nuts)	5 eggs
	1 teaspoon vanilla
	½ cup soaked dried apricots
1 teaspoon Rumford baking powder	1 cup honey-dipped papaya, chopped
½ teaspoon sea salt	1 cup raisins
¾ cup butter	1 cup dried pineapple, chopped
1¾ cups honey	1⅓ cups chopped pecans

1. Sift 3½ cups flour with baking powder and salt. Cream the butter separately until it is light, then add honey and blend the two together.

2. Beat the eggs into the flour mixture one at a time. Add the vanilla and stir in honey-butter mixture. Beat until thoroughly mixed. Then fold in fruit and nuts.

3. Butter the bottoms of two 4″ x 8½″ loaf pans. Divide batter between the two pans. Preheat the oven to 350 degrees, then bake batter one hour. If the loaves crack on top during cooking reduce the heat to 325 degrees. Cool loaves in pans for 30 minutes before disturbing, then remove the loaves and allow them to cool on racks. Wrap in brandy-soaked cheesecloth and foil to store.

CHUTNEY MADE WITH HONEY

5 pounds peeled tomatoes	2 pounds raisins
1 large onion	1 pound honey
Juice of 3 lemons	½ teaspoon ground cloves
½ cup apple-cider vinegar	½ teaspoon cinnamon
½ teaspoon sea salt	1 pound dates

1. Slice the tomatoes and onion and mix them together. Pour the lemon juice over mixture while stirring.

2. Mix in vinegar, salt, raisins, dates, honey and spices. Stir until everything is well homogenized. Then place on medium to low heat, cover, and cook for about two hours, or until the mixture has a soft, syrupy chutneylike consistency. Pack the mixture into airtight jars. Refrigerate. Use with chicken, rice dishes, curries, etc.

HONEY CAROB FUDGE

1 cup honey	¼ cup dates
1 cup carob powder	½ cup finely shredded fresh
1 cup unsalted natural peanut	coconut
butter	½ cup sesame seeds
¼ cup raisins	1 cup finely chopped walnuts
¼ cup finely chopped prunes	1 tablespoon butter (approx.)

1. Mix the honey, carob powder and peanut butter together in a saucepan. Place on low heat, stirring gently. Then mix in the raisins, prunes, dates, coconut, seeds and nuts, and stir until the mixture reaches an even consistency.

2. Lightly rub the butter along the bottom of a square cake pan. Pour the ingredients into the pan and refrigerate for the rest of the day. Then cut the mixture into regular fudge-like squares and serve.

Fructose

Sometimes called fruit sugar or levulose, fructose has recently come to prominence as a sucrose replacement, and it is easy to see why. Being extremely concentrated, fructose gives you more sweetness for less sweetener. Because it digests in the liver rather than in the small intestine, and because it is broken down by different enzymes than used by sucrose, fructose requires no insulin for digestion. This means it does not unbalance the blood-sugar level. Hypoglycemics and diabetics generally report no adverse side effects.

Too good to be true? In some ways. Fructose by itself, like sucrose, provides no nourishment. It is empty calories. Some people find it just too sweet, or they don't care for its particular taste. (It is often placed in yogurt to jazz up the fruit flavors; if you like the taste of sweetened fruit yogurts you'll probably like fructose.) In large amounts it is known to cause gastrointestinal upset, and certain varieties contain substances that may induce allergic reactions. Still, fructose is less harmful than sucrose, if no less addicting, and the prospects for it as a table-sugar surrogate are promising.

Barley Malt

Still another good bet is barley malt. Like fructose it doesn't cause big fluctuations in blood-sugar level. It is composed mainly of the disaccharide maltose, which breaks down far more slowly and evenly in the digestive system than sucrose. Like fructose, barley malt has its own particular flavor, a kind of nutty, mild taste that is much less sugary than either fructose or sucrose. It also has a thick viscosity like honey, and it looks wonderful in the jar. Try it.

Mirin

Lovers of Oriental food will quickly recognize the unique, only slightly sugary taste of this rice syrup used to sweeten a number of Japanese dishes. Both barley malt and mirin may be hard to find. Look for them at Oriental food stores and occasionally at natural food stores, especially those that maintain a department for macrobiotic foods.

Is Sugar Our Roman Lead Vessel?

In the past few years scholars of Roman civilization have come up with a rather surprising theory. The decline of Rome in the first centuries after Christ, they claim, was due not entirely to politics or moral degeneracy. There were biological reasons too.

It was around the time of Christ, they tell us, that molded lead receptacles became popular in Rome among the masses. Up to this time pottery vessels had been the vogue. But by 100 A.D. metalworking had achieved new levels of sophistication. Cups and plates made of lead became a kind of status symbol that no up-to-date Roman household would be without.

Now lead, as everyone knows today (but no one realized in 100 A.D.), is a slow poison. Take a little every morning with your breakfast, lunch and dinner and you'll slowly start to fall apart, both physically and psychologically. Keep a whole civilization on the stuff for a century or more and you have the makings of a major decline and fall.

No doubt attributing the degeneration of an entire society to a single obscure cause is simplistic history at best. The point, however, is that it *is* possible for a particular ingested substance to adversely influence masses of people without their awareness—witness cigarettes before the 1960s —to weaken them, diminish their effectiveness, and in this way influence the subtle twists and turns of their history.

Could sugar be such a substance for us? We have seen how harmful it is to the human mind and body alike. There is no question that our entire nation is heavily addicted to sugar, that every year the hook sinks deeper, and that the increase is mirrored by ever-climbing rates of degenerative disease. Again, while it is naïve to blame a complex situation on a single factor, is it not feasible to believe that sugar is *one* of the reasons Americans are so prone to diseases that in some other parts of the world are practically unknown? Is it not possible that a society that lives on a substance so admittedly unhealthy is basically a society that is poisoning itself to death?

What to do?

Stop eating sugar. Or at least cut down on it to a significant degree. Fanaticism on the subject can of course reach ridiculous extremes, and it should be said that you do not have to eliminate every last grain for the rest of your life to stay healthy. A little sugar taken once in a while as the special treat it was originally meant to be will do no one much harm. In the last century, Americans ate around four pounds per person per year. Just about right. Let's head back in that direction.

How to cut down? Will power and common sense mostly, aided by the understanding that after a period of struggle the craving for sugar *will* diminish, like any craving, and that the game is well worth the candle. Here are a few ways and means that might help in the struggle.

1. Fruits are a perfect substitute for sugar. When you are trying to kick the sugar habit keep some grapes around (15 percent natural fruit sugar), or figs (65 percent sugar), raisins (70 percent) or dates (75 percent). These are all well endowed with natural sweetness, as the percentages show. Later on, when you're more thoroughly weaned, reach for less sugary fruits like oranges (11 percent), apples (15 percent), bananas (23 percent) or even for vegetables—the sugars in carrots or in squash

will more than quench your need for a lift in blood sugar, which is what sugar craving is really about anyway.

2. Keep temptation at a distance. Get rid of the sweets in your house immediately, the candy, the cakes and cake mixes, the table sugar, the pancake syrup. What the eye doesn't see the heart doesn't yearn for.

3. If you are addicted to cola drinks here's an especially good tip. Take some naturally carbonated mineral water (club soda in a pinch). Fill a glass two-thirds full, then fill the rest with unsweetened grape juice, orange juice, or unsweetened apple juice. The result is an amazingly delicious "spritzer." You'd be proud to serve this drink to the most critical guests, or even to a seven-year-old connoisseur of grape soda.

4. Try cooking without sugar. This means (1) making dishes that don't call for the usual ½ cup of sugar, etc.; (2) devising alternate ways of making your favorite dessert without sweeteners; (3) substituting honey, barley malt, molasses et al. in the desserts you absolutely cannot live without.

5. If you've ever tried to stop smoking, you know that the desire for a cigarette tends to wax and wane. There is a lesson here that may carry over to sugar addiction. Next time the urge comes and the only thing in the world you want is a gooey confection, just remember: In a few minutes the urge will pass. Guaranteed. It will pass. Focus your attention on something else, a small chore, perhaps. If you can get through this momentary period of desire, the craving *will* go away. It has to, because your blood chemistry will change, and the craving with it. Then you'll have this conquest to feel good about. It will help you next time the craving arises.

6. Don't get discouraged. If you slip from your resolve and fall into a chocolate sundae, enjoy it. Then try again. You've been stuck on sugar a long time, probably since you were a baby. It may take a few tries till victory is yours.

VEGETABLES

Each society has food priorities that it passes along from generation to generation. In ours, for whatever complicated reasons, vegetables have earned a rank low on the totem pole. There's not a great deal we can do about this fact except improve on it in our own kitchens and pass something better along to our children. At the same time, however, there are vegetables, and then there are VEGETABLES.

What does this mean? Well, on the one hand there are the vegetables we purchase in cans or frozen in boxes. Vegetables preserved in sugar or salt. Vegetables with the last increment of life cooked out of their souls. Vegetables overboiled, overspiced, overpeeled and oversliced. Vegetables that sit three weeks in a railroad car before seeing the fluorescent light of day. Vegetables grown in soil so depleted that their vitality is a whisper and their taste a whimper. No wonder people shun such things.

Then there are VEGETABLES. These are the fresh-picked garden kind, unadulterated, nonrefined, nonfrozen, nonovercooked, nonoversliced. And with luck, nonchemically grown. Between these two varieties there is an infinite gap. The first category stands to the second as a cardboard picture of a carrot stands to the real thing.

What Makes a Vegetable a "Good" Vegetable?

By "good" we mean a vegetable that is nourishing *and* delicious. And as nature would have it, the two almost invariably come together. If a food tastes dull and flat there's probably not much nutrition in it either. If it tastes juicy and sweet and fresh it's good for you too. Why? Because it's the nutrients in what you eat, the vitamins, proteins, enzymes, and so forth that bring life to food in the first place and make it taste good. When these nutrients are missing, as they are in refined, overprocessed food, there's not much left over to taste good.

But don't take our word for it. Try it. With just a few modifications in your shopping and cooking habits you'll quickly agree that vegetables have been given short shrift in the modern world and that the really fresh, unadulterated kinds can be the best part of the meal. Here are some simple rules for maximizing the natural taste of vegetables.

1. Buy fresh vegetables. Avoid the canned, packaged and frozen kind. If you must go to the packaged route, frozen vegetables are better than canned.

2. If possible buy organic. Vegetables grown this way really do taste better, and they're probably healthier for you. Better yet and cheaper yet, start your own garden. Grow your own organic foods. Even if you live in a city it's amazing how many tomatoes will come off a single well-loved vine kept on the fire escape or window ledge. Or how many herbs you can cultivate in a small flower box. Or how nice a garden you can hoe on a ten-foot-by-ten-foot piece of unused backyard soil.

3. When you get your vegetables home make sure they're stored properly, sealed in airtight bags or containers, and eaten promptly. The length of time vegetables keep their nutritional integrity differs from plant

to plant. Root vegetables like potatoes, carrots and onions store especially well and keep their vitamin quotas for long periods of time. The same for squash, cabbage and turnips. A schedule of storage times for different vegetables is listed a little farther on.

4. Delicate leafy greens should be kept refrigerated in a sealed bag or container. Celery, carrots, peas, radishes, broccoli, cauliflower and tomatoes also. Cucumbers, beans, eggplant and summer squash can be left uncovered. Fresh peas and beans should be stored in their pods and not shelled until minutes before cooking.

5. Vegetables keep best in a cool, dark, quiet place. The refrigerator or root cellar is best. As soon as they are exposed to light, air, heat and handling, enzymes that oxidize vitamins and turn sugar to starch are stimulated within the cellular structure. Heat, sunlight and the human touch are therefore the principal enemies of stored foodstuffs. Another trick to note: When you store foods keep the vegetables and fruits in separate areas. Fruits emit a gas (methane) as they ripen which speeds up the deterioration of any vegetable in the vicinity.

6. Try to eat green, leafy vegetables the day you purchase them. The ritual of visiting the open-air market each morning and buying the day's food is a time-honored one, and still alive in parts of the world where refrigeration is not readily available. Such shopping labors are rewarded in the long run, for the sooner food is eaten the more nutrients it provides.

7. Leave the skins on vegetables when cooking. Except in cases where the skin is chemically coated, as with cucumbers that are waxed before being put on the store shelf, try not to peel or skin a vegetable or remove its healthy outer leaves (as with lettuce).

8. Wash all vegetables *quickly*. Don't soak them. Overwashing leaches out nutrients and washes away vitamins, especially the water-soluble kinds like B and C.

9. Imperfect-looking fruits and vegetables are not necessarily unac-ceptable. This doesn't mean you should buy wilted produce, of course, but neither should you automatically shy away from an apple, say, that's a little lopsided or imperfectly colored. Blemishes, odd shapes and un-even color may even indicate that the produce has not been dyed or artificially colored, or that chemicals are not used to improve its shelf appearance. Growers learned long ago that consumers buy food more on the grounds of how it looks than on how it will taste and how healthy it is. And so they willingly oblige. A large, shiny, ridiculously perfect-looking vegetable or piece of fruit will, you may notice, often taste mealy and bland. This is because its mineral goodness has been sacrificed to achieve its spiffy appearance.

10. Cook vegetables in as little water as possible. Usually only the bottom of the pan should be covered. No more than a half inch at most. Steaming vegetables is highly recommended, as is pressure-cooking or stir-frying in a wok. Whatever method, the faster the better. Keep the lid tight and don't remove the vegetable while it's cooking.

11. Treasure the water you've cooked the vegetables in. It's rich in the water soluble vitamins that have been driven out during the heating. The "pot liquor" of any cooked vegetable has no calories, no roughage (which makes it an ideal brew to feed the sick), and it may be added to soups, stews, gravies, sauces, practically anything. Just don't throw it away.

12. Be wary of peeling, cutting, grating, slicing, dicing. Each time you make a cut on a vegetable another internal surface is exposed to the light and air, and more nutrients are put at risk. It's preferable to cut vegetables into a few chewable chunks and to do it immediately before cooking time. Even better, cut them up *after* they've been cooked. This second method will be easier too. If you're going to pare and shred, at least save the peelings to put into a soup.

13. Spice your vegetables with moderation, if at all. Unless you're using a recipe that calls for specific spices, the subtle, undoctored taste of fresh garden vegetables will stand on its own quite well, thank you. Be especially careful with salt, sprinklings of which have an absorbent effect on the water content of vegetables, sucking out vitamins and minerals you'd prefer left in. For the same reason, try not to salt vegetables while they're cooking. Spinach that is treated this way loses almost 50 percent of its iron.

The Vegetable Honor Roll:
Notes on How to Get the Most from the Best

Botanically speaking, vegetables are classified in the following way:

1. Flower vegetables (broccoli, Brussels sprouts)
2. Root vegetables (beets, turnips, carrots)
3. Stem vegetables (celery, asparagus)
4. Tubers (potatoes, Jerusalem artichokes)
5. Bulbs (onions, shallots)
6. Leaf vegetables (watercress, parsley, spinach)
7. Legumes (peas, beans)
8. Fruits of vegetables (tomatoes, squash)
9. Fungi (mushrooms)
10. Seeds and nuts

If you look at all ten types of vegetable as a kind of single composite plant, it's apparent that every part of this plant is a source of nutrition. Bear this in mind next time you chuck out the green tops of turnips or cut off too much of the asparagus stalk. Many of the most healthful parts of our favorite vegetables, as we are about to discover, are the parts we don't preserve.

Now to some vegetables. If there are newcomers here to your list, why not give them a try?

1. Flower Vegetables

Broccoli—A powerhouse of vitamin A plus thiamine in the flower and leaves and vitamin C throughout. Potassium, calcium and iron are all present in goodly amounts. When cooking, many people throw away the stem of the broccoli and the outer leaves, thus losing the most nutritious parts. Cut off only the woody bottom part of the stem, remove only the thickest outer leaves, and eat the rest. When preparing, slow cooking (as with most flower vegetables) may produce flatulence. It may also reduce the vitamin content of the final product. Better to cook the broccoli quickly in a minimum of water. Steaming is best. Broccoli is a coarse vegetable with lots of roughage. This makes it excellent for people who eat a lot of refined foods, bad for people with digestive difficulties. In the second case, purée the plant into a fine mush, then serve. Broccoli goes well garnished with cheese or with any crunchy item like sunflower seeds or ground nuts. Store in the fridge, and eat as soon as possible.

Cauliflower—Its most potent vitamin is thiamine, followed closely by vitamin C. Lots of calcium too, as much as 35 mg. a serving when properly prepared. Perfect in a crudité or as an appetizer, as the vitamin B content stimulates the appetite. Also good for diets; it has one of the lowest calorie counts of any food, less than 10 calories per serving, cooked or raw. When buying cauliflower avoid discolored, dirty brown plants, plants that are splayed, plants with yellowed buds or yellowed leaves. Look for tight, white, happy-looking flowerlets and full green leaves. Use no salt when preparing, as it depletes vitamins. Cook quickly, preferably in a steamer. The leaves of the cauliflower are nutritious and make excellent filler in soups. Plenty of roughage here. If cauliflower produces too much flatulence try cooking it in milk at low heat. Milk neutralizes plant acids and prevents the breakdown of sulphur compounds that cause intestinal gas.

CAULIFLOWER CARROT DELIGHT

1 head cauliflower	2 cups whole milk
5 carrots	½ teaspoon honey
2 tablespoons butter	Pinch of nutmeg
1½ tablespoons whole-grain flour	

1. Steam the cauliflower until tender.

2. Cook the carrots until they are pulpy, then purée them in a blender.

3. Make a roux of the butter and flour. Add milk, carrot purée and honey. Cook mixture over medium heat, stirring constantly, until well thickened. Pour the carrot sauce over the cauliflower, add nutmeg, and serve.

Brussels sprouts—Avoid sprouts with yellowed leaves. Look for young, firm, deep-green produce. The smaller the sprout the sweeter the taste. While Brussels sprouts may appear intact after several weeks of refrigeration, they lose most of their vitality, if not their good looks, after four or five days. So eat them right now if you can. Though they can be purchased year around, they are at their tastiest from October through December. Brussels sprouts have a slightly diuretic effect. They're extremely low in calories, with less than 20 to a typically sized serving. Cook them in as little water as possible, but *do* cook them, as raw Brussels sprouts may have too much oxalic acid for comfort. The strong flavor of Brussels sprouts can be reduced by cooking them quickly (eight to ten minutes) in a little water, or cooking in milk for ten minutes at temperatures below boiling.

BRUSSELS SPROUT SURPRISE

1 pound Brussels sprouts	¼ cup water
1 tablespoon corn oil	Bread crumbs
1 large onion, diced	½ cup grated Cheshire cheese
4 tomatoes	
½ teaspoon sea salt	

1. Slice the Brussels sprouts in half and sauté them in oil, along with the onions, for 5 minutes.

2. Remove the skins of the tomatoes by immersing them in boiling water, then peeling.

3. Into a medium-sized oiled casserole place the Brussels sprouts, tomatoes, salt, onions and water. Sprinkle bread crumbs on top. Be sure the cover of the casserole is tight, then bake in oven at 325 degrees for approximately 45 minutes.

4. Remove. Sprinkle cheese over top of the casserole. Place back in oven until cheese has melted. Serve.

2. Root Vegetables

Turnips—Save the tops and use them in soup or as a cooked green. The tops are one of the richest—and least known—sources of vitamin C in nature. Though not particularly popular in the United States, turnips are one of the most nutritious of all vegetables, and like all root vegetables they are less exposed to pesticides than their grown-above-ground cousins. Turnips are rich in calcium, iron, phosphorus, and vitamins A and B. The white kinds are the best-tasting, especially those ripened in the fall. Be sure when purchasing that they are fresh and crisp, not spongy, cracked, split at the top, or fibrous in the roots. Turnips can be baked like potatoes, ten to fifteen minutes. Try steaming them too, then garnish with a little paprika and grated cheese. Keep them stored in a cool but not overly dry location. Young, fresh turnips make an excellent crudité. They also stand alone as an hors d'oeuvre.

Kohlrabi—A little known and absolutely delicious vegetable. Its fresh, crisp taste lies somewhere between a carrot and a head of cabbage. Kohlrabi is a wonderful source of vitamin C. A single serving provides far more of this nutrient than the minimum daily requirement calls for. It also has a bit of thiamine, a touch of vitamin A and lots of calcium. Kohlrabi is harvested as a bulb-shaped root and can be eaten raw, sliced up in a salad, or boiled for five minutes as a main vegetable dish. Store it sealed in the hydrator.

Carrots—One of the most popular of all vegetables, though not necessarily one the most nutritious. While carrots are famous for their carotene supplies, other vegetables such as broccoli, parsley, turnips, beet greens, spinach and radishes have a good deal more. Carrots, nonetheless, are a good source of B-1 and sulphur, and cuisinewise they have a thousand uses. Many of the nutrients in a carrot are in the skin, so try not to scrape or peel them. Just scrub carefully and serve whole. As a rule, smaller, younger carrots are more nutritious than large, while the green tops of the carrot are almost as good for you as the fleshy part, rich in iron, trace minerals and roughage. Add the tops to salads—they don't stand alone very well—or use them in slow-cooking soups and stews. When shopping avoid cracked or limp carrots, as well as those with a dusty, discolored look. Scrub them with a vegetable brush for best cleaning. Carrot juice, incidentally, is reputed to have medicinal value, especially for increasing the body's resistance to infections. It is said to improve breast-milk quality and to have a cleansing effect on the liver. If you own a juicer, mix eleven ounces of carrot juice with five ounces of cabbage juice and take the concoction once a day for a week. This drink is good as any overall tonic. A glassful, with some of the tops juiced in, will provide as much as 40,000 units of vitamin A.

Beets—Beets have a high amount of vitamin B-1 plus a rapidly oxidizing sugar that makes them a quick-energy food. They're fairly good in the calcium department; and while low in vitamin A, their tops make up for this and should not be neglected in soups. The tops, in fact, are actually more nutritious than the root, especially as far as the B vitamins, iron and calcium are concerned, Try cutting them up along with the root and sautéing them together. Good beets are crisp and hard, deep red, without ridges or cracks. Keep beets no longer than a week, and eat the tops within a few days after purchase. Steamed beets will maintain their nutritional integrity if not cooked too long. Garnish the finished product with tarragon, thyme, mint or yogurt. Beet juice is a tonic for anemia and poor circulation. While preparing the juice, include some of the beet tops. Take this drink in moderation though, as it's strong stuff, once a week at most.

Radishes—Extremely high quantities of vitamins A and C, followed by supplies of B vitamins, calcium, iron and phosphorus. One of the healthiest of all vegetables, pound for pound, though their strong, pungent taste prevents most people from eating many of them at a time. Shop for the firm, deep-red varieties minus black spots, softness or pitting. Especially large radishes are apt to be fibrous and tasteless. Try the daikon radish for a change of pace, available at most Oriental food stores.

3. Stem Vegetables

Celery—An old saw among dieters has it that "Celery has minus calories; only five per stalk, and six that get used up in the chewing." Allergics should be careful of uncooked celery. It contains allergens that may occasionally trigger sneezing attacks. Celery with green leaves is nutritionally preferable to the variety with yellow leaves, though both taste the same. Trim off the root, serve raw in salads. Or serve braised and creamed with milk and butter. Use the leaves for garnishing or place them in soups and salads. Store celery in the hydrator. If you want to make celery extra-crisp before a dinner party, and don't mind losing a few of the nutrients, place the stalks in ice water an hour before serving.

COLD GAZPACHO SOUP

¼ cup scallions
½ cup carrots
½ cup cucumbers
½ cup celery
½ cup green peppers
¼ cup radishes

2 cloves garlic, chopped
¼ cup unrefined oil
1 teaspoon sea salt
2 tablespoons vinegar
1 large can tomato juice

1. Chop the fresh scallions, carrots, cucumbers, celery, green peppers and radishes, and place them in a large mixing bowl. Stir, then add chopped garlic.

2. Make a separate vinaigrette of the oil, salt and vinegar, and add it to the chopped vegetables. Stir, then slowly add the tomato juice.

3. Place the mixture in the icebox for at least two hours before mealtime. Gazpacho is at its best if allowed to sit a day before serving.

Asparagus—Strong in both C and B vitamins. Before purchasing check that the stalks are not too stiff or woody, a sure sign of old age. When preparing, remove the lower part of the stalks and cook the asparagus in a double boiler for ten minutes or until soft, then serve with lemon squeezed over it. If you boil asparagus, the water you cook them in can be added to soups to give them extra body. Also, try cooking asparagus in half a cup of milk thickened with several tablespoons of whole-wheat flour. Store asparagus in the refrigerator, no longer than four or five days. Peak season for this delicious vegetable runs from February through June.

4. Tubers

White potatoes—A staple in many parts of the world. If cooked and eaten in the skin they provide a good dose of vitamin C, especially when unsliced. The skin has iron; the flesh, vitamin B, phosphorus, and small but high-quality protein. Add raw egg or soy sauce to mashed potatoes to improve on this protein supply. Potato water is also good to add to bread dough. If you must slice your potatoes before cooking, put them in the refrigerator first for several hours. This will slow down the enzyme action that dissolves vitamins when the potato is exposed to air. Potato chips, French fries, potato sticks and kindred sorts are worthless from a nutritional standpoint, as the combination of slicing and overcooking removes about 90 percent of the good stuff. Try never to boil potatoes, and if you must, be aware that salt added to the water removes most of the vitamins that prolonged heating misses. Potatoes with green sprouts growing out of them should *never* be eaten. They contain a substance called solanine, which can cause vomiting, diarrhea and worse. Store potatoes in a dark place away from extremes of heat. Room temperature is best. Don't refrigerate. When purchasing look for potatoes that are firm, cool, without wrinkles or soft spots. Russet, Idaho or Maine potatoes make the best baking. California, Pontiacs and Red Bliss are not as good, but are usually lower in price.

Sweet Potatoes—A potato in name only (it is part of a different vegetable family), the sweet potato contains more vitamin A than white potatoes and is considerably easier to digest. Their high endowment of natural sugars makes sweet potatoes an excellent source of quick energy too. When purchasing, odd-shaped sweet potatoes are best. Look for uniformly colored skins free of soft spots and bruises. Avoid those with cracks at the ends. Unlike white potatoes, sweet potatoes store for short times only, and *never* in the refrigerator. Purchase only as many as you're prepared to eat within a few days.

Jerusalem artichokes—Popular in many parts of the world, Jerusalem artichokes have somehow been largely passed over by the American palate. All the worse for Americans, since this delicious, versatile, nutty-tasting tuber grows wild throughout vast stretches of the country and sits by forest and roadside just waiting to be picked. It can be identified by its six-foot-high straight stem and the large, sunflowerlike yellow flowers that crown it (commercial growers have tried to rename this vegetable the "sunchoke," presumably because of its physical similarity to the sunflower plant and because botanically the plant itself is neither an artichoke nor a native of Jerusalem). Jerusalem artichokes are rich in vitamin C, protein and iron. They can be eaten raw, sliced into salads, or added to a mixture of stir-fried vegetables. They are especially popular in Chinese cuisine.

5. Bulbs

Onions—The vegetable of a thousand uses. Their strong, biting taste is dissipated by quick cooking, while their most prominent nutrient, vitamin C, is—surprise—*increased,* just as long as the onions are not overcooked. The younger, smaller onions are usually more digestible and richer in nutrients than the large. Peel under water or with water on your knife to reduce tears. Also, try putting a small slice of onion under your tongue as you slice the onion. (For onion breath, mix in parsley with onions; it will neutralize the odor.) Though you'd never know it from their taste, onions are 15 percent sugar, and hence are an energy food, especially when mixed up raw in salads. Onions have an antibacterial effect too and are taken in many parts of the world as a remedy for colds. Try boiling a sliced onion in milk, straining off the pulp, and drinking a glassful of the liquid next time flu strikes. If nothing else, the vitamin C will help. As a rule, onions store well and last for many weeks, but only if kept in a mesh bag and stashed in a cool, dry place. Do not store with potatoes, as the two will quickly exchange flavors. Different kinds of onions include:

Leeks—Good source of vitamins A and B plus sulphur. Should be kept in the refrigerator or in a cool place. The tops make an unusual and delicious addition to any salad. Leeks taste like regular onions, only sweeter and less harsh.

Bermuda—Sweet, mild onion with red or white skin. Delicious cut into salads.

Spanish—Larger than Bermudas. Sweet and succulent.

Shallots—Grow in cloves like garlic, with green tops. A gourmet treat, available from November through April.

White—Used especially for boiling. Also good for making creamed onions, and in stews.

Scallions—Long-stemmed and delicate to the taste. Excellent cut up in salads. Unlike other varieties of onions, they should be refrigerated.

6. Leafy Vegetables

Spinach—A favorite of natural cooks. If prepared quickly, say five to seven minutes in less than a half inch of water, then garnished with crumbled hard-boiled egg or tiny slices of garlic, it can be a taste delight. Spinach leaves are especially sensitive to water. After washing, quickly spin the leaves in a salad spinner or dry with paper towels. Even a few minutes' exposure to water will dissolve out the important sugars, vitamins (especially A and C) and minerals of which spinach has amazingly large amounts. While the debate is still unsettled concerning whether the high oxalic-acid content of spinach does or does not combine with calcium to form indigestible salts—thus robbing the body of this precious mineral—it is probably wise to play it safe if you eat a lot of spinach and supplement your diet with other foods strong in calcium. Store spinach in an airtight container and keep it in the fridge. Eat within two or three days of purchase for maximum nourishment.

Watercress—A wonderful, if little appreciated, body cleanser and blood cleaner, especially when taken as a juice. According to Korean tradition, watercress juice is a cerebral tonic and is used in that country by students before examinations and other mind-taxing challenges. Like most other green-leaved vegetables, cress is strong in vitamin C and has heaping amounts of calcium. Since it is highly sensitive to pollutants and can grow only in pure water, most watercress comes to the table fairly innocent of sprays and insecticides. Unlike other greens, it should be stored in clear, clean water. Change the water every other day. Watercress does not store well though, and should be served a day or so after purchase. It makes any salad a gourmet delight, and goes especially well with onions, tomatoes, dandelion greens and bits of feta cheese.

Parsley—Like watercress, parsley is another nutritional sleeper. This humble green, usually used only as a garnishing, has more vitamin C *and* vitamin A than practically any other vegetable in the world, ounce for ounce. It is also rich in B vitamins, has tremendous stores of iron and calcium, and is not bad in the phosphorus and trace-element departments either. All in all, a neglected and highly nutritious food. Start putting more of it in your salads. Note though that a lot of the life gets washed out of parsley when it is randomly tossed into the stew. It's better when eaten raw. Next time you have a hunger, grab a bunch of parsley leaves. There are practically no calories here, and the roughage will help clear out fat too. Before eating, keep it fresh in the hydrator.

Cabbage—Another powerhouse vegetable with plenty of B and C vitamins, calcium, iron, sulphur, phosphorus and iodine. When taken raw, cabbage acts as a cleanser of the mucous membranes in the stomach and intestines, and the juice is also an appetite stimulator. Cabbage is one of the gassy vegetables, however, and may sit hard in a delicate stomach. Quick, low-heat cooking will help relieve this problem. Cook cabbage in a half inch of water at a low heat for no more than ten minutes. If a gassy, sulphurous smell is emitted you'll know the heat is too high. Cabbage will keep in the refrigerator for about a week. A delicious and easy sauerkraut can be made of it in the following way:

HOMEMADE SAUERKRAUT

1 head cabbage   **5 tablespoons sea salt**
1 gallon spring water

1. Slice the cabbage into sauerkraut-sized strands. Fill a large, wide-mouthed glass or pottery crock with water, add the salt, and mix the water until all the salt has dissolved. Place the cut-up shreds of cabbage into the water. You can add a few carrots and onions to the mixture if you like.

2. Take a round stone or appropriate weight and place it on top of

the cabbage. This will keep the shreds totally submerged. Otherwise they will have a tendency to float to the top, become exposed to the air, turn yellow, and spoil.

3. Cap the crock, leaving the cap slightly ajar so that gases can escape. Set the full crock aside for at least a week to 10 days. After a while the fermenting process will cause the brew to smell a bit, so keep it in some far-off corner of the house or yard. After the third or fourth day of fermentation a bubbly yellowish scum will rise to the surface of the water. This is a healthy sign. The cabbage is fermenting. Remove the scum with a spoon, give the cabbage a healthy stir or two, replace the stone and set the crock aside again. Check in this way every day or so. After 8 or 10 days the sauerkraut will ripen and turn a bit yellow. Taste it and see if it's to your liking. If not, let it ripen a few more days.

4. When the sauerkraut is ready, place it in a glass jar with about half the original water and half freshly added water. Cap tightly and keep refrigerated while using.

Swiss chard—Another green leafy vegetable strong in vitamins A and B. It has a rather pungent flavor, which makes it better cooked than raw, though some people like a few leaves mixed with other greens in a fresh summer salad. The best way to cook chard is to steam or stir-fry it with a drop of oil and a little garlic. If you must boil it, do so quickly. Like most greens, chard will become nutritionally depleted if cooked in water more than ten minutes. Chard, by the way, is extremely easy to cultivate. If the winter snows aren't too deep, it will grow straight through December.

Kale—Second only to parsley in Vitamin A. Also lots of C. Goes best cooked in the company of other greens; mixes especially well with spinach or standard salad greens—dandelion leaves, romaine, endive, escarole. When purchasing avoid kale with yellowed leaves or a wilted appearance. Droopy kale tastes just as it looks. Bronzing on the leaves, however, comes from cold weather and may even improve the taste. Store airtight in the fridge.

Dandelion greens—Very high in vitamins A, B and C. Dandelion greens are delicious in salads too, though for some odd reason they're neglected in our country. This is even more puzzling when you consider they're free. This spring go out and pick a bunch of the smaller, pluckier-looking leaves in your backyard or in a nearby park or meadow (by midsummer the larger leaves are usually hairy and tough; keep an eye out for the smaller tender shoots). Take them home, wash, and put into a salad. The leaves will stand on their own with oil and vinegar. They also mix perfectly with other salad greens. Dandelion leaves are particularly good for people with poor digestion. Also for convalescents, as they are one of the few leafy vegetables that are low in roughage. They have plenty of protein too; in fact, greens in general are far more fortified with this nutrient—and others too, like calcium—than is ordinarily supposed. Look at the following comparison of green vegetables versus milk.

Greens Compared with Milk As a Source of Nutrients

Food*	Protein	Calcium	Ribo-flavin	Iron	Vitamin B-12
	gm.	mg.	mg.	mg.	mcg.
Milk	7.0	234	340	0.2	1.2
Soy Milk	6.0	60	120	1.5	0.6
Broccoli	7.2	206	460	2.2	0.6
Turnip Greens	6.0	490	480	3.6	
Greens, Average†	6.7	305	390	3.0	
Soybeans‡	19.6	120	260	5.0	

Taken from U. D. Register and L. M. Sonnenberg, "The Vegetarian Diet." Quoted in Dr. Ioannis S. Scarpa and Dr. Helen Chilton Kiefer, *Sourcebook on Food and Nutrition* (Chicago: Marquis Academic Media, 1978).

* 1 cup or 220 gm.

† Greens included: broccoli, Brussels sprouts, collards, dandelion greens, kale, mustard greens, and turnip greens.

‡ Commercial.

Lettuce—There are many varieties of lettuce, most of them moderately well endowed with vitamins and minerals (though not as richly as, say, broccoli or parsley or turnip greens). Generally speaking, the darker green the lettuce the more nutrition there is in the leaf. The most popular variety, iceberg, is absolutely the most anemic and uninspired of the lot. Better-tasting and better for you are:

Ruby red—Once exotic, now rather easy to find, even in the supermarket. The leaf has a pretty dark-red fringe. Lots of vitamins A and C, and especially good taste.

Romaine—High in roughage, very alkaline. Especially low in calories and good for dieters. Is known by its long, dark-green leaves.

Butterhead—Rich in phosphorus, a lighter-color leaf than romaine.

Cos—Very similar to romaine.

7. Legumes

Though technically part of the vegetable family, legumes constitute their own subsection in this grouping. Literally, a legume is a pod with seeds inside it. Think of peas, beans and lentils as prime examples. Legumes are especially high in protein and when mixed with grains make a complete and hearty meal. Some of the most common and nutritious legumes are as follows.

Peas—The much-loved pea is a versatile food, rich in potassium, magnesium, iron, phosphorus, vitamins A, B complex and C. Its protein, vitamin *and* mineral content all increase considerably when the pea is dried, especially when it is then made into soup, and particularly when made into split-pea soup.

SPLIT-PEA SOUP

1 cup dried peas	½ teaspoon thyme
2 carrots, sliced	6 cups water
3 stalks celery, diced	½ cup milk (optional)
1 onion, sliced	Salt and pepper to taste
1 bay leaf	

1. Wash the dried peas well and separate out any stones. Dried peas do *not* have to be soaked before using.

2. Place the peas, fresh vegetables, bay leaf and thyme in a soup pot, cover with water (vegetable cooking water would be ideal if any is available). Bring mixture to a boil with top off pot and skim off any foam that rises to the surface. Turn down heat, cover, and allow soup to simmer for 1 to 2 hours. Stir frequently and add more water if necessary. (You can also add a little milk to the mixture while it is cooking to make it richer and thicker.) The dish will be ready when the vegetables are pulpy and the soup has that famous thick pea-soup consistency. Stir in salt and pepper and serve.

Peas are a highly concentrated, filling substance that are best complemented by light foods such as carrots, cucumbers, celery, salad and fruits. Well endowed in the roughage department, they are believed by some to help constipation. The other side of this coin though is that peas produce flatulence as well, especially the dried varieties, and so should be eaten sparingly by those with tendencies toward such problems. While the shelled and boiled varieties of peas are the most popular in Western countries, so-called "sugar peas" or "snow peas" are widely employed in Oriental cuisine where they are eaten raw or cooked and served directly in the pod. Fresh peas are also used in Middle Eastern cuisine, and in India where they are frequently a main ingredient in curries.

VEGETABLE CURRY

6 onions, chopped	1½ tablespoons sea salt
1 tablespoon ghee (see page 164)	2 fresh green chilies or chili powder to taste
1 tablespoon turmeric	1 cup chopped carrots
¾ tablespoons curry powder (or better, garam masala, available at Indian grocery stores)	1 cup fresh peas
	1 tablespoon lemon juice

1. Fry onions in ghee until they become transparent. Then add turmeric, curry (or garam masala), salt, and chilies or chili powder. Add carrots and sauté for several minutes.

2. Cover saucepan and cook for another 15 minutes, then add peas. Mix well, cover and cook until the peas and carrots are dry and very tender. Add lemon juice a few minutes before the vegetables are ready. Serve with rice and lentils.

Beans—Dried beans are on top of the list as far as fiber and roughage go and make excellent antidotes for constipation. Medical tests also tell us that dried beans reduce blood fats, a major cause of hardening of the arteries.

There are, of course, many varieties of dried beans, almost all of them high in protein (as much as 20 percent) plus B vitamins, phosphorus, calcium and iron. If you eat a lot of dried beans it is sound nutritional practice to feast on them in the company of grains. That's the way it's done in most countries: rice and beans (the Orient), rice and lentils (India), tortillas and beans (Mexico), black beans and rice (Cuba), soybeans and bulgar (Middle East), brown bread and baked beans (New England), and so forth. The amino acids in the legumes and in the grains complement one another, combining to form a complete protein. More on this in the section on protein.

Unlike other vegetables, dried beans can and should be cooked for long periods of time before serving. Cooking increases their nutritional value and makes beans more digestible. Soybeans, for instance, should be washed and allowed to soak several hours or, better, overnight before cooking. Same with black-eyed peas, navy beans, adzuki beans and most others. If overnight soaking is not possible the beans can be quickly brought to a boil and then allowed to simmer for an hour or two. If you are plagued by flatulence when eating beans the best antidote is to combine both the above methods, soaking overnight *and* boiling and simmering the next day. The gassy quality of beans is due to two starches, stachyose and raffinose. Neither can be broken down by the enzymes in the small intestines. Both combine with other bacteria to make gas. As a rule, these maverick enzymes can be made quiescent by the one-two punch of soaking and then boiling. A further method is to remove a quarter of the cooking water after the beans are half-cooked and replace the water with apple-cider vinegar. Then continue to cook until beans are soft. For a more detailed description of this method see the chapter on "Beans, Nuts and Seeds" in Fred Rohé's worthy book *The Complete Book of Natural Foods* (Boulder: Shambala Publications, 1983). Some people, by the way, drop a pinch of baking soda in with the beans to reduce flatulence, but this is not recommended, as soda steals nutrients from vegetables, just like salt does.

A gallery of beans would include:

Mung—Small, unassuming beans grown mostly in India. They are often used for sprouting. Next to soybeans they have more protein than any other member of their family. Soak for several hours before cooking. Boil one cup mungs in three cups water for a half hour to an hour.

Adzuki beans—Especially popular in Japan, adzuki beans are tasty and easily digested. A small dark-red bean with a stripe down its side, wonderful when mixed with grains or on its own. Use the water they're boiled in for kidney disorders. Soak for an hour before cooking, then cook one cup beans in three cups water for about an hour. Adzukis can be added to boiling rice and cooked (and served) together.

Garbanzo beans—Better known as chick-peas. Lots of good roughage and a fine source of protein. Very similar to the so-called "yellow-eye" and "cranberry" beans. Soak for two hours before using. Mix one cup garbanzos to five cups water. Cook for about three hours, or until tender. They go nicely with pungent goat cheeses, in a fresh salad, in rice, in vegetable soups, and above all in a famous Middle Eastern dip, hummus.

HUMMUS

2 cups garbanzo beans
½ cup sesame-seed oil
3 cloves garlic, finely chopped
½ cup sesame tahini
⅓ cup fresh lemon juice

½ teaspoon sea salt
Pinch of paprika
½ teaspoon cumin
¼ cup water (optional)

1. Soak the beans overnight to make them soft. (If you're in a hurry use the precooked, somewhat less nutritious canned varieties.) Next day mix all the ingredients together except the garbanzos and the water, and place in a blender. Purée until smooth.

2. When the paste reaches a thick but workable consistency blend in the garbanzos a few at a time. If the mixture becomes too thick while you're blending, add the water until dip reaches an agreeable consistency. Refrigerate and then serve with pita bread.

Fava Beans—Large, lima-shaped beans rich in vitamin B and calcium. Rather bland in taste. They go best mixed with rice or in a casserole. Soak for two hours, then cook one cup of beans in two cups water for about an hour, or until beans are tender.

Kidney beans—A red or white kidney-shaped bean rich in protein. (The white kind are sometimes referred to as cannelli beans.) Try mixing the white and red together with a little oil and serving them cold for a delicious summer salad. These are the beans you enjoy best in chili and in many Mexican dishes. Soak for two hours, cook for about the same amount of time, one cup beans to three cups water.

Black beans—As the name says, black. These are very popular in Cuban, Chinese and Caribbean dishes, and have a full, hearty taste. Soak for about two hours, then cook one cup of beans in four cups water for about an hour and a half.

BLACK-BEAN DIP

2 cups black beans
2 medium onions, diced
1 clove garlic, chopped
Sprinkle of fresh dill

Sprinkle of basil
Dash of pepper
¼ teaspoon sea salt
Juice of 1 lemon

1. Boil the black beans until they are tender.
2. Combine the onions, garlic, dill, basil, pepper and salt in a mixing

bowl and add the lemon juice. Stir, then add the beans and put the whole mixture into a blender. Blend until finely puréed. Serve on fresh bread, whole-wheat crackers, or as an hors d'oeuvre.

Lima beans—One of the most familiar on the list. A bit bland perhaps but with plenty of phosphorus and protein. When eaten with dairy products or eggs they make a perfect meatless, high-protein meal. But beware, they tend to be more caloric than many other varieties of bean. Soak for two hours, cook one cup beans in two cups water for an hour to an hour and a half.

Navy beans—A rather inferior protein but good taste and good source of minerals, including magnesium, iron, copper, sulphur and phosphorus. Also lots of roughage. The dried kinds are particularly gas-producing. Soak for two hours, then cook one cup beans in three cups water for an hour.

Soybeans—The number-one protein-bearing bean, and just about the best source of protein after meat, eggs and dairy products. Widely used in the East, especially in the form of tofu, or bean curd. At their best when served with soy or Tamari sauce. Soak four hours or overnight. Then cook one cup beans in four cups water for three to four hours.

Pinto beans—A speckled Mexican specialty with a good protein. Excellent with rice. Serve with a grain to bring out their subtle taste. Soak three hours, cook three hours in three cups water.

Lentils—Need only a few minutes of soaking to soften them. Then clean them carefully: Lentils for some reason are especially apt to have stones or sandy debris. More acidic than other beans, they are also more digestible when well cooked. Lentils are a traditional accompaniment to rice and curry dishes in India.

Black-eyed peas—Really a bean, not a pea. Small, oval, with a black spot on the side (hence the black eye), they are a favorite in the American South. Usually served as a main vegetable dish, they are referred to as "cow beans" in some parts of the country. Delicious in almost any concoction, especially with rice. Soak one hour, cook one hour in three cups water.

Green beans—The *vin ordinaire* of beans, green beans are easy to cook, easy to find in the market, simple to grow, and like all other green and yellow vegetables, full of carotene and vitamin A. Unlike most members of the bean family, however, green beans need not be dried before they are cooked but can be plucked and eaten right off the vine. They freeze well too, especially if garden-fresh. Blanch them quickly, seal them in an airtight bag, and place them in the freezer immediately. Green beens go perfectly in a summer salad or as a side dish of their own.

MARINATED GREEN BEANS

1 medium onion, chopped	**½ cup water**
¼ cup unrefined olive oil	**1 pound fresh green beans**
2 tomatoes, peeled and sliced	**1 tablespoon sea salt**

1. Sauté the onions in oil several minutes, then add tomatoes, water, beans, and salt. Cook mixture until the beans become soft and tender.

2. Place in a bowl and refrigerate for a day. Always serve cold.

8. Fruits of Vegetables

Certain so-called vegetables are actually the seed-bearing parts of the plant, the ovaries, and as such are technically a fruit. This differentiation is hairsplitting for all but botanists, perhaps, though the fact that these fruit/vegetables constitute the fecund parts of the organism tends to make them especially succulent and nutritious. Among the fruits of vegetables are the following.

Cucumbers—Not as strong as many other vegetables in the nutrient department, though well fortified with thiamine and some vitamin A. If you are eating a meal with heavy meats an enzyme in the cucumber called erepsin will help you digest animal protein. Most supermarket cucumbers are covered with wax as a preservative and should be thoroughly peeled. It's better to purchase this vegetable unwaxed from a health food store. Keep in the refrigerator and eat as soon as possible.

Tomatoes—The perennial favorite, tomatoes are especially easy to grow, even in a flowerpot. A strong source of vitamins C, B and A. Those allergic to tomatoes will tolerate them better if the tomatoes are boiled. Hothouse tomatoes, the kind you usually get in the market during the winter, are notoriously bland and drained of vitality. Best to eat these only occasionally and enjoy your tomatoes in the summer when they're vine-ripened. Fresh tomatoes will mature better and faster if you rest them stem side down in a warm place. When fully ripened store them in the refrigerator.

Eggplant—Like the tomato, eggplant botanically belongs to the nightshade family, and like the tomato, it was up to the middle of the nineteenth century considered a deadly poison. Large, watery, somewhat bland in taste and not excessively endowed with nutrients (eggplant's actual vitamin content has never been accurately determined), eggplant serves primarily as a backdrop for other foods. It goes best in casseroles, meat stews, mixed vegetable dishes or covered with a substantially flavored meat or cheese sauce. Eggplant's low calorie count makes it an ideal food for dieters. Keep it stored in the refrigerator, and after slicing, eat it right away.

Squash—Several good varieties here, including butternut, Hubbard, banana and buttercup. A good heavy squash means it has a thick wall and hence better-tasting meat. Its easily digestible qualities and high water content make it excellent for convalescents. Thick-skinned varieties will store well in cool, dark places. The ideal temperature is about 55 degrees. The thin-skinned kinds must be eaten immediately. Popular varieties of squash include:

Zucchini—A thin-skinned green summer squash. Easy to grow, looks like a long cucumber, but has its own succulent taste. Wonderful sautéed in oil or in a casserole.

Patty pan—Popular greenish-white, round, thin-skinned variety with scalloped edge.

Acorn—Round, brownish, thick-skinned squash. A familiar sight and taste in the fall. Will store for long periods of time but is sweetest if eaten during the first weeks after harvest.

Butternut—Thick-skinned fall squash. Familiar yellow pear shape, sometimes grows a foot long. Especially good when baked.

Pumpkin—Hard-skinned. Use the flesh for pie. Remove the seeds, wash them, spread them out on a cookie sheet and dry in the oven for an hour at about 200 degree heat. The seeds are munchy, crunchy, and a lot better for you than potato chips.

Green peppers—The much-neglected green pepper is, though most people don't realize it, one of nature's best sources of vitamin C, having quantities of this important substance far in excess of that possessed by lemons, limes, grapefruits or even oranges. Fresh green peppers are primarily a supplementary vegetable, going perfectly as part of a fresh salad, or added to any dish of mixed cooked vegetables. When shopping for green peppers look for plants that are heavy and thick-walled, and that show no puncture marks, watery spots, or crinkled, wilted skin. Peak season is June to October. Peppers do not keep for long periods of time, so buy them in small quantities, keep them refrigerated, and eat them within a few days after purchase.

9. Fungi

Mushrooms—Mushrooms have a fairly healthy supply of minerals, especially phosphorus and iron, plus a fair amount of vitamin B. They are easy to digest and go well with a variety of other foods. Avoid those that look too ripe, are discolored or have pitted caps. A few drops of lemon juice over mushrooms after washing and before refrigerating in a sealed bag will help keep their crunchy, earthy taste intact. A particularly nutritious mushroom variety, especially popular among the followers of macrobiotics, is the dried shiitake mushroom. Among its many virtues it is said to have a strong antitumor effect and is used in various forms of Japanese traditional medicine to fight cancer. Shiitakes will keep indefinitely when stored in a well-sealed container.

CLEAR MUSHROOM SOUP

½ tablespoon curry powder
1 onion, chopped
2 tablespoons butter
1 clove garlic, chopped
½ pound fresh mushrooms
1 cup soup stock
1 tablespoon fresh-squeezed
  lemon juice
1 cup water
1 tablespoon Worcestershire
  sauce (optional)
¼ tablespoon basil (fresh if
  possible)
2 green onion tops,
  chopped

1. Sprinkle the curry powder over the chopped onion, place in a skillet and sauté in butter until brown. Add garlic and mushrooms and sauté another 5 minutes.

2. Add soup stock, lemon juice, water, Worcestershire, basil, and simmer the whole mixture for 2 minutes. Serve garnished with chopped green onion tops.

10. Seeds and Nuts

Technically not vegetables, seeds and nuts inhabit their own categories, both biologically and nutritionally. Both are enormously substantial foods; it's a pity they have been relegated to the snack department. Some varieties of nuts have almost as much protein in them as meat, and are hence a heavy staple on vegetarian menus. An added bonus too is that since their texture is crunchy and snappy seeds and nuts make an excellent substitute in a child's lunchbox for junk munchies. Indeed, mixed with a selection of dried fruits, seeds and nuts comprise an irresistible taste treat and as such they are presently being marketed along with the standard commercial chocolate bars at many candy-store counters. Don't, however, eat too many nuts at a sitting, as they contain a great deal of oil and are high in concentrated fats. A few nuts here, a few more seeds there, is best. Try not to overdo.

Here's a list of some favorites in both categories:

SEEDS

Pumpkin seeds—Sold in some parts of America as "pepitas," endowed with a relatively rich amount of iron, protein, varieties of vitamin B and some calcium, dried pumpkin seeds are as crunchy as chips and as easy to procure as your Halloween pumpkin. Next October, when you're scooping out the tangled innards of a pumpkin, separate the seeds, place them on a metal tray, dry them in the oven at a low heat for about an hour and keep them on hand for a salty treat. If you don't care for the chewy outer shell, you can hull them yourself, a rather burdensome task, or simply purchase the shelled variety at any natural food store.

Sesame seeds—A staple food in many parts of the Orient and the Middle East, sesames are grown mostly in East Asia and Africa, and were originally introduced to the West by African slaves. Like many other seed varieties, sesame seeds contain ample supplies of potassium, iron and protein. They taste best when toasted; try them sprinkled over slices of cold bean curd dipped in Tamari sauce (add some chopped scallions and grated ginger too). Or, for that matter, sprinkle them on just about anything: a salad, meats, cooked vegetables, cookies, breakfast cereals. They have a quiet, subtle taste that blends with a large number of different foods (see page 102 for an excellent sesame-seed hummus recipe). And the next time you sauté vegetables try cooking them in sesame oil. The oil has a stronger taste than the seeds themselves, but it is a good taste and goes especially well with fried carrots and bean curd.

Sunflower seeds—Another health food standard. You can grow your own, of course, but shelling is a problem and the shells have jagged edges that tend to catch in the teeth and throat. Better to purchase the fresh hulled varieties from the natural food store. They are often sold in bins by the pound. Toast them first, if you like, and then sprinkle them over salads or mix the nuts with hamburgers for an interesting "seed burger." Salted varieties make an excellent party snack or lunchbox treat. There's plenty of protein, phosphorus and potassium here for all.

Pine nuts—Not nuts at all but seeds from certain varieties of pine tree, pine nuts, or pignolis as they are sometimes called, are mostly imported from Mediterranean countries and are relatively high in protein and iron. They do not really stand on their own as a separate snack food but are best added to cooked dishes: chopped onto soups, added to vegetables or included in omelets.

Flaxseeds—The linseed oil we mix with our paints is distilled from these humble little seeds, but their value is more than industrial. The ground seeds, though they do not have a particularly strong flavor, add a tasty *je ne sais quoi* to breakfast cereals along with a nice supplement of protein, iron and phosphorus. You can also grind your own flaxseeds in a food processor or mortar and pestle, and then sprinkle them over yogurt or cottage cheese. A tea brewed from these seeds has been a standard for many centuries as an aid for constipation and flatulence; the bulk they provide when added to cereal will help in this department also. You can use them medicinally too by simply letting them sit in a cup of water overnight, straining the next morning, and drinking the liquid. Flaxseeds can be purchased at almost any natural food store.

Nuts

Walnuts—The best and most familiar are English walnuts, sold practically everywhere. Black walnuts are both more nutritious and more accessible (most walnut trees in America are of the black variety), but their meat is bitter and they are difficult to crack. Walnuts offer a good source of iron and potassium, like most members of the nut family, and go well in just about any dessert, pudding, or with soft cheeses. Most commercial brands have been bleached with lye to produce those pretty gray shells and have been exposed to certain toxic gases to make shelling easier. Buy the untreated kinds if possible.

Cashews—Be careful, the shells of cashews are poisonous—which is why they are first steamed after picking, then sold shelled and bagged. (These nuts are actually a rather close relative of poison ivy.) Cashews are high in certain proteins, magnesium, iron and sodium. Eat them alone or on top of desserts, in pies and puddings, or ground up into a delicious nut butter.

CASHEW BUTTER

1 pound cashews	sesame oil

1. Grind the cashews in a blender, food processor or electric nut grinder.

2. Mix in several teaspoonsful of sesame oil, blend again. Add more oil; continue blending and adding oil until the ground nuts take on a peanut-butter-like texture. Serve on toast or on fresh bread.

Almonds—A highly nutritious, delicious, all-round nut, almonds contain large amounts of vitamin B, calcium, protein, magnesium, iron and phosphorus. Its oil is not usually considered edible, though it is used extensively in tanning preparations and in skin creams. The seer and healer Edgar Cayce considered almonds to be one of the finest foods the earth has to offer, and went so far as to claim that "an almond a day keeps cancer away." For some people, though, the outer skins of almonds are irritating to the digestion. If this proves to be the case for you, the skins can be removed by placing the nuts in a pot, pouring boiling water over them and letting them soak for several minutes. The skins will then loosen and can be slipped off with relative ease.

Peanuts—Botanically, peanuts are not nuts at all but members of the legume family. In taste and consistency they are so nutlike though that such distinction seems academic at best. Peanuts are rich in vitamin E and niacin, and are a sound if relatively incomplete source of proteins. Toasting and salting makes them especially delicious, of course, but if heated too much peanuts lose some of their nutritional properties. At best they should be roasted no longer than a minute, preferably in a frying pan with a few teaspoons of oil. Even then they will lose some of their potency. When shopping for peanut butter, keep away from commercial kinds unless the label tells you they contain no additives, preservatives, emulsifiers to stop the peanut butter from sticking to the roof of your mouth, and so on. The really natural kind comes with the oil separated on the top. Don't be put off by this—it's a sign that the substance has not been too tampered with. Simply give it a minute's good stir and enjoy. You can also grind your own peanut butter using any of the many commercial machines presently on the market.

Pecans—A very rich, fatty nut, its high calorie count makes it a nemesis to dieters, its wonderful taste a temptation to gourmets. It has an especially high count of vitamin B-12, as well as iron and protein. Buy the unshelled kind if possible, thus assuring yourself that they have not been tampered with and that they will keep (shelled pecans do not last very long).

Sea Vegetables

It has been estimated that three-quarters of plant life found in the ocean is eatable, and that a majority of this vegetation is more nutritious than 95 percent of the foods we normally eat. Indeed, all the major sea vegetables contain the entire spectrum of mineral elements required by the human organism. Quite an endorsement, and add to this that almost *all* major vitamins are present in sea vegetables, including vitamin B-12, the vitamin most needed by nonmeat eaters, plus niacin, thiamine, riboflavin, pantothenic acid, betacarotene, and on and on.

But the prejudice against sea vegetables prevails. About the only place you'll find them in the United States and Europe is at Oriental grocers or at the back counters of natural food stores, usually in odd plastic packages bearing unpronounceable names like wakame or hijiki.

Yes, sea vegetables do have a somewhat exotic taste at first for the uninitiated, and yes, for some they are a bit difficult to digest. It has even been suggested that Orientals have special enzymes in their intestines that allow them to eat sea vegetables with impunity.

All may be the case, but only up to a point. Taken raw or poorly prepared these foods are difficult to love. But when properly cooked they can be delicious and even addictive, like oysters and clams and sushi. In fact, anyone who enjoys Japanese dishes, especially sushi or sukiyaki or yosenabe, is already eating and appreciating them: The maki-type sushis come wrapped in seaweed, and many of our favorite Japanese dishes contain some form of nori, wakame or arami. If you're intrigued there are many cookbooks on the market describing fine and inventive ways of integrating sea vegetables into the daily menu. A list of these books will be found in Books for Further Reading.

Sea vegetables come to the consumer in many varying sizes and shapes. Some are short and stringy; some are long and tentaclelike; some are tubelike; some are commercially pressed into flat greenish sheets; they are as varied as sea life itself. If you're interested in opening yourself up to this new world, keep an eye out in the natural food stores or Oriental markets (especially the Japanese and Korean markets) for any of the following:

Arami—A wiry, black seaweed relatively mild in taste. Loaded with protein, vitamins A and B, it goes nicely in vegetable soup or served as a side vegetable. It can also be boiled, then served cold with sesame seeds sprinkled over it.

Hijiki—Stringlike and wiry. The taste is saltier than arami and takes some getting used to. Soak in water for at least a half hour before using, then sauté in sesame or corn oil for about a half hour or until the hijiki becomes soft and pliable. It can then be added to soups or served with rice or vegetables. Add Tamari sauce to improve taste. Hijiki is especially rich in iodine and helps lower blood cholesterol levels. If you take it regularly you'll never need iodized salt.

Nori—Nori is more than two-thirds protein, has more calcium than a glass of milk, and contains almost no fat—the natural dieter's delight. It comes in pressed square sheets that are sometimes formed a foot wide.

In Japanese cuisine it is often used as a kind of wrapper to keep pastries and rice balls together. Nori leaves can be toasted or crumbled up and sprinkled over rice or noodles.

Wakame—In the aftermath of Hiroshima and Nagasaki, many patients suffering radiation poisoning were kept alive with a special diet heavily concentrated in sea vegetables. Wakame was one of the varieties most commonly used, and its radiation-reducing qualities have since been well established by Japanese scientists. It is said to be especially good if you've just received heavy doses of X rays.* Rinse wakame under cold water and let it soak for about ten minutes. Then slice this long, thin green sea vegetable into pieces and boil for about a half hour or until it turns soft. Wakame goes wonderfully in soups, especially miso soup, and in seafood soups or stews. It can be toasted at 350 degrees for a quarter of an hour, then crumbled over noodles or rice. Like other sea vegetables, it is vastly rich in minerals, especially iodine.

Dulse—A dark-red seaweed that can be added with great effect to salads. It can also be eaten dry or boiled in soup. Dulse has an extremely high iron content, which makes it especially good for menstruating women and those suffering from anemia.

Kombu—A dark-green sea vegetable with many uses: It can be soaked for several hours, then boiled with soups, served with vegetables, even frosted with icing and made into a candy. It is often served with rice and meat as a side dish in Japan. A popular Japanese tea called kombu-cha uses kombu as the primary ingredient. When baked for twenty minutes in a 350 degree oven and then ground up in a mortar and pestle, kombu can be sprinkled directly into soup as a salt substitute.

Specialty Items

There are more interesting, unusual natural foods available today than ever before, though some are less popular or less conspicuous than others. The following items are all super high in the nutrition department, yet of largely unknown or at least obscure reputation. Several of them, like carob, for instance, make excellent food substitutes (in this case for chocolate). Most can be purchased at specialty food stores, natural food stores or Oriental groceries.

Carob—Sometimes called St.-John's-bread, carob comes in a seed-pod straight off the carob tree. The pods have plenty of important nu-

---

* See T. Akizuki, M.D., *Documentary of A-Bombed Nagasaki* (Nagasaki: Nagasaki Printing Co., 1977), as quoted in Michio Kushi, *The Cancer Prevention Diet* (New York: St. Martin's Press, 1983), pp. 211–213, 220–221.

trients, including vitamins A and B plus calcium, iron, phosphorus and magnesium. They can be chewed alone or ground into a powder and used in practically any confection where chocolate is called for. By itself, however, carob is only slightly sweet and bears but a distant flavor resemblance to chocolate, so don't suppose that without another sweetener like honey added in, it will carry the day. It is at its best in baked goods like brownies or in a sweet chocolatelike drink such as:

CAROB MALTED

5 cups whole milk	5 tablespoons carob powder
1 tablespoon malt	¼ teaspoon pure vanilla
2 tablespoons honey	extract

Put all the ingredients into a blender and purée until smooth. Put in the refrigerator and serve chilled.

Tempeh—Tempeh is a fermented soybean concoction that has been a staple in Indonesia for many centuries. Recently brought to the West, it can now be purchased in either cake form or, more commonly, as a starter culture to help you make your own. Tasting something like bean curd, tempeh nonetheless has its own rich flavor and its own array of nutrients. Because of its high protein content and its liberal vitamin B-12 supply it can serve as a meat substitute. Unlike bean curd, it does not cause intestinal gas. It makes an excellent food for convalescents and people with weak stomachs.

Soba noodles—Also available at either Oriental grocery stores or natural food stores, soba noodles are made from whole wheat rather than refined pasta dough, yet they taste just as good and are certainly better for you. A Japanese staple, these are the spaghettilike strands you like so much in Oriental soups and noodle dishes. They are now packaged and sold by several American natural food manufacturers, and these varieties are recommended over the Japanese commercial brands that frequently use preservatives.

Tahini—A favorite in the Middle East and in certain parts of the Orient, tahini is made from sesame seeds that have been ground, crushed, then bottled or canned along with the sesame oil extracted in the grinding process. Tahini can be purchased at Middle Eastern grocery stores and at natural food shops. By itself tahini is rather oily and bland; its primary use is as a mixer; the hummus recipe given on page 102 is a good example. Tahini can also be mixed with peanut butter, yogurt, miso (see page 113) and especially with honey.

TAHINI-HONEY DIP

1 cup tahini   **4 tablespoons honey**

Mix the honey and tahini together and serve on crackers, bread or eat as is for a candylike treat. The 4 tablespoons of honey are an arbitrary measurement, by the way. You may like to expand or reduce the amount according to your tastes.

Acidophilus milk—A tart, tangy-tasting liquid made from cultured milk with acidophilus bacteria added. The taste is not unlike yogurt, though stronger, and the digestive action that the helpful acidophilus flora introduce to the intestines is as helpful. Acidophilus milk is, in fact, a stronger digestive than yogurt, especially since many of the commercial brands of yogurt are manufactured with sugared additives and inferior cultures. Acidophilus milk can be found in the dairy section of many food shops. It should be kept in the refrigerator and used within a day or two of purchase, as it spoils even more quickly than regular milk. (See page 203 for more on acidophilus.)

Burdock root—When you walk through a meadow in late summer numbers of little spiky burrs will sometimes stick to your clothing. Their needles lock so firmly into the fabric that they must be yanked off one at a time. These burrs come from the burdock plant. And while the burrs may be a nuisance, the stem of the plant, when uprooted, peeled and cooked, makes delicious eating and is used in many parts of the world, especially Japan and Hawaii. Burdock root contains many minerals and vitamins, including vitamin C and potassium, and is reputed to have an overall strengthening effect when regularly included in the diet. Either pick your own fresh root (in the spring the young leaves can be steamed and eaten too) or purchase it pickled or fresh at Oriental groceries and macrobiotic food stores.

Miso—A fermented soy bean paste, extremely popular in Japan where an entire folklore has gathered around it (see *The Book of Miso*, William Shurtleff and Akiko Aoyagi, Brookline, Mass.: Autumn Press, 1976). Miso is a good source of vitamin B-12 and contains no fiber or cellulose, making it easily digestible. Since it includes four digestive agents —lactic-acid bacteria, salt-resistant yeasts, fermentation-producing molds and enzymes—its action in the bowels is believed to help break down foods efficiently and assimilate them quickly. In Japan miso is even looked upon with a kind of supernatural awe and it is widely believed that a steady diet of it will increase the life span. Miso can be found in all

Oriental and natural food stores. Hatcho miso, because it is highest in protein, is generally considered the most nutritious.

BASIC MISO SOUP

1 quart water	Sea vegetable (optional)
1 onion, sliced	Slices of tofu (optional)
3 tablespoons miso	

1. Place water and onion in a pot and bring to a boil, then reduce to a simmer.

2. Place miso in a separate bowl with small amount of hot water and mash it with a wooden spoon until miso is thoroughly mixed. Add miso to soup and cook for several more minutes. A sea vegetable like wakame or arami, or slices of tofu, can be added to taste.

Tofu—Bean curd. By now a relatively well-known commodity, tofu has been a favorite in the Orient for thousands of years. One four-ounce serving yields roughly 8 grams of protein, the same as many varieties of fish, and it mixes well with hundreds of other foods: Put a slab of it in soup, crumble it over noodles, sauté with vegetables, mash it into cottage cheese or dice it into salads. Today tofu is available at most supermarkets. Be sure to keep it in water when storing, and change the water every day if possible.

TOFU MAYONNAISE

2 tablespoons vinegar	Juice of a lemon
1 clove garlic, minced	1 teaspoon Dijon-style mustard
½ cup yogurt	2 teaspoons Tamari sauce
½ pound tofu	2 tablespoons unrefined olive oil

Place all ingredients in a blender and purée. Can be used as a spread, on sandwiches, in salads, wherever ordinary mayo is used.

Soy milk—The liquid extracted from crushed soybeans during the production of various soy products, such as bean curd. Because of its high vitamin and protein content, soy milk can be used as a cow-milk substitute for children with allergies to dairy food. Purchase *fresh* soy milk whenever you can, as the canned varieties are often adulterated. (See page 204 for more on soy milk.)

Chia seeds—These small black seeds, which come mostly from Mexico and the American Southwest, are extremely well endowed with protein. They make excellent seeds for sprouting. Or grind them in a mortar and pestle and sprinkle them over cottage cheese or into bread dough. Since they have little taste of their own, high-protein chias are an excellent way to slip some extra protein into the family peanut butter or breakfast cereal.

A Last Word About Preparing Vegetables

Much has so far been said concerning methods of preparing and cooking vegetables to insure their highest natural goodness. Here are some last thoughts: recaps, reminders and reiterations.

• With the exception of beans and some leafy greens, vegetables should be cooked as *quickly* as possible. The more cooking that vegetables are forced to endure—this is almost an axiom—the more of their nutrients will be wasted. Vegetables that are ordinarily boiled can be parboiled instead; or steamed. Rather than deep-frying try stir-frying in a wok; or sautéing.

Vegetables: Steaming Versus Boiling

Vegetable	Cooking Method	% of Protein Loss	% of Calcium Loss	% of Magnesium Loss	% of Phosphorus Loss	% of Iron Loss
Asparagus	Boiled	20	16.5	9	26	34
	Steamed	13	15	1	10	20
String Beans	Boiled	29	29	9	26	34
	Steamed	17	16	21	19	24.5
Cabbage	Boiled	61.5	72	76	60	67
	Steamed	31.5	40	43	22	35
Carrots	Boiled	26	8	22	19	34
	Steamed	14.5	5	6	1	21
Cauliflower	Boiled	44	25	25	50	36
	Steamed	8	3	2	19	8
Spinach	Boiled	29	5.5	59	49	57
	Steamed	6	0	18	10	26
Average for All Vegetables	Boiled	43	32	45	46	48
	Steamed	16	11	19	17	21

• Use as little water as possible when cooking vegetables. Water pirates out the water-soluble vitamins, especially B and C, and evaporates minerals. Steaming, pressure-cooking, sautéing and stir-frying are the best methods to conserve water *and* to speed up the vegetable cooking process. The table on page 115, adapted from *Commercial Vegetable Processing,* by J. Woodruff and B. Luh (Westport, Conn.: Avi Publishing Co.), tells all.

• Many gas-producing vegetables can be cooked at low temperatures in milk instead of water. Milk has a neutralizing effect on certain plant enzymes and has a gentler cooking action on delicate vegetables. Try it. The champion of this method, Adelle Davis, has lots of good tips on milk boiling in her book *Let's Cook It Right* (New York: New American Library).

• Again: Don't overslice. Some vitamins are light-sensitive. Others are air-sensitive or heat-sensitive. Almost no vegetables need or enjoy prolonged exposure to the elements. If you are going to chop and dice, know that (1) the larger the pieces the better the conservation of vitamins will be; (2) you should cut and chop immediately before cooking; (3) you should slice the vegetables *after* they are cooked, not before.

• Learn the spoilage schedule for different vegetables. Some, like onions and potatoes and thick-skinned squash, will last for months if kept in the proper environment. Others, like lettuce, tomatoes and cucumbers, spoil in a week. Check the storage information given on page 117, and experiment on your own. The refrigerator is usually, *but not always,* the best place to keep foods. Sometimes a dark, dry cellar is better; sometimes a warm, damp closet. Try it yourself and keep track.

• Whenever it's feasible, serve vegetables raw or slightly steamed. If necessity doesn't demand that you bake or fry or boil them, don't. Vegetables are the gift of the earth and need no improvement. Why tamper with what is already perfect?

About Natural Cooking Utensils

Get yourself a steamer, a pressure cooker, a good cast-iron or stainless-steel skillet, and a wok. Avoid aluminum if possible. Since aluminum is both toxic and soft, cooking with aluminum utensils will increase your intake of this metal. Iron, on the other hand, is fine; the natural iron in cast-iron cooking equipment actually helps supplement the body's need for this precious mineral. Steer clear too of Teflon and copper. Teflon is obviously not something you want to ingest, but if you insist on using it, throw out any Teflon item that's chipped or peeling and try to stick to the newer, harder synthetic coatings like SilverStone. Copper is an essential

Storage Schedule for Vegetables

Food	Storage Life	Optimum Temperature for Storage
Beans (dried)	a year	dry atmosphere, around 35 degrees; as antiweevil and moth protection first keep in fridge for several days before storing
Cabbage	5 months maximum	40 degrees
Carrots	half a year	freezing to 40 degrees
Cauliflower	2 months maximum	just above freezing with some moisture in the air
Celery	several months	just above freezing with some moisture in the air; store away from cabbage
Kale	1 month maximum	just above freezing in highly moist atmosphere
Leeks	1 to 3 months	just above freezing in moist atmosphere
Onions	3 to 6 months	just above freezing in a dry atmosphere; keep in mesh bags or basket so onions can breathe
Peas (dried)	a year	freezing to 40 degrees
Peppers	2 to 3 months	45 to 50 moist degrees; will rot below 40 degrees
Potatoes	3 to 4 months	35 to 40 moderately moist degrees; be sure to keep in dark place; late potatoes store best
Pumpkins	several months	55 dry degrees; cure for 2 weeks at 80 degrees (near heater, for instance) before storing
Squash	3 to 5 months	55 dry degrees; cure as with pumpkins (above) before storing (don't cure acorn squash this way)

mineral, but only in minute amounts; it's easy to overdose. Enamel is okay. So are glass, wood and nonleaded ceramics.

For stirring, stainless-steel utensils are good. Better though are wooden forks, spoons, spatulas, skewers and so forth; all have a natural and "right" feeling about them when used with food. Wooden plates are nice to eat from too. When you slice, cut on a wooden cutting board, making sure you wipe it thoroughly when finished. If they are not well cleaned, wooden cooking utensils can breed bacteria.

COOKING WITH A WOK

A wok is a round-bottomed iron or steel cooking pan designed for quick stir-frying. Its main virtue is its curved shape, which helps disperse the heat evenly over the entire surface, making it easy to move foods around and mix them with liquids at the bottom of the pan. Woks can now be purchased at standard kitchen supply stores. When you get your wok home, season it before using by filling the bottom of the pan with oil or fat and placing it over low heat for several minutes. Remove pan from heat and allow the oil to cool. Then throw out the oil and give the wok a good washing. Dry thoroughly. Now it's ready to go. To clean wok after use, remove from stove while still warm, place it in the sink, and wash with warm water, tilting water around the bowl and scrubbing off debris with a soft-bristled brush. Never store a wok that has not been thoroughly dried. It will quickly rust. To use your new utensil for cooking, place oil in the bottom and heat until it's extremely hot. Add sliced vegetables (solid ones like carrots first, soft ones like greens last). Simmer with the lid on until they're done, stirring the vegetables with a watchful eye to prevent sticking and burning.

Grains, seeds, beans and other storables are best kept in glass jars away from light, or in wooden barrels or bins. Covered ceramic containers are good too. Investigate bamboo: bamboo steamers, bamboo strainers, bamboo ladles, colanders and mixing instruments. They're available at gourmet kitchen shops and in Oriental grocery stores. Also, marble mortars and pestles for slow, careful grinding jobs. Look for real wooden-handled Japanese and Chinese knives. They are beautifully honed and balanced instruments, especially the paring knives and cleavers. A kitchen simply feels more natural and more in tune with natural foods when the utensils are made of substances like wood, rattan, stone, bamboo, clay. High tech may have its place, but not—as much as possible—in the natural kitchen.

USING A STEAMER FOR VEGETABLES

Place the steamer in the bottom of a pot into which just enough water has been added to keep the water level slightly below the bottom of the steamer. Add vegetables and place cover on the pot, making sure the top is seated securely. Turn on the heat. As soon as the water comes to a boil, reduce heat to a simmer. Steam the vegetables for several minutes, ten at most, two or three at least. Use the pot liquor when you are finished for soups and stews.

Freezing

Frozen vegetables are second-best only to fresh, and home freezing is an easy art to master. If you happen to grow your own vegetables you can enjoy local produce all year around this way, especially if you own a deep freezer or have access to one. Otherwise use the freezer compartment of your fridge. Just follow these rules for home freezing and you'll be on your way.

1. Wash everything thoroughly in cold water before freezing it. The dirt you overlook will amalgamate into the very fiber of the frozen produce and it will be twice as difficult to remove after the vegetable is thawed.

2. Most vegetables should be blanched before freezing. This process slows down the enzymatic reactions that cause the vegetables to toughen, discolor and decay. It also softens the vegetables and makes them more pliable. To blanch, place the vegetables in a blancher or any mesh holder or wire basket. Boil a gallon of water for each pound of vegetables, and place the basket into the boiling water. Cover, and let boil according to the schedule on page 120. (Add one minute to the blanching time if you live 5,000 feet or more above sea level.)

3. After the vegetables have been blanched, quickly remove the container from the boiling water and plunge it into a pot of cold water. Let the contents thoroughly cool, changing the water several times in the process.

4. Remove the vegetables, drain, and quickly pack them in plastic bags or tight-lidded containers. If you do use plastic bags, press out as much of the air as possible before storing to make them airtight.

5. Place the produce into the freezer immediately after packing. Below 0 degrees is best for long-term storage. Many foods last only six months, even in deep storage.

Blanching Schedule for Vegetables

Vegetable	Blanching Time
Asparagus (40 sticks)	3 minutes
Green beans (1 quart)	2 minutes
Lima beans (1 quart)	2 minutes
Beets	not necessary
Broccoli (15 stalks)	3 minutes small plant, 4 large (can also be steamed instead of blanched)
Brussels sprouts (2 cups)	3 minutes for small buds, 4 for large
Carrots (10 carrots)	3 minutes
Cauliflower (3 cups)	3 minutes
Corn (4 ears)	7 for small, 10 for large
Peas	not necessary
Peppers	steaming is sufficient
Pumpkin	steaming is sufficient
Spinach (1 quart)	3 minutes
Squash (3 cups)	4 minutes
Sweet potatoes	steaming is sufficient

FRUITS

Nutritionally fruits pack a wallop, much more than most people realize. They are easily digested, packed with vitamins, and contain goodly amounts of bulk, mainly cellulose and hemicellulose, to help along the peristalsis. Some fruits, such as prunes, have a laxative effect for this reason. However, this laxative effect, while good in moderation, can become excessive if large amounts of fruit are eaten at a sitting. And many fruits tend to be acidic, upsetting the stomach when taken in quantity (orange juice is especially guilty in this department). The high sugar content of certain fruits, especially grapes and dried fruits such as figs, apricots, and raisins, makes them hard on the teeth and not ideal for people with blood-sugar problems.

Generally speaking, therefore, fruits should comprise about 5 percent of your daily food intake, and probably not much more. They achieve their best effects when taken in small doses on a daily, regular basis. Fruits go well with the breakfast meal—don't sugar them, for heaven's sake—and for dessert. Their high water content makes them good summer eating. Some fruits, especially melons, are more than 90 percent water.

Try to eat fruits that are local and freshly picked. Oranges are best in winter; watermelons, in summer; grapes, in the fall, and so forth. One of the wonders of modern transportation is that a wide range of fruits and vegetables is available to us at all times of the year, regardless of their natural growing season. This is a big temptation, of course, but nature has something to say in the matter too. You can store an apple for ten months in a cold room all right, but somehow the taste and vitality are not the same when the time comes to eat it. You'll find this to be true too for grapes bought in May, or for a hothouse tomato, or for a January peach. Such fruits are mealy and somehow out of sorts. The general rule of thumb should be: every fruit according to its season.

Buying and Handling Fruits

Each fruit has its own special language of ripeness. With a bit of practice that language can be easily learned.

To begin, there is the basic vocabulary. For starters, stay away from overripe fruits. The stepped-up enzymatic activities in late stages of ripening run away with most of the nutrients.

Learn how a ripe fruit smells. Aroma is one of the most important signs of a ready-to-eat fruit. It should emit a *fragrance*, fresh and fruity, but not too sweet, not too pungent.

Each fruit has its own color and texture that tell you when it's ripe. If your fingers leave pucker marks as you squeeze, this generally means the fruit is over the hill.

Be wary of fruits that are very green or very unripe. They were picked too early and will never mature to their nutritional potential as a vine-ripened or tree-ripened fruit would do. In fact, vine- and tree-ripened fruits are the ideal, but you're not very likely to find them at the supermarket. Try local fruit and vegetable stands, or, better, your own backyard.

When you get fruit home, let it ripen at room temperature and handle it as little as possible. Once it has reached maturity pop it into the fridge.

Unless you enjoy the aesthetic of the fruit bowl in the middle of the table, it's also a good idea to keep the fruit covered while it's coming to maturity. Otherwise vitamins will be lost to the light and the air. Once a fruit reaches ripeness, fermentation speeds up, starch turns quickly to invert sugar, and the food loses its goodness in a matter of a few days. Learn to recognize that moment of peak ripeness, and seize the eating opportunity.

The best teacher is experience. If you're unsure just what makes a cantaloupe or a banana ready for the eating, shop with someone who knows. A little guided practice and you'll soon get the sense of it. Here are more pointers to keep in mind about each individual fruit.

The Fruit Honor Roll

Apples—Among the most popular of all fruits, apples have been overbred in the West for hundreds of years, and apple growers have so commonly hybridized these fruits for appearance at the expense of nutrition that one cannot depend on them too heavily for all-round nourishment. Apples tend to be somewhat low in the mineral department, and though often touted as a source of vitamins B and C, most species apparently contain only trace amounts of both. It can even be said that apples are most useful simply for their zesty taste, as a sweet, crunchy dessert (they're great to eat in lieu of a sweet whenever you get a sugar craving), or, even more, as a medicinal boon, their fruit-acid salts serving to stimulate the intestines and their roughage aiding the digestion (unsugared apple juice, in moderation, helps in this department as well).

There are, of course, innumerable varieties of apples to choose from. The more popular ones are not necessarily the best-tasting or even the best-looking; more commonly they are the apples that store best and hence have the longest shelf life. Still, the picking season comes in the fall, and apples are at their sweetest and most nourishing at that time of year. Some common and popular varieties include:

Jonathan—A small, deeply red apple with a tangy, tart taste. Makes especially excellent applesauce or apple juice.

Delicious—One of the better eating apples, it is bright-red in color and exceedingly sweet though somewhat mealy if not eaten fresh. Don't use it in pies as it tends to fall apart too easily when heated.

McIntosh—Another favorite, a bit tangier, crisper and smaller than the Delicious, and available at most markets all year around.

Rome—At their best when baked or used in pies. Romes are bright red and have a strong, distinctive aroma.

Golden Delicious—Another common variety, mostly yellow or greenish-yellow, extremely sweet and a bit mealy if not perfectly fresh. Their claim to fame is that they go equally well baked in a pie, cooked in a sauce, sliced into a fruit salad, or standing alone as a dessert.

Some less well known varieties worth seeking out include:

Northern Spy—Recommended by many connoisseurs as the most delicious of all eating apples. Their slightly tart taste makes them an excellent apple either alone or mixed into a fruit salad.

Winesap—A very dark red apple with a tangy taste that is indeed reminiscent of fruit wine. Will go in a pie or confection but is best when eaten alone.

Cortland—Another excellent eating apple, the Cortland is a speciality of the eastern part of the United States. Their taste is more subtle than many other apples, delicately tart and tartly delicate.

Newton-Pippin—A yellow-and-green variety, its tangy flavor goes especially well in apple pie, some say better than any other apple on the market.

Granny Smith—A yellow variety that matures a month earlier in the summer than other apples. It is extremely sweet tasting, though somewhat softer than many other species.

Apricots—These imports from the Middle East are amazingly high in vitamin complex B and vitamin A, and when dried their vitamin content increases even more. Apricots are also full of minerals, especially calcium, phosphorus and iron, and are delicious in the bargain. Serve fresh apricots uncooked—they lose nourishment if heated. When cooked, however, they are said to serve as a mild natural laxative. The best time of year to purchase apricots is June through August. Look for plump yellowish-orange fruits. Avoid those with greenish streaks or tinge, as well as apricots whose yellow color seems just a little too bright and gaudy (they are probably dyed). When ripe store in the refrigerator.

Avocados—Though sometimes spoken of as a vegetable, avocados are botanically very much a fruit. They are almost always served raw, either on their own, sliced with lemon juice squeezed on them, or as part of a salad. Avocados can also be mashed and used as a spread on good whole-grain bread. Avoid fruits that are rock hard or those with bruises, discolored skin, and puncture marks near the stem. Signs of perfect ripeness include soft but not mushy feel when squeezed, deep-green skin and yellow meat, especially near the pit, and a weighty, solid feel. Avocados can be ripened at room temperature, then kept in the refrigerator or in a cool, dry area. Once you have sliced the avocado quickly wrap the remaining parts in plastic wrap. Exposure to air will cause avocados to quickly spoil. Sprinkling the meat with a little lemon juice will prevent it from turning black. Avocados are grown in California and Florida on staggered growing schedules, and are thus available almost all year long. The oil of the avocado can be mixed with other oils and used for cooking, though its primary value is in cosmetics as a skin softener. Avocados are heavy in the fat department, and though they are sometimes included on diet menus, they will do your waistline no favors.

HEALTHY GUACAMOLE SPREAD

1 ripe avocado	¼ cup freshly chopped onion
½ teaspoon freshly squeezed	½ teaspoon sea salt
lime juice	Dash pepper
1 fresh tomato, finely chopped	

1. Blend or hand-mash the avocado until it is finely mashed. Mix in the lime juice and stir.

2. Add the tomato, onion, salt and papper. Mix. Refrigerate for several hours, then serve as a spread or dip for crackers.

Bananas—Bananas are very sweet, and they make a good sugar substitute. They have an especially high supply of potassium for those who are potassium-starved. (If you crave bananas check your diet. See if you are getting enough potassium-bearing foods.) They are also excellent fare for weak stomachs. Mash them into a fine pulp, strain them through some cheesecloth, and feed to convalescents or to babies as an early solid. They have lots of vitamins A, C and even some B along with respectable amounts of iron and phosphorus. Be careful of especially green bananas though, as they can trip off food allergies. When shopping for bananas, look for the extra-ripe ones in the bargain bin. If you eat them that same day they're often tastier and better for you than the green ones. Let bananas mature at room temperature. They need some heat to ripen. After they get to the eatable stage slow down the aging process by storing them in the refrigerator. While you're at it you can make a natural banana "Popsicle." Peel a firm but not overripe banana, wrap it in aluminum foil, and place it in the freezer for twenty-four hours. Remove and eat. The banana will have congealed into a firm consistency that has a sweet, creamy taste something akin to ice cream.

Berries—Highest in vitamin C in the berry family are strawberries, followed by raspberries. Blueberries and blackberries trail considerably behind, though they have some stores of vitamin B to make up for it. Berries should be purchased when plump, fresh and firm. Any sign that they are overripe (such as purple- or red-stained containers, indicating spoilage and leakage) means this particular batch should be avoided. Blackberries turn jet-black when ripe in August. Blueberries get a silvery sheen around the same time of year. Strawberries turn dark red in the spring, without any green or white visible at the stems. Avoid overly large strawberries; they are often mealy and tasteless. Store berries on a plate or shallow pan in the refrigerator without washing them; wash only before eating. Most berries spoil quickly, even when kept cold, so eat them as soon as possible. As with apples, one bad berry spoils the lot, so before refrigerating pick out the rotten ones. When cleaning strawberries, hull them *after* they've been washed to prevent the juices from washing away.

Cherries—Stay away from the canned varieties, especially Maraschino, which are heavily dyed and sweetened. The fresh kind are well endowed with precious minerals, iron, copper and manganese. Cherries store well when immersed in water and kept in the refrigerator. They should be eaten fairly soon after purchase, however, at least within a week. Their low roughage content makes them excellent food for people with poor digestion. Avoid those that are too soft, sticky, or with a light-colored skin. Cherries stand alone as a refreshing dessert or they can be used in pies, cakes, tarts and as a garnishing for meats. Their season is rather short, running from May through June. Popular varieties include:

Royal Ann—Large yellow cherry with a somewhat heart-shaped contour. Very juicy and firm, they are best used for preserves and canning.

Bing—One of the most popular, they are very large, with dark-red skin and an especially sweet taste.

Lambert—Very large cherry with dark-red meat.

Montmorency—Known for their tartness, they go best in pies, tarts and confections.

Black Tartarian—Very sweet cherry with thin skin and purplish-red meat.

Republican—A small heart-shaped cherry with dark-colored meat. Somewhat tart or sour, goes well in preserves and puddings.

Dates—Among the sweetest of fruits, date meat can be placed in a blender, ground up at high speed, and used as a sweetener, sprinkled over cereals or added to confections. Nutritionally, dates are a reasonably good source of vitamins A and B-1 and contain respectable amounts of calcium and iron too. They are almost always purchased in preserved form, either loose from a bin or sealed in a package. Though many consumers are not aware of the fact, a number of date species are available to the discerning buyer. The small, pale-brown, dried-out, nut-sized packaged commercial varieties we have become accustomed to are often the only types available at the supermarkets, and as a rule these have been heavily processed. Try the natural food stores, food co-ops, or fresh farm stands for a wider selection of varieties. Look for dates with a plump body and a very dark brown or black, slightly sticky skin. Dates make an excellent candy substitute, but because of their sweetness they should be eaten in moderation.

Grapes—Grapes are rather heavy on the calorie side, around 70 per cup, so use them sparingly when on a diet. If you're trying to kick the sugar habit, they make a satisfying substitute. Grapes do not store well. Keep them in the refrigerator for best results. And note that grapes stop ripening the moment they're picked, so if you harvest your own be sure they're vine-ripened before removing. Grapes are a mild, natural diuretic and have a wonderful cleansing effect on the whole body, especially the kidneys. They are excellent for removing uric acid from the system and stimulating the bowels. For this reason some people begin and end a fast with a grape diet. When purchasing grapes, look for moist, plump, deeply colored fruits without bruising or spoilage on the skin. Avoid grapes with whitish coloration around the stems. Some of the twenty-five varieties grown in this country include:

Red Malaga—Large, seeded grapes, available from midsummer to October.

Concord—Somewhat tart, with thick skins that slip off easily. Very popular for juice and preserves.

Niagara—A large white grape, very juicy and sweet. Most varieties are seedless.

Thompson—Seedless. Excellent for drying and making raisins.

Tokay—Available from the end of summer through January. Large, round, firm grape with a tough skin and slightly sweetish flavor.

Delaware—Tender, small, delicate grapes, seeded and very sweet. Available at the end of summer.

Almeria—Large, dry, seedless white grape.

Emperor—Light-red grape with a somewhat purple blush on ripe skins. A pungent, sweet taste and tough skin.

Olivette Blanche—Early summer white grape with sweet flavor. Does contain seeds.

Melons—Best known in the melon family are cantaloupes, honeydew, crenshaw, Persian and casaba. Melons have an extremely large supply of vitamin C plus some vitamins A and B. Their high water content gives them a slightly diuretic effect, helping to wash the kidneys and bowels, and making them a happy treat on steamy summer days. Try adding chunks of chilled melon to a cold fruit salad containing grapes, oranges and bananas. Melons are an especially seasonal fruit, so beware of cantaloupes in January; they may be available, but they will rarely be good. Melons should be kept at room temperature till ripe, then refrigerated until eaten. Each melon has its own ripening schedule. Cantaloupes are usually picked green from May to September and are not really ripe until the stem ends become slightly soft and the skin takes on a yellowish tinge. They will also smell fragrant when ripe. Honeydews are available through the summer and into the fall. Those with a whitish or greenish hue still have a way to go. Honeydew is ready when it takes on a creamy yellowish color. Unlike most other melons, it is at its best served at room temperature. Persian melons are quite expensive but are a great taste treat. They are available through the summer and are at their best in July. Casabas are larger and turn a yellowish color when ripe. They are at their sweetest in the fall. The same is true with crenshaws, which come on the market from July through November.

Oranges—Oranges, of course, have lots of vitamin C. This has been their claim to fame for many years now, a claim, incidentally, exaggerated to a considerable degree by the citrus-fruit growers. True, oranges have almost twice as much vitamin C as grapefruit and several times more than limes, lemons and even tangerines. They also have good stores of vitamin B. And while not particularly strong in the mineral department, there are substances in oranges that seem to help the body retain its calcium, especially in children. But if you really want good doses of vitamin C, parsley, broccoli, cabbage, Brussels sprouts, kohlrabi, kale, peppers and many other vegetables will treat you twice as well. And be wary of imbibing too much orange juice. Many people drink it every day as if it were water, which it decidedly is not. One can overacidify on too much of a good thing, and there is strong evidence that overconsumption of O.J. can be harmful to the teeth (all that citric acid, day after day) and even more to the gums. A glass or two of fresh-squeezed orange juice a week should be maximum. When shopping for oranges, beware of varieties with conspicuously bright-orange skins. They are probably dyed. Look for firm, heavy fruits without soft spots, mold or wrinkling. You can store orange juice in the refrigerator for several days without losing any of its nutrients. The oranges themselves will do well there too and will mature more slowly when kept cold.

Papayas—Papayas are among the most healthful of all fruits. Both the meat and the juice of this food are reputed to be excellent for stomach and digestion problems; it contains a sizable amount of protein; and the vitamin A content is so high that one papaya at mealtime generally supplies an adult with the full requirement for the day. Papaya extract, moreover, which is sold separately at the vitamin counter, is taken by many people because of its enzymatic qualities, which are said to stimulate the gastric juices and increase the appetite. The fruit is, as well, one of the most delicious of all tropical foods and one of the prettiest when cut into slices and added to a fruit salad. The only problem you may have with this wonderful fruit, if you live in a cold climate, will be finding it in the first place. Generally, winter is the time of year it will be most available, but even then you may have to search it out at a specialty store or put in a special order.

Peaches—As peaches bruise easily, they are almost always picked green and allowed to ripen on the shelf. Avoid those with brown spots, pockmarks, blemishes or spongy skins. Allow peaches to ripen at room temperature, then quickly place them in the refrigerator. A nice golden color with a red blush plus a slightly soft texture means they are ready to eat. The *clingstone* variety has a flesh that adheres tightly to the pit, and is best for canning. the *freestone*'s flesh falls away easily and makes excellent fresh eating. Sprinkling sliced peaches with a drop or two of lemon juice will delay discoloration and help bring out taste. Peaches contain a respectable supply of vitamins A and B (the supply increases when the peaches are dried), and are known to build up hemoglobin in the blood. Like most fruits, they are not high in minerals though they do contain small amounts of potassium, calcium and iron. Once ripe, keep them in the refrigerator and eat within two weeks. Season runs June through September.

Pears—An August to December treat. Don't worry about whether or not they are tree-ripened. Pears mature best when they are picked early and then allowed to age in a dark, cool place. If you're dieting, pears are not the least fattening fruit you can eat, bearing around 100 calories per fruit and more when they're dried. When purchasing pears press the stem end to be sure the fruit is pliable but not mushy. A ripe pear should have a fragrant smell. They ripen from the inside out and thus should be eaten while still a little firm. Stay away from fruits that are discolored, bruised or have soft brown spots. Pears make an excellent natural dessert. Try:

STEWED PEARS

6 medium-sized pears	½ cup water
6 cloves	Sprinkle of cinnamon
⅓ cup honey	

1. Wash and pare fruit. Cover each pear, pincushion style, with the cloves. Place pears in a shallow saucepan. Pour the honey over them. Add water.

2. Cover the pan and simmer until the pears are soft (but not too

soft). Sprinkle with a little cinnamon. You can serve this dish immediately or refrigerate it for several hours, then serve cold.

Pineapples—Like papayas, another tropical fruit, pineapples are regarded as an aid for digestion plus an excellent source of vitamins, especially vitamin C. When purchasing pineapples stay away from the canned varieties; they are usually kept in a thick syrup of dextrose and water; fresh pineapple is far better and in many cases, interestingly, less expensive ounce for ounce. You can tell if a pineapple is ready for eating by tugging at one of its central leaves. If the leaf slips out easily the pineapple is ripe. Also, a good pineapple should have a rich brown color, be fairly heavy, with a surface that does not dent easily or give when you press it. Stay away from pineapples that have black spots on them or that smell sour. Once ripe, pineapple meat should be eaten quickly. Keep pineapple slices refrigerated at all times.

Watermelons—Used frequently by fasters taking the "fruit cure" to clean out their digestive system, watermelon serves up generous shares of vitamin C plus reasonable amounts of B and A. It has a stimulating effect on the kidneys and is a mild diuretic. A tea made of the seeds boiled ten minutes in fresh water is said to help reduce hypertension. Watermelon is, of course, best eaten when chilled, and is a favorite summertime food, not only as a dessert but as the main ingredient of fresh salad. When you bring the watermelon home let it sit a day or two before refrigerating, especially if it's on the unripened side. Look for well-shaped oval melons, without too many dents or troughs, and with nicely rounded ends and a creamy-colored (not pale-green) belly. Shun melons that are too green or that have soft spots anywhere on their surface. When tapped a ripe melon should sound a bit hollow. The skin should peel off easily when scraped with a fingernail. Try mixing watermelon slices with a fresh salad made of grapes, apples and bananas. If you purchase a cut melon be sure the exposed flesh is a deep pink and that the seeds are jet-black. Whitish seeds are a no-no. Place the sliced pieces in the refrigerator immediately after purchasing with the exposed flesh covered tightly in plastic wrap.

Dried Fruits

The main advantage of dried fruits is that they keep, and that they tend to have more fiber than the fresh kind. The main disadvantage is that in the drying process most fruits become more fattening than before. This felony is compounded by the fact that dried fruits are compressed and bite-sized, less obvious in their bulk, so that one tends to eat more of them at a sitting. Witness raisins. They're half the size of grapes, but ounce for ounce, more fattening. A small handful here and a small handful there quickly add up to the equivalent of a large-sized fresh grape cluster. While dried fruits are especially delicious and make excellent snacks, several things should be considered before you eat too many.

1. A fruit becomes very sugary when it is dried. Some become almost like candy, and for this reason they aren't a good deal better for those who suffer from blood-sugar problems than white sugar itself.

2. Dried fruits are often commercially preserved with harmful chemicals. Many, for instance, are sulphured. This means the fruit has been exposed to sulphur dioxide, a poisonous gas. Though this process locks in some of the nutrients, especially the A vitamins, and gives the fruit longer shelf life, the exposure may be harmful. Early in this century when sulphuration was widely used, several doctors working for the FDA studied its effects and found they were indeed harmful for human consumption. The reports were quickly buried, misquoted and maligned, however, and since then no upper limit has ever been established for sulphuring.* Raisins, pears, apples and apricots all regularly get the sulphur treatment before going to market.

3. Dried fruits are expensive. Usually a lot more than their fresh counterparts.

You can avoid all these problems by drying your own. Arrange the fruits on a spacious tray so that there is plenty of air space around each. Place the tray in the sun for several days until the fruits are thoroughly dehydrated. Then place them in glass or pottery crocks and store in a cool, dark place. This is an ancient preservation method and it works fairly well for most fruits. Be sure a netted cover or mesh screen is kept over the tray to protect against the birds.

You can also dry fruits in the kitchen. Heat the oven to around 160 degrees, put the fruit on a tray, and place the tray in the oven, leaving the door open several inches. Aim a fan at the opening so that fresh air is kept circulating.

Apples need about three or four hours in the oven; bananas, about six; grapes, up to twenty-four hours; apricots, seven or eight hours; figs, ten to fifteen hours; plums, about twelve hours; pineapple, about ten to fifteen hours. It is difficult to be precise concerning drying times, as much depends on how juicy the particular fruit is, how steady the oven heat, and how well the air is kept circulating.

As a final alternative you might consider investing in a dehydrator.

* Beatrice Trum Hunter, *Fact Book on Food Additives and Your Health* (New Canaan, Conn.: Keats Publishing Co., 1972).

This is a mechanism something like a smoker. It creates dry heat that completely evaporates all water from anything you put in it, including meat if you want to make your own jerky. You can buy a dehydrator, or you can build one yourself. A good commercial model is available from:

Cache Manufacturers
Box 692
Logan, Utah 84221

Plans for building your own dehydrator are available from:

Solar Survival
Box 275
Harrisville, New Hampshire 03450
Plans cost $10.75. They pay postage.

Rodale Press
Plans Department
33 East Minor Street
Emmaus, Pennsylvania 18049
Plans cost $14.95.

FIBER

Fiber is the nonmetabolized residue of plant tissue, the parts of the plant that pass through the body undigested and exit largely intact. Mainly it comes from the cell walls of the plant. Within the plant itself fiber serves to contain the cellular protoplasm and to support the plant's shape.

You won't find fiber in meat or fish or dairy products. It comes exclusively from plant matter. A high-fiber diet can thus be achieved only by eating a high-natural-carbohydrate diet.

For many years fiber was a part of just about everyone's daily meals, and this was a very good thing for reasons we will presently come to. Then in the nineteenth century commercial refining techniques came along. White bread, polished rice, refined sugar, refined cereals. And then canning. Straining. Clarifying. People ate more and more meat, fewer and fewer fruits and vegetables. The diet became softer, heavier in fats. Sweets intake increased drastically. Milk and cream and butter became staples. Synthetic foods made their appearance. The result of all this was the amounts of natural fiber eaten decreased dramatically. And so did the national health.

Fiber Makes a Comeback

But no one seemed to notice. Fiber was, after all, indigestible matter. What good could cellulose do? Better to get it out of the food beforehand and save our organs all that extra digestive effort.

Then at the end of the 1960s two British scientists, Dr. Denis Burkitt and Dr. Hugh Trowell, made news.

Their controversial medical findings were founded on a central observation: certain intestinal ailments, cancer of the colon and diverticulosis (a chronic inflammation of the colon) in particular, had increased dramatically over the past sixty or seventy years, a time span that coincided neatly with the arrival of large-scale food-processing techniques. These and other degenerative diseases were still rare in underdeveloped countries where such processing techniques were unknown, Burkitt and Trowell pointed out. Only in the industrialized countries had such diseases become epidemic.

Burkitt witnessed this phenomenon firsthand while serving as a field doctor in Uganda. Despite the meager and at times nonnutritious diet the Ugandan people consumed, he observed, degenerative gastrointestinal diseases were almost unknown.

Fiber, Burkitt and Trowell agreed, was the reason. Or more specifically the absence of fiber.

Continued research turned up plenty of evidence to back up this idea. In countries where the upper classes ate refined foods and the lower ate nonrefined foods, it was observed, the upper classes developed degenerative intestinal diseases and the lower classes did not. During World War II, German soldiers who served in the front lines and who lived on raw vegetables developed none of these ailments. Those behind the lines who ate refined foods got sick. American prisoners of war fed polished rice in Japanese prison camps developed stomach diseases. Those who ate brown rice kept their healthy digestive systems. Jews from Syria and Iraq who subsisted on traditional Middle Eastern grains and legumes were free from chronic intestinal problems. When after World War II they moved to Israel where a more refined diet is eaten, symptoms started to develop. Everywhere one looked a similar pattern emerged.

The conclusion was clear: Processing food robs people of more than just the nutrients. It steals away the bulk, or roughage, as fiber is sometimes called, from the food. This bulk, though it supplies no nutrition per se, performs physiological duties in the digestive tract that the body can scarcely do without. In its own way it is as important as vitamins or minerals or any of the fundamental nutrients that food provides.

Burkitt and Trowell's finding met with disbelief and ridicule from the scientific community. But by and large the evidence was convincing, and it wasn't long before public consciousness began to take notice. Today the importance of fiber is clearly recognized, and there is even something of a bandwagon effort to put fiber *back* in the food. Perhaps ultimately we will learn to leave it there in the first place.

Not All Fiber Is the Same

Fiber is made up of several varieties of nondigestible plant matter, chief among them being nature's most common vegetable substance, *cellulose*. Cows and other multistomached ruminants can digest cellulose and live on grass alone. In man's single-stomached digestive system the cellulose passes through the mill and out, and with it goes *lignin,* with its woody consistency, along with a coarse substance called *hemicellulose*. Also the *pectins,* found mostly in fruit and familiar to anyone who has done any canning. And soft substances like *gums* and *mucilages*—note that all plant fiber is by no means fibrous or even solid.

Added together, these different types of fiber comprise what is called *total dietary fiber.* This is the sum of all fiber taken into the body via a particular carbohydrate.

Seems like a simple enough measuring device. Just add up the amounts of coarse and soft fiber in the food and derive the sum, which then represents the total dietary fiber. But there's a catch, and as is often the case, it's in the terminology.

The problem is to avoid mistaking the phrase "total dietary fiber" for the term *"crude fiber,"* which specifically describes the harder, coarser, less dissolvable components of roughage. The two are different.

The term "crude fiber" describes only a certain percent of the total fiber in a plant. It includes the tough, woody kinds of fiber like cellulose, hemicellulose and lignin. It does *not* include the soft, more easily dissolved gums and mucilages and pectins.

The softer varieties of fibers are more difficult to separate and hence more difficult to weigh and examine than is the solid crude fiber. For this reason laboratory analysis has traditionally measured crude fiber only, while the softer fibers, more difficult to quantify, are ignored.

When fiber content is listed on a commercial label it is usually the crude fiber only that is presented, not the total dietary fiber. This is an unfortunate omission, because there is a good deal more soft fiber in most carbohydrates than crude, and because soft fiber is generally more useful in the digestive tract than hard. In fact, indications are that too much crude fiber can be as harmful as too little.

Some manufacturers, to compensate for this incomplete labeling, estimate the total dietary fiber by multiplying the crude fiber content by four. This method is entirely arbitrary, however, as the ratio of crude fiber to soft in any carbohydrate varies according to the fruit, nut, seed or vegetable in question, plus how fresh it is, when it was picked, what the season is, how it is cooked and seasoned and stored, and so forth. An old carrot tastes hard and woody, because it *is* woody, thanks to the increase with age of its lignin content. The same carrot when young will be resilient and pliable, and will contain more of the softer fibers, less of the lignin. In other words, fiber content changes as the plant changes. It is by no means a figure carved in stone.

Thus, be aware: When checking a label for the fiber content be sure the figure represents *total dietary fiber* and not just *crude fiber*. Recent developments in laboratory technique now allow testing for the softer fiber as well as for the crude. There is no longer any excuse for this important figure to be missing from any label or table or list. So watch for it.

Why Is Fiber Good for You?

As fiber moves through the stomach into the small intestine and the colon it performs not one but a series of beneficial actions. It is these that make fiber so important. What are they? Note:

1. Fiber and Constipation

Perhaps fiber's most touted function is as a natural laxative.

When food is commercially refined its bulk is removed. What remains tends to be soft, pulpy, without coarseness or body. Witness white bread or white sugar.

Inside the digestive tract this mealy, denatured residue moves ponderously along on its journey to excretion. Because it contains no fiber, it does not irritate the linings of the gut in the way that food with plenty of fiber does, and it therefore digests slowly. Soon it stagnates and grows hard. Constipation is the inevitable result.

Those who eat adequate amounts of unrefined carbohydrates, on the other hand, studies have frequently shown, move food through their systems with considerably more dispatch than those who do not. The difference can be profound. Food that takes four days to pass through a person who eats no fiber is likely to digest in a quarter of this time in someone who does.

Another reason fiber keeps the digestive tunnel functioning so well is because unrefined carbohydrate material, and fiber in particular, exerts a strong absorbent action, drawing local stores of water into the feces and swelling their size and weight. These stores provide the feces with the double gift of bulk and softness. Both make the stool transit more swiftly through the gut, and more easily. Those who eat a high-fiber diet, tests show, not only eliminate more frequently than those who do not, but their feces are larger and fuller, and more wastes are excreted at each bowel movement.

High-fiber food, in short, is a laxative, some would say of the best and most natural kind. If you're plagued with ordinary constipation problems, try going on a high-fiber diet for several weeks and observe the difference.

2. Fiber and the Health of the Colon

One of the really insidious side effects of constipation is that when fecal residues stagnate in the system for long periods of time, they impact the colon. Certain kinds of bacteria, bifidobacteria in particular, are then given the chance to breed.

Bifidobacteria contain enzymes that when allowed to remain too long in the gut transmute bile salts into toxic residues. Some people believe that the toxins deposited by these dangerous substances—along with the slow process of internal self-poisoning they produce—induce cancer of the colon. Some studies have demonstrated that people who have at least one and preferably two bowel movements a day develop colonic cancer less frequently than those who eliminate less than once a day.

In this instance roughage is preventive medicine. By stimulating peristalsis and speeding up digestion, fiber helps the system remove the poisons. This prevents the buildup of harmful bacteria, especially in the colon. Impacted feces, moreover, have a tendency to fasten onto the walls of the large intestine and remain there, making this area into a veritable breeding grounds for disagreeable microbes. Fiber has a cleansing effect on these pockets of infection. It helps get rid of toxins that have accumulated over time, sometimes for years and years.

3. Fiber and Diabetes

Recent reports indicate that by doubling or tripling the amount of fiber in the diabetic diet, the need for insulin may be reduced considerably or *even eliminated entirely.* In light of the fact that diabetes has so long been considered incurable, this is a startling discovery. In one study more than *half* the diabetic subjects discovered that by increasing stores of fiber in their food they could cut down on their insulin intake.

The reasons why fiber works so well against diabetes is something of a mystery. One theory has it that since fiber is not digestible, it remains intact within the gut where its absorbent qualities trap nutrients like a sponge and delay the rate at which sugar is released into the blood. Whatever the cause, there's a good chance that in the next few years we will see more and more links forged between diet and diabetes, and that fiber will be featured in all of this, center stage.

4. Fiber as a Medicine

Peptic ulcers, gallstones, appendicitis, spastic colon, varicose veins, ulcerative colitis, hemorrhoids, all at one time or another have given laboratory evidence of responding positively to increased fiber intake.

While there is more evidence in some cases than in others of fiber's healing effects, the most conservative physician today will agree that fiber is a direct aid for many gastrointestinal problems and especially for diverticulosis. Both Burkitt and Trowell were in fact originally alerted to the relationship between diet and disease while studying diverticular patients. Since then high-fiber diet has been an almost automatic prescription for this ailment.

More speculative perhaps is the relationship between fiber and atherosclerosis. Still, it *is* known that in laboratory tests subjects given a diet heavy in pectin-bearing fruits and gum-bearing beans develop significantly lower blood cholesterol. And that vegetarians generally have lower cholesterol levels than meat eaters.

It is also known that the more quickly food transits the system the less opportunity there is for bile salts from the liver to be reabsorbed through the intestinal wall. Bile salts carry a great deal of cholesterol. And fiber is known to have a binding effect on bile salts, which means the salts "stick" to the fiber, are absorbed into it, and are given a quick heave-ho via elimination.

Lowering the intestinal reabsorption of bile salts, moreover, means that much less plaque-building cholesterol is deposited in the system, and this reduces the chance of blockage developing in the arteries. Countries that live on a diet high in fiber almost invariably have low rates of atherosclerosis. In countries where fiber is missing from the diet, like ours, the disease is rampant.

5. Fiber and Weight Loss

It's in the weight-loss department above all that fiber has achieved its real glamour. These days there is scarcely a new diet on the market that does not in some way refer to fiber's fabled ability to keep us slim. Fruits and vegetables have finally become fashionable.

How can fiber help control excess poundage? First, through simple chewing. High-fiber foods are bulky foods. Think of fresh apples, a piece of celery, a plate of baked beans. You have to chew them for a while, longer than you would if you were eating the same food in its refined rendition. So you eat less.

Chewing also uses up calories. Don't laugh! It does. The more you chew your food the sooner you feel full. And the slower you eat while you're doing all this chewing the less food you'll want.

Fiber absorbs water too. So you're likely to feel fuller sooner. It also contains no calories. So while the fiber's giving you that satisfied full feeling, it's also leaving no traces, fatwise.

Studies indicate that fiber causes fats to be metabolized and eliminated faster than when the fats are eaten on their own. The sooner fats are rinsed out of your system, of course, the less chance there is of their lodging in the wrong places. Make it a rule of thumb when dieting to eat fats in the company of high-fiber carbohydrates such as carrots, beans and whole grains.

Fiber also seems to produce some kind of mysterious "blockade" effect in the intestines against calories, slowing down the rate at which the calories are absorbed and increasing the speed at which they are eliminated. Little is understood about this mechanism, but it has been frequently noted and observed.

What About Bran?

After fiber's rediscovery, a rare coalition of commercial food manufacturers and the health food movement promoted the idea that fiber could be *returned* to food once it had been removed. Though there are many ways this can be done, including actually dropping ground wood cellulose (read: sawdust) into the food, the most popular method came to be supplementing defibered foods with bran.

Bran, of course, is the outer chaff of the wheat kernel removed during the refining process. It can also be rice polishings, though in this case such residues are usually referred to specifically by name as "rice bran."

Bran has nourishment in its own right, especially vitamin B and trace minerals. Most of the bran, however, is composed of roughage, and it is a roughage that it stands or falls. Under this name it is commonly added to commercial breakfast cereals, and is sold separately in packages and in bulk supplies. It is also taken as a natural laxative. A teaspoonful in the morning and at night is the standard amount. It most decidedly works.

But there are problems. Many people take several spoonfuls of bran each morning to insure a proper daily fiber intake. There is, however, some evidence that bran's powerful binding qualities cause it to combine with minerals, especially calcium and iron, and to "steal" these minerals out of the body via elimination. Bran is also known to slow down protein metabolism and to cause excessive intestinal gas. For people already bothered by chronic flatulence bran sometimes proves more of an irritant than an aid. Bran absorbs water and expands inside the colon, like any good fiber material should. This means that if too much is eaten over a period of time it will form massive, watery lumps in the gut. The larger these lumps become the more of a burden they exert on digestion. Eventually they may stop all forward motion, and the bran then ends up constipating the bowels rather than unbinding them. In extreme instances serious blockages can occur and surgery becomes the only recourse.

This happens only when people take excessive quantities of bran, or when they introduce it to their diet too quickly and in large doses. If you plan to use bran, begin by taking small amounts and then build up. A half teaspoon a day will do. Later on, if it's really necessary, you can increase the dose.

If you're using bran for constipation, know that if you don't get results right away you won't get them at all. One teaspoonful in the morning and one before bed should give you relief by the second day. Surely the third. Absolutely the fourth. If not, better find another method.

If you insist on taking a fiber supplement, bypass the somewhat problematic bran and use fresh wheat germ instead. Wheat germ has a lot more nutrition in it than bran and it tastes good too. Sprinkle it on cereal in the morning and have it on your salad at night.

Still, the real issue is: Why add bran or any other extra fiber to your food in the first place? It's simply not necessary, if you think about it. Surely the best way to get roughage into your diet is to eat natural foods that already have it. Easy. That way supplements are no longer necessary. You have the real thing.

High-Fiber Foods

The following table provides a representative sampling of the natural fiber content in common foods.

Fiber Content in Different Foods

Food	Amount	Grams of Total Dietary Fiber
Apple	1 whole	3.0
Asparagus	4 spears	.9
Avocado	1 whole	4.4
Banana	1 whole	1.8
Beets	1 cup	4.2
Bran	1 cup	23.0
Broccoli	1 cup	2.2
Cabbage	1 cup	2.2
Cantaloupe	½ fruit	1.6
Carrots	1 cup	2.1
Cauliflower	1 cup	2.2
Corn	on cob, 1 ear	5.9
Cracked-Wheat Bread	1 slice	2.1
Cucumber	1 ounce	0.1
Figs	1 medium	2.4
Grapefruit	½ cup	0.6
Grapes	12	0.3
Green Beans	1 cup	3.9
Green Pepper	1	0.8
Grits	½ cup	9.1
Kidney Beans	1 cup	2.0
Lentil Soup	1 cup	5.5
Lettuce	1 serving	1.5
Mango	1	3.0
Mushrooms	1 cup	1.8
Okra	½ cup	2.6
Orange	1	2.5
Parsnips	1 cup	6.2
Peach	1	1.4
Pear	1	2.6
Peas	1 cup	7.9
Pickle, Dill	1	1.2
Pineapple	1 cup	2.2
Plums	1	0.2
Potato, Baked in Skin	1	3.0
Prunes	1	1.0
Pumpernickel Bread	1 slice	1.2
Radish	5	0.2
Raisins	2 tablespoons	1.2
Raspberries	1 cup	9.2
Rice, Brown	1 cup	1.1

Fiber Content (*cont.*)

Food	Amount	Grams of Total Dietary Fiber
Rice, White	1 cup	0.4
Rolled Oats	½ cup	4.5
Spinach	1 cup	11.4
Strawberries	1 cup	3.4
Tomato	1	2.1
Watercress	1 serving	0.7
Whole-Wheat Bread	1 slice	2.4

You should have at least a bit of fiber every day, preferably from fresh, nonprocessed foods. Exactly how much you need is difficult to say in grams and milligrams. Ten grams a day is the standard amount nutritionists have come up with, though twice this figure wouldn't hurt. Americans have gone from eating an average of 8 grams a day in 1884 to 3 grams a day in 1984. Not good.

On the other hand, some of the fiber we eat is invisible—colorless, tasteless, without odor—and is artificially added to our foods by the powers that be so they can feature their food line as being "fortified with natural fiber." The processors, at it again.

Since the 1960s, for example, wood pulp and cotton have been slipped into such foods as ice cream (it stops the crystals from freezing), salad dressing (as an emulsifier), reconstituted seafoods (to keep the fish sticks from falling apart in your hands) and whipped cream (as a stabilizer). They also add "body" to diet colas, stop the chocolate from settling to the bottom in soft drinks, and add bulk and weight to white bread. The wood itself has absolutely no nutritive value and is not particularly good for you, although manufacturers proudly list the amounts of pulp poured into their product under that old ubiquitous title "crude fiber." So once more, there's good reason to steer clear of commercial food brands and to search out the fresh, natural, untampered-with foods that Mother Nature so gladly gives to those who are willing to receive.

CHAPTER THREE

Fats

Fats are the second basic member of the carbohydrate-fats-protein trio. They are the least important of the group nutritionally, and the most controversial. Let's have a look.

Fats: Buzz Word of the Eighties

In our time the word "fat" has become a disgrace on two rather crucial counts. First, as in overweight; blubbery and unsightly. Second, as in cholesterol; hardening of the arteries and heart attack. Not a very good combination. No wonder fats are out these days.

And perhaps they should be, though not altogether, for they are still a basic part of the human diet and should be understood as such.

Body Fat and Dietary Fat

Let's start by making a distinction between body fat and dietary fat. The two are not the same.

Body fat is the adipose tissue that covers much of the contours of the human body. It serves several functions. First, it protects the internal organs from shock, wrapping around them in a protective jacket. Second, the layer of fat just below the skin surface is an insulator against heat and cold alike, sheltering the body from extremes of temperature the way insulation packed into a wall protects a house. Third, fat cells participate in the regulation of skin texture, and in keeping the cell membranes in good health. Lastly, fat is stored energy, lodged mainly in the body's storage system we call the fat cells. As an architectural feat these cells are a model of efficiency and space. Since form follows function in nature as in engineering, each pleasingly rounded cell is designed to fit snugly next to its neighbor, causing that curiously compact yet spongy bulge that fat makes at the midriff and containing enough energy supplies within it to power an organism for many days. A gram of fat supplies 9 calories. That's a good deal more than a gram of carbohydrates might ever boast, or a gram of protein. When the body needs extra supplies of nutrition it always has these vital energy packets at its disposal.

Dietary fats, on the other hand, are a basic nutrient, found in just about every kind of food we know. Animal dietary fat, for instance, comes with almost every kind of meat, even fish and lean meats, dairy products, and eggs. And vegetable fats are derived from various sources, including most nuts, many seeds and fruits, vegetables and grains like olives, avocados, soybeans and corn. Many foods have a surprisingly high amount of dietary fat. Note the following table.

Table of Fat Content in Common Foods

Food	Fat Content (approx. %)
Milk	25
Cheese	30
Beef	15
Lamb	15
Lard	25
Pork	25
Olive Oil	100
Butter	80
Peanut Butter	50
Cashews	60

Over the past century, consumption of dietary fat has risen at rather amazing rates. Today it makes up approximately 40 percent of our daily nutritive intake, and it is not unusual to find individuals whose diet includes 60 percent or even 70 percent fats. The average teen-ager's daily fare, as anyone who knows one will agree, regularly includes helpings of ice cream, peanut butter and jelly sandwiches, slabs of American cheese, buttered white bread, sausage grinders, pizza, spaghetti and meatballs, bologna heroes, hot dogs, shakes, chocolate bars, foods that are all brimming over with fats. And the lunch menu at any local high school may be little better.

If the truth be known we are an entire nation, young and old, of fat addicts. We have grown used to fats; we crave them. Fats bring an aroma to the kitchen. They are part and parcel of Mom's apple-pie, down-country standard American fare. A large number of our common grocery items are laden with fats, some exposed, others hidden. Foods like commercial bread, canned tuna fish, cottage cheese, breakfast cereals, sardines, peanut butter, salad dressings and many more are all made many times more fatty through the addition of oils, fillings, lard or additives. Even though the past years have witnessed the cholesterol scare, with its accompanying emphasis on exercise and sane eating, it has not been enough. The national level of fat consumption has dropped a few notches, true, and in 1977 the Senate Select Committee on Nutrition and Human Needs stated quite clearly that Americans include far too many fats in their diet. It recommended that we reduce our intake, cutting the 40 percent daily ration to 30 percent.

But this is still high. Much too high.

What Are Dietary Fats Good for, Anyway?

Despite the claims of some nutritionists that we can live contentedly without *any* fats in our diet, fats do play their part, especially as carriers of both fatty acids and of fat-soluble vitamins, such as vitamins A, D and E. Without fats these vitamins would never reach their destinations. Fats are also a great appetite quencher. In a Yukon stew or in a slice of gooey cheese, they tend to satisfy the appetite longer than either protein or carbohydrate, imparting a rich flavor to other foods. In fact, their appetite-satisfying factor has become increasingly crucial in our national diet, where refined foods play such an important part and where manufacturers will invariably take the path of least resistance to improve the taste of their product. If the natural nutrients are filched from a food via refinement won't the eater soon discover what pap he is really getting? Of course he will. So it becomes necessary to disguise these skeleton victuals with something that *does* stick to the ribs. Remember, it's the nutrients in a food that ultimately make it tasty. Method: Add fats to refined foods. The weighty presence of a fat, especially an animal fat, blended with white flour gives the bread the weight it's missing. For this reason lard is often used in commercial cakes, crackers or bread. White rice has little body of its own. So the cook boils it in chicken stock and adds several sizable pats of butter when serving to make up for the deficiency. The fact is that wherever you find a diet heavy in refined foods you'll also find plenty of fats with them, mixed in or served in the company of.

Chemically speaking, the fat family is predominantly populated by a complex molecule known as a *triglyceride*. Each arm on this three-limbed structure is in turn composed of one *glycerol* and three *fatty acid* molecules. The way these fatty acids combine with one another and with the glycerols determines what kind of fat they will be.

While there are many varieties of fatty acids, the three important ones are *linoleic acid, linolenic acid* and *arachidonic acid*. (The first two were so named because they were originally discovered in linseed oil.) For years it was believed that the body could not produce its own supplies of these three acids, which is why they were termed essential. Further study showed that only linoleic acid needs to be taken in directly from the food supply, and now some scientists believe even that can be manufactured by the body. Above all, we know that fats are included by nature in most of the foods we eat anyway, and that only small amounts, perhaps as small as a pat or two of butter or a spoonful of oil, are actually required to meet the day's minimum need. The notion that we must devour mountains of meat or oceans of oil to keep our bodies going strong is hogwash, pure and simple.

Saturated, Monosaturated, and Polyunsaturated Fats: What Are They? What Do They Do?

No doubt like all of us you have been regaled by advertisers through the years with the wonderful news that their product is *polyunsaturated*. Whatever that means. You know that polyunsaturated, for some vague reason, is supposed to be good for you, and saturated bad for you. That's about all.

What these terms really mean, briefly speaking, is this: Certain fats are said to be "saturated" when they are solid at room temperature, like beef fat. They are "polyunsaturated" when they are liquid, like oil. That's it. Polyunsaturates include vegetable and fish oils. Saturates include most animal fats, such as tallow or cheese. According to popular dogma, the unsaturates are better for your health because they contain all the three essential fatty acids, linoleic, linolenic and arachidonic, and because they have no cholesterol. The problem, however, is a bit more complex.

To get a clear picture of the simple chemistry behind all this, especially the difference between polyunsaturated and saturated, think of the fatty acid molecule as being a Tinkertoy model, the kind you assemble yourself. Let's put it together, stick by stick.

First take several wooden Tinkertoy wheels with the holes on the rim, and some straight Tinkertoy sticks. Make a series of connecting crosses out of them, like this:

```
        H    H    H
        ‖    ‖    ‖
  H ═══ C ═══ C ═══ C ═══ H
        ‖    ‖    ‖
        H    H    H
```

The wheels each represent carbon atoms, the sticks are the stems, the *H*s at the end of each stem are atoms of hydrogen—now you have a fundamental molecule of a fatty acid. The one shown here is saturated because all its stems are filled with hydrogens; there is no room for another. Full house. Saturated.

Now take a few more of the sticks and several round wheels. Attach them so that they make a straight, more complex structure, like this:

```
      H    H              H    H
      ‖    ‖              ‖    ‖
H ═══ C ═══ C ═══ C ═══ C ═══ C ═══ C ═══ H
      ‖    ‖    ‖    ‖    ‖    ‖
      H    H    H    H    H    H
```

Note that most of the stems have *H*s on them for hydrogen, but that two are empty. The fact that these two stems are free makes this into what is called a "monosaturated" fatty acid, something halfway between saturated and unsaturated. (Monosaturates seem to have no effect on blood fats one way or the other.)

Finally, here is a model of a polyunsaturated fat:

```
      H    H    H    H    H    H    H
      ‖    ‖    ‖    ‖    ‖    ‖    ‖
H ═══ C ═══ C ═══ C ═══ C ═══ C ═══ C ═══ C ═══ H
      ‖              ‖              ‖
      H              H              H
```

Note that *four* stems are empty. "Poly" means many—many empty carbon stems. A polyunsaturate is a fat molecule with several free stems. This particular Tinkertoy model could, by the way, represent any polyunsaturate from corn oil to mayonnaise.

Now none of this information about saturates and unsaturates would have anything more than classroom interest to us did it not touch on one of the major issues of our time. That issue needs little introduction. It is cholesterol.

CHOLESTEROL: THE PHANTOM INGREDIENT

Some call it a hall of mirrors, and justly so. Around the beginning of the twentieth century, atherosclerosis in the United States began to rise sharply, accompanied by a parallel increase in the use of dietary fats. Few people in the United States noticed the correlation until the 1950s and 1960s, at which time evidence began to accumulate that people who indulge in high-fat diets frequently show large accumulations of a substance called plaque in their blood. Plaque is composed mostly of cholesterol.

Up until then, hardening of the arteries was considered to be a natural by-product of aging. Then along came laboratory findings that linked the plaque to diet, and to cholesterol in particular. This pale waxy material, it seemed, likes to lodge in arteries, which transport oxygen-rich blood through the organism, and to camp there permanently in stubborn defiance, blocking the passageway and ultimately stopping the blood flow entirely. Scarcely anything can be done to remove it once it's there. When vessels in the brain develop this kind of blockage, stroke results. When arteries near the heart are narrowed through plaque buildup, count on angina pectoris. When plaque causes blood clots, sudden, deadly heart attacks can result. Such a condition is called hardening of the arteries—atherosclerosis. It kills about half the people in America.

As soon as scientists caught on that cholesterol and heart failure are associated they put out an all-signals alert. In 1964 the American Heart Association made it official, publishing literature with such headlines as: "All Americans Now Urged: Change Fat-Eating Habits." As yet there was no conclusive proof of the link between fats and atherosclerosis, but in test after test the evidence mounted. Shortly after World War II the work of Dr. Ancel Keys at the University of Minnesota suggested a strong relationship between food fats and heart attack. Follow-up experimentation at Highland-Alameda County Hospital in Oakland, California, and at the Rockefeller Institute in New York City narrowed the problem down to animal fats in general and to cholesterol in particular. The famous Framingham Heart Study, meanwhile, had already demonstrated that a person with a high cholesterol count, say 260 milligrams per 100 milliliters of blood, has three times the chance of dying from a heart attack as one with 195 milligrams, and that a person with double this 260 rate has a *five times* greater chance of death.

Further tests seemed to confirm these early revelations. Cross-cultural studies were done and these too checked out, showing that people who lived in places like Guam or Korea, where the diet is low in saturated fats, have negligible amounts of heart disease, while those who come from countries like Finland and the United States, where large amounts of saturated fats are eaten, have it aplenty.

Great excitement arose in the medical community, and for a while it looked as if heart disease was cornered. Overnight a spate of new food products appeared at the supermarket, aimed at eliminating demon cholesterol from the American chow line. Skim milk, nonfat dry milk, low-fat cheese and yogurt, nondairy creamer, all became new words in the vocabulary and took their place in the American vernacular. Before too long the term "polyunsaturate" became a household word along with them.

Polyunsaturates come from plants, never from animals. And unlike animal fats, polyunsaturates are cholesterol-free. This fact was immediately greeted as a great discovery, and polyunsaturates were hailed as the new health food by just about everyone. Preliminary tests then indicated that polyunsaturates actually do seem to reduce the amounts of cholesterol in the blood system and do play a part in the reduction of plaque buildup.

Before too long margarine, made from vegetable fat and without cholesterol, started giving butter a run for its money in the marketplace, while the so-called miracle polyunsaturated oils were touted as preventing about everything from heart attacks to corns. Meanwhile, old standbys like eggs, high in cholesterol and impossible to decholesterol, suddenly appeared on everyone's hate list. Doctors began to speak of polyunsaturates in hushed tones, and to *insist* that anyone with high triglyceride levels switch to them immediately. From 1960 to 1980 the use of polyunsaturates tripled.

What Is Cholesterol?

Amidst all the hoopla few people bothered to ask what cholesterol was in the first place or to inquire about its function in the body's chemical factory. Those who did discovered that it was a benign, ubiquitous and highly necessary part of the human organism. Cholesterol, they learned, is technically not a fat at all but a solid alcohol, a complex hydrocarbon. Manufactured in many parts of the organism, though primarily in the liver, it is a basic ingredient in the making of bile, in the synthesis of vitamin D and in maintaining the balance of sexual hormones. Most crucially, its waxy consistency serves as a sheathing to protect both nerve tissue and the delicate interior linings of blood vessels. Think of how the oil from lamb's fat greases your fingers when you touch it, and how it repels water when you try to wash it off your hands. Cholesterol has something of the same consistency and acts in much the same way, as a protective coating for membranes throughout the veins, shielding them from the friction of moving fluids, especially from the wearing effects of ever-rushing blood.

Cholesterol, in other words, is as necessary to the running of the human organism as oil is for an automobile. Public opinion to the contrary, it is also a required ingredient in the human diet. If we don't get enough of it in our food, our bodies manufacture their own supplies to compensate. Like it or not, there will always be plenty of cholesterol inside us.

To make matters even more complicated, it is now known that not all forms of cholesterol are necessarily harmful. A type of cholesterol known as HDL (high-density lipoprotein), it was discovered several years back, in some little-understood way helps in the recycling of insoluble fats and cholesterol by removing them from the arteries, returning them to the liver for processing, and generally keeping the body free of fatty gluts. So-called LDL (low-density lipoprotein) and VLDL (very-low-density lipoprotein), on the other hand, have been found to carry cholesterol from the liver *to* the veins and to deposit it there. People with high HDL levels of cholesterol in their systems seem to have a profound resistance to strokes and cholesterol-induced problems in general; those with high LDL and VLDL levels are above-average risks for heart attacks and strokes. HDL levels, it is worth noting, are highest in those who do not smoke, who are not overweight, and who exercise regularly.

For those who understood these facts it thus came as no shock when the public was informed that enthusiasms over cholesterol findings had been a bit hasty. Nor were they surprised when scientists one day announced to the world that, ahem, the value of polyunsaturates as a cure-all for heart disease was now, ah, under further scrutiny.

Preliminary studies demonstrating that polyunsaturates lowered blood fats were re-evaluated and in some instances discredited. To the surprise of researchers, there was no consistency in test data. Some experiments showed that polyunsaturates *increased* blood-fat levels.* In many parts of the world where saturated and unsaturated fats are eaten in equal amounts there was a minimum of artherosclerosis. Sometimes people who ate *more* saturated fats suffered *fewer* circulatory disturbances. Sometimes it was the other way around. It seemed to vary from community to community and from person to person.

The more surveys that were run the more puzzling the feedback became. Dietary studies done of Trappist monks revealed that more than half of these peace-loving vegetarians suffered from some form of athero-

*A. Gattereau and H. Delisle, "The unsettled question: butter or margarine?" *Canadian Medical Association Journal* (1970) pp. 268–271.

sclerosis or high blood pressure. Benedictine monks, who were also sur-
veyed, had approximately the same levels of cardiovascular disease,
though their diets regularly included heaping portions of red meat. Autop-
sies performed on the bodies of Nazi concentration camp victims showed
that many of them had developed hardening of the arteries during their
imprisonment. Their typical meals consisted of thin vegetable gruel and
bread. People from Swiss mountain towns in the Loetschental Valley
thrive on diets high in milk and cheese. They have almost no heart
disease. The same is true for Jews living in Yemen; but these same
people, when they move to Israel, experience a rapid increase in heart
disease. The Masai tribesmen of Central Africa, a cattle-raising, heavy
milk-drinking and meat-eating people, have a diet that is more than half
comprised of animal fats. Yet atherosclerosis is exceedingly rare among
them. Such contradictory studies abound.

While many doctors had at one time solemnly warned patients they
must avoid saturates and eat only polyunsaturates if they wished to avoid
hardening of the arteries, new findings demonstrated that polyunsaturates
had a somewhat unpredictable effect on the connective tissue of the
body, destroying proteins and reducing overall elasticity in both joints
and veins.

A process known as "cross-linking" became especially apparent to
researchers. Here the oxidation of digested polyunsaturated oils encour-
ages a chemical reaction called "polymerization," which in turn produces
a number of free radicals, renegade molecules run wild. These freewheel-
ing particles join up with certain protein molecules forming a new, trans-
muted molecular structure that has a hardening effect on skin tissue and
that undermines the flexibility of arterial walls. Some researchers believe
that because of this cross-linking effect excessive use of polyunsaturates
promotes premature aging rather than retards it and, ironically, clogs
rather than heals constricted arteries. Many popular commercial oils, further, were found to have an anti-vitamin-E action in the body. Prolonged
usage was proclaimed to cause deficiencies, sometimes serious deficiencies, of this important substance.

Particularly ironic was the discovery that while some people who
follow a diet high in polyunsaturates do indeed show a lesser incidence
of atherosclerosis, these same individuals tend to be more susceptible to
cancer. Out of the frying pan and into the fire.

There is, in fact, information showing that people who eat a high
number of fats *of any kind* are more prone to cancer than those who
avoid them. According to data collected by the United Nations in 1964,
heavy fat eaters, and especially those who take many unsaturates, show
a significant increase in cancer of the colon. Breast cancer is not far

behind, along with cancer of the prostate, rectum, ovary and blood (leukemia). All seem to be in some way expedited by fats.

Why this is so no one is quite certain. One theory has it that bile acids produced by fats tend to be broken down in the colon by strains of lingering toxic bacteria (the kind that a colon without proper fiber intake is likely to breed). These acids are then transformed into carcinogenic substances. Another theory claims that when polyunsaturates are oxidized they alter human chromosomes, leading to cellular mutation. This process of sudden, violent mutation, some believe, is the same process that causes cancer. But no one knows for sure.

Due to the onslaught of all this negative information concerning polyunsaturates, the FDA finally banned commercial manufacturers from claiming that their polyunsaturated products were in any way helpful for preventing cardiovascular diseases.

Yet even today all that food merchants have to do is *mention* the word "polyunsaturated" on a product label. That's all. No special claims are necessary. The consumer's conditioned response will take care of the rest. The fact remains, however, that no conclusive evidence has ever been found proving that unsaturates reduce cholesterol buildup in the arteries. There is even some evidence implying the opposite. And while all the laboratory feedback on polyunsaturates is not so bleak—unsaturates do seem to reduce the frequency of heart trouble under certain conditions anyway, and there is some evidence that in moderation they may help keep blood pressure from going too high—the point is that vegetable fats are surely no panacea for *anything*.

What then are we to believe concerning the cholesterol story? Should fats be avoided entirely? Is one fat better than another? Is an unsaturate healthier than a saturate? Or vice versa? Does it matter how much cholesterol we eat? Is dietary cholesterol really related to atherosclerosis? Why is it that despite the fact that Americans are using half the amount of butter, whole milk and eggs than they did thirty years ago, and despite the fact that polyunsaturate use has increased 40 percent during this period, the incidence of heart disease has nonetheless *doubled* over this period of time? The answer is: Nobody knows.

An Alternate Explanation of the Cholesterol Question

Twenty years ago a book was published that broke fresh ground in the world of natural nutrition. It was called *Food Is Your Best Medicine* and was written by a physician named Henry G. Bieler.

Bieler had practiced orthodox medicine for some years before he decided that conventional medical theory really didn't seem to get to the bottom of questions concerning health and disease. So he struck out on his own. After much experimentation he reached certain conclusions that he shared with readers in the beginning of his book. In Bieler's own words:

> The first conclusion is that the primary cause of disease is not germs. Rather, I believe that disease is caused by a toxemia which results in cellular impairment and breakdown, thus paving the way for the multiplication and onslaught of germs.
>
> My second conclusion is that in almost all causes the use of drugs in treating patients is harmful. Drugs often cause serious side effects, and sometimes even create new diseases. . . .
>
> My third conclusion is that disease can be cured through the proper use of correct foods. This statement may sound deceptively simple, but I have arrived at it only after intensive study of a highly complex subject: colloid and endocrine chemistry.*

Bieler sticks to his guns. In *Food Is Your Best Medicine* he makes a strong case for the power of food as both stabilizer and destroyer of human health. In his chapter on heart disease, for instance, he has much to say concerning the relationship of cholesterol to hardening of the arteries. Perhaps most crucial is his belief that the eating of fats themselves is not particularly hazardous. What is dangerous, he claims, is when natural fats are *altered* through the process of commercial refining and especially by heating. "Overeating of fats and oils, as long as they are in their natural state, cannot cause arterial disease," he writes. "The body merely stores the excess as fat. It is only when *unnatural* fats, or *natural fats which have been altered by being overheated, are consumed as food, that the trouble arises.*" In other words, the trouble is not in the quantity of fats, Bieler maintains, but in the quality—what is done to the fats before they reach the consumer. This is where the real trouble lies. An interesting view of the question, certainly, and one worth some consideration. Bieler supports his case by citing the eating habits of the premodernized Eskimo culture. Among these hearty people the diet once consisted almost exclusively of whale and seal blubber, the fattest of the fat. Yet the health of their cardiovascular system was, by all reports, phenomenal. As soon as the Eskimos began eating refined fats, however, or fats cooked with starch, their health declined. "I have found," Bieler writes, "that it is impossible for the liver to synthesize a perfect cholesterol from a fat that has been heated with starch. The resulting cholesterol is used by the body

* Henry G. Bieler, M.D., *Food Is Your Best Medicine* (New York: Random House, 1965), p. i.

for arterial lining, but being an unnatural or altered cholesterol, it fails to wear well, soon breaks down and is corroded, resulting in various forms of arterial disease and degeneration." As to the question of saturated versus unsaturated, Bieler cuts through the Gordian knot. It matters little, he claims, how saturated or unsaturated a fat may be, *as long as it is a natural, unprocessed, unadulterated fat.* In this sense, he maintains, animal fats, marrow fats, brain fats, organ fats, all have their value. So does fat in beans, in avocados, in seeds, in nuts and in tropical fruits such as coconuts. All are useful, provided the liver is healthy enough to synthesize them, *and* provided they have not been artificially altered. "Fats," Bieler writes, "saturated or unsaturated, do their greatest harm to the body when they are used as shortening or cooking oil, that is, when they are heated with other foods, especially the starches. Fried bread or potatoes, donuts, hot cakes, pie crust, cakes and pastries—all offer *altered* cholesterol. And when you eat these highly regarded confections, the result is imperfect artery lining, erosion of the arteries, atherosclerosis." The worst offenders of all, he believes, are doughnuts and potato chips, with popcorn heated in cooking oil trailing along as a close third. We often hear that foods prepared in such ways are bad for our health. We hear less frequently plausible reasons *why.* If we are to believe Bieler, modern medical research is looking for answers to the cholesterol dilemma up the wrong tree. The problem is in what is done to the fats before they are eaten, he tells us, not in how many fats are eaten over a year's time or how full or empty their molecular chains may be. These considerations may go a long way toward explaining why the results of cholesterol testing is so often erratic and contradictory. Since testers invariably overlook the vital question of *how refined, unrefined, processed, preserved, heated and otherwise altered* the fats given to test subjects are, it makes a certain obvious sense that their findings will be inconsistent. Without considering the crucial variable of *quality* in the substance being studied, test results must inevitably be incomplete. But once again, this very question of quality is glossed over by modern researchers. A fat is a fat is a fat, they might say. An oil is an oil is an oil. But is it?

How to Deal with the Cholesterol Dilemma

As you were warned, a hall of mirrors. Men like Bieler and others who have presented unorthodox theories concerning the relationship between fats and coronary problems sometimes score solid points with the logic of their reasoning.

At the same time, it would be flip to dismiss the many medical findings that do point a finger at fats, especially animal fats, as contributive to cardiovascular problems and to other diseases as well. From all we can tell, fats in quantity simply aren't very good for you.

What then to do? Where is the happy medium?

The fact is that there *are* some commonsense measures that a person can take until absolute proof of one sort or another comes down the pike concerning the question of fats. None of these measures are too extreme. None are too taxing on time, or on the pocketbook, or on the nerves. They include the following:

1. Avoid margarine. Nutritionally it's empty, and by and large it is made of chemicals. Butter is better. You can avoid the butter/margarine dilemma entirely by using other spreads in their place. Try, for example, the tofu mayonnaise recipe on page 114. Or place fresh hummus on the table where the butter/margarine usually sits. Its wonderful, pungent taste becomes quickly addictive. Hummus is especially fine on pita bread, though it also goes nicely on crackers and whole-wheat bread (see hummus recipe, page 102).

2. Or try something entirely different. Go to the natural food store and purchase a package of miso. (See page 113 for information on miso.) Take it home and prepare a most delicious spread that is far better for you than either butter or margarine, and far lower in fats.

MISO SPREAD

¼ cup water   ½ cup tahini
½ cup miso   1 small onion, chopped

1. Heat the water until it is lukewarm. Add the miso and stir until it dissolves. Miso is a bit chunky and it will take some stirring and prodding to get it to liquefy.

2. Gradually add the tahini to the liquefied miso, stirring all the time. Aim for a batterlike consistency. Taste the mixture frequently. If it is too bland—that is, if it tastes too much like pure tahini—add a bit more miso. Some people prefer the taste strong on the miso, some like it strong on the tahini.

3. When the mixture reaches the desired consistency, mix in the onion and serve. Miso and tahini go wonderfully on whole-grain bread. Keep it refrigerated.

3. If you eat meat, eat lean meat. Stay away from pork especially. Interestingly, dried beef and chipped beef have a good deal less fats in them than the fresh varieties. Some organ meats and especially liver also

tend to be relatively low in fats. But the spoiler is that they are *higher* in cholesterol than most other meats.

4. Keep meat portions small. Try cutting back. Instead of eating 5 ounces of meat at a sitting put a half-sized portion of steak on your plate, 2½ ounces, say, and then compensate for the smaller amount by taking high-protein carbohydrates like beans with your meal.

5. Eat more chicken. Watch out for duck though; there's more fat on those little bones than meets the eye. The same for goose. Turkey is better; but ounce for ounce chicken is your best bet, especially if you remove the skin before cooking. Frog's legs, by the way, have almost *no* fats, if you're interested.

6. The harder cheeses like Swiss and Cheddar tend to be higher in cholesterol than the soft. Mozzarella, for instance, has about 66 mgs. cholesterol per 100 grams, while the harder Cheddar has 99 and Swiss 100.

7. Polyunsaturates are present in foods that are far better for you than the heavily processed vegetable oils. If you want to get polyunsaturates into your diet concentrate on eating such items as nuts—almonds, walnuts and pecans are all polyunsaturates. Also sesame and sunflower seeds. And beans, particularly soybeans and bean curd.

8. Eat high-fiber foods. They reduce blood-cholesterol rate by binding with bile salts, the carriers of cholesterol, and flushing them out via elimination.

9. Fish is an excellent source of animal protein and is much lower in dietary fats than meat. This is *not* true of shellfish. Scallops, for instance, though containing only trace amounts of fat, have almost as much cholesterol as corned beef. A helping of shrimp has even more.

10. When making soup, use bouillon cubes instead of meat stock. Your soup won't have as much body this way, but you can compensate by adding hearty grains like barley, rice or whole-wheat noodles. Organic vegetable bouillon can be purchased at most health food stores.

11. If you are an habituated meat eater, try substituting vegetable protein once or twice a week in place of meat. Beans are an especially good meat surrogate. They are filling enough to be eaten as a main course, and despite the poor press they've gotten, they are *not* fattening. Bean curd—tofu—also makes an excellent meat stand-in. See the book *Diet for a Small Planet*, by Frances Moore Lappé (New York: Ballantine Books), for excellent meat-substitution recipes.

12. Avoid fried foods, especially deep-fried foods. Also avoid using fats to flavor your vegetables. Try fresh herbs and spices instead.

13. When you use oil use it sparingly. A drop or two in the bottom of the pan is fine for sautéing; you don't have to saturate everything in

sight. When making salad dressing make dressings that don't call for oil. An exotic Oriental substitute for the oil-and-vinegar standard is made as follows:

TOFU DRESSING

2 umeboshi plums	**1 onion, chopped**
1 tofu cake	**½ teaspoon sesame oil**
¼ cup water	**¼ teaspoon sea salt**

Mash the umeboshi plums till they are finely pulped (umeboshi plums are a standard Japanese salted plum and can be purchased at the macrobiotic section of any natural food store). Mash up the tofu and add it to the plums along with the water, onion, oil and salt. Stir the mixture until it reaches a creamy consistency. Use on any fresh green salad.

14. If you're eating eggs, soft cook, hard-boil or poach them. Don't cook them in oil. Only the yolk of the egg, by the way, has cholesterol. The whites may be used as desired.

15. Eat low-fat desserts. Fruits are perfect. Stay away from cakes, ice cream, pies, etc.

16. If you have cardiovascular problems, it's best not to load your system with large amounts of food at each sitting. Better to take smaller portions at frequent intervals. The digestion of big, bulky meals can be a strain on the heart.

17. Try to include no more than 10 percent fats in your diet, and try to take in less than 300 mgs. cholesterol per day. It's two sides of the same coin and each effort leans on the other; reduce your dietary-fat intake and you'll automatically reduce your cholesterol, especially when you eliminate or cut down on animal fats. Ten percent fat is the equivalent of around two tablespoonfuls of butter a day. You don't need any more than that to stay fit.

18. Learn which foods are high in fats, which foods low. Then shop accordingly. The following lists can be used as guides.*

---

* Note that certain items like fish and potatoes are listed on both the high-fat list and the low-fat list, depending on the variety and method of preparation. Be sure to check both when looking up values for any particular food.

High-fat Foods

Food	Approximate Measure	Fats per Gram (%)
Almonds	⅔ cup	54
Bacon	12 strips	55
Beans, Soy	⅔ cup	18
Beef, Rump	3½ ounces	32
Beef Flank	3½ ounces	23
Beef Hamburger	3½ ounces	30
Beef Steak (Porterhouse)	3½ ounces	27
Brazil Nuts	⅔ cup	66
Butter	½ cup	81
Cheese, Blue	3½ ounces	31
Cheese, Camembert	3½ ounces	25
Cheese, Cheddar	3½ ounces	32
Cheese, Cream	3½ ounces	37
Chocolate	3½ ounces	34
Coconut	1 cup shredded	35
Cream	½ cup	20
Doughnuts, Plain	3	21
Eggs	2 medium-sized, cooked	12
Fats, Vegetable Cooking	½ cup	100
Fish, Herring	3½ cups	13
Fish, Salmon	3½ ounces	17
Fish, Sardines in Oil	3½ ounces	11
Fish, Shad	3½ ounces	10
Ice Cream	¾ cup	13
Lamb, Rib Chop	3½ ounces	35
Lamb Roast	3½ ounces	19
Lard	½ cup	100
Margarine	½ cup	81
Mayonnaise	½ cup	78
Milk, Whole	1 cup	12
Milk, Whole Dried	1 cup	27
Oil, Salad	½ cup	100
Peanuts	⅔ cup	44
Peas, Split	½ cup	25
Pork, Chops	3½ ounces	26
Pork, Ham	3½ ounces	33
Potato Chips	20 chips	14
Potatoes, French-fried	20 fries	19
Potatoes, Hash-Browned	½ cup	12
Sausage, Bologna	3½ ounces	16

High-fat Foods (*cont.*)

Food	Approximate Measure	Fats per Gram (%)
Turkey	3½ ounces	20
Veal	3½ ounces	28
Walnuts	1 cup, halved	64

Low-fat Foods

Food	Approximate Measure	Fats per Gram (%)
Apple	1 small	trace amounts
Applesauce	½ cup	trace amounts
Asparagus	½ cup cut	trace amounts
Banana	1 medium-sized	0
Barley, Pearled	3½ ounces	1
Beans, Green	½ cup	trace amounts
Beans, Kidney	½ cup	trace amounts
Beef, Dried or Chipped	3½ ounces	6
Beets	½ cup	trace amounts
Blackberries	⅔ cup	trace amounts
Bouillon Cubes	1 cube	trace amounts
Bran	2½ cups	2
Bread, Rye	1 slice	trace amounts
Bread, White	1 slice	2
Bread, Whole Wheat	1 slice	1
Broccoli	⅔ cup	trace amounts
Brussels Sprouts	⅔ cup	trace amounts
Cantaloupe	¼ melon	trace amounts
Carrots	1 cup, grated	trace amounts
Cherries	1 cup	1
Chicken, Broiler	3½ ounces	7
Clams	3½ ounces	1
Corn	⅔ cup	1
Corn, Popped	½ cup	trace amounts
Cornmeal	½ cup	trace amounts
Crabs	3½ ounces	3
Dates	½ cup, pitted	1
Farina	½ cup	trace amounts
Fish, Bluefish	3½ ounces	4
Fish, Cod	3½ ounces	trace amounts
Fish, Flounder	3½ ounces	½

Low-fat Foods (*cont.*)

Food	Approximate Measure	Fats per Gram (%)
Fish, Haddock	3½ ounces	trace amounts
Fish, Halibut	3½ ounces	5
Fish, Tuna	3½ ounces	8
Grapefruit	½ cup	trace amounts
Grapes	⅔ cup	trace amounts
Honey	1 tablespoon	0
Lemon	1 medium-sized	1
Liver	3½ ounces	5
Lobster	3½ ounces	2
Mushrooms	½ cup	trace amounts
Noodles, Egg	⅔ cup	1
Oatmeal	⅔ cup	1
Onion	1 medium-sized	trace amounts
Orange	1 medium-sized	trace amounts
Papaya	1 medium-sized	trace amounts
Peach	1 medium-sized	trace amounts
Peas, Green	⅔ cup	trace amounts
Pickle, Dill	1 large	trace amounts
Pimiento	1 medium	trace amounts
Pineapple	1 medium	trace amounts
Potato, Baked	1 medium	trace amounts
Potato, Flour	1 cup, sifted	1
Pretzels	5 stick pretzels	trace amounts
Prunes	⅔ cup	1
Pumpkin	1 cup	trace amounts
Raisins	⅔ cup	1
Rice, Brown	½ cup	2
Rice, White	½ cup	trace amounts
Rye Flour	1¼ cups sifted	1
Sauerkraut	⅔ cup	trace amounts
Scallops	3½ ounces	trace amounts
Shrimp	3½ ounces	1
Squash	½ cup	trace amounts
Sugar	½ cup	0
Tomato	1 medium-sized	trace amounts
Watermelon	3½ ounces	trace amounts

What about specific high-fat foods like butter, cooking oils and eggs? Foods that are condemned by most authorities as cholesterol builders but that are rich in vitamins and nutrients? Foods that the human race has eaten for thousands of years without any apparent difficulties until the advent of the twentieth century? Must they be sacrificed? Must we give up all these good comestibles forever and ever if we are to avoid atherosclerosis? Not necessarily.

BUTTER, MARGARINE AND A LITTLE-KNOWN SUBSTITUTE FOR BOTH

Around the first decades of this century margarine appeared on the market as a cheap substitute for butter. Not an imitation yet; a substitute. Its natural color was a kind of greasy white, and for years it came this way out of the package. Some consumers liked it like this. Most didn't. Butter continued to prevail as the number-one spread.

But the margarine manufacturers were an ambitious lot. From the beginning they objected to the heavy taxes that the government, in its attempts to protect the dairy industry, had levied on sales of colored margarine. One such, the famous Oleomargarine Act of 1886, had forced outrageous tariffs and license fees on all margarine retailers, and had subjected the sale of colored margarine to dozens of niggling restrictions.

Through all this the margarine manufacturers knew intuitively that their product would sell better if it was dyed yellow to look like the high-priced spread and they continued to push for change. Already they were packaging their product in cute butterlike blocks, and selling it at the dairy counter as if it was a milk and cheese product. And the price was right; at most stores it cost half as much as butter. But there was still that problem —the coloring. How could you fool the public into thinking they were eating pure creamery butter when the stuff you peddled looked like cold cream? And if the consumers wanted to give it a butter-yellow hue they had to do all the artificial coloring themselves; the yellow dyes were usually sold along with the margarine in a separate package. So the margarine people continued to push for the untaxed right to dye their product, an unabashedly deceptive dirty trick, when you think about it.

Legal battles ensued. The dairy industry, no small lobby itself, fought back with a slew of litigation, and for a while it was anyone's ball game. Then came World War II and the folks on the home front turned more and more to synthetic foods when the real ones weren't available. Pretty soon they got accustomed to them. After the war the question of synthetic coloring thus seemed less of an issue to just about everyone, with the exception perhaps of the Dairyman's Association, and before long the laws were reversed, making it (in most states) legal to dye margarine any color a marketer liked, tax-free.

Early versions of margarine in the United States had been composed mostly of lard. But meat has always been an expensive commodity, and so animal fats were soon replaced with vegetable oils. The trouble was that these oils were liquid, not solid, and even when treated with hardeners and emulsifiers it was impossible to get them to stand tall and well cubed like the competition. So the process of "hydrogenation" was introduced.

To hydrogenate you force hydrogen gas through a fatty substance under enormous heat and pressure, activating the process with a metallic catalyst such as platinum, copper chromite, or most commonly nickel, a highly poisonous substance in its own right. The hydrogen atoms are then compelled to bond with the available empty carbon atoms, producing a more heavily saturated compound. The process is especially useful in making soap. And gasoline.

To hydrogenate margarine the process is more or less the same. The liquid vegetable oil is cooled under pressure, the hydrogens are forced through the substance as it bubbles in the vat, and the oil is transformed from a liquid into a semisolid fat that has the same density and texture as butter. It's not butter or anything like it, of course. But since the consistency is similar (if a bit more like Vaseline), and since artificial butter flavoring is added, the wonders of modern chemistry fool the human senses once again.

The irony of all this is that by hydrogenating an oil *the oil no longer remains a polyunsaturate.* Remember the Tinkertoy model. If you fill all those empty stems with hydrogen atoms you change a polyunsaturate into a saturate. And this is exactly what happens when the hydrogen is bubbled up through the oil. The polyunsaturated vegetable oil gets transformed into saturated margarine.

Many manufacturers, in fact, continue to promote their so-called "polyunsaturated" margarine as if it still has all the so-called cholesterol-fighting virtues of polyunsaturated oils, when in fact these virtues have been cooked out during the hydrogenation.

The problem, moreover, does not just stop with the hydrogenation. After the vegetable oil has been saturated, it must then be cosmeticized and made presentable to the buying public. Now follows an orgy of straining, deodorizing, cooking, dyeing and filtering, which, presto!, transforms the greasy gumbo into neat yellow patties for the dairy counter. In the process the vitamins and minerals in the oil are depleted, and essential proteins and fatty acids are altered beyond recognition. Almost nothing of any nutritive value is left.

Next, to add insult to injury, cheap (and saturated) coconut oils are combined in the concoction, along with hydrogenated soybean oil, artificial butter flavorings, coal-tar dyes, diacetyl (to make it smell like butter), plenty of salt, isopropyl as a stabilizer, chemical emulsifiers and benzoate of soda as a preservative. And since there is absolutely no nutrition in this mixture, supplies of vitamins A and D are added back to it artificially.

The final product is then shipped off to market where it is sold under the name of margarine, that good old American favorite spreadable spread. Its official identity, however, under the federal Food, Drug and Cosmetic Act, is not as a natural food product at all, but as—this is what they truly call it—a "plastic food." Really. That's the official government term for margarine and numerous other artificial foods.

Fred Rohé tells an amusing story along the lines of foods plastic and artificial.* Interested to learn how many days margarine would last without spoiling, he placed a fresh margarine stick on his windowsill and left it there, exposed to the elements, the flies and the California sun. Now as we all know, real butter will melt into a gooey mess after several hours. In two or three days, if the bugs leave anything at all, it will become a smelly, moldy hunk of rancidity. .

Not so the margarine. Two *years!* later, Rohé tells us, he finally decided that his experiment had made its point: The margarine on his windowsill had only half melted in all this time. Its shiny yellow surface showed no mold, no signs of insect life, no rancidity, nothing. Like plastic itself, it was veritably eternal.

So the next time you're about to purchase margarine as a low-fat substitute for all those "unhealthy" foods—like butter—give it a second thought. Recall how the margarine was made, and all the hype and half-truths that surround it. Then decide if you really need such a useless substance to confuse what is probably already an overconfused digestive tract.

What then about butter? There's no doubt that butter is a high-content fat, and that it's loaded with cholesterol. Assuming that cholesterol buildup in the arteries is actually attributable to high-fat foods (which question, as we've seen, is still far from settled), might it not be wiser to avoid butter entirely? Perhaps. But not necessarily.

Butter, for example, contains many nutrients and also accelerates the synthesis of vitamin B-6 in the intestine, a vitamin that is known to be friendly to cardiac tissue and to aid in the removal of excess cholesterol from the blood. In many cases, frying foods in polyunsaturates has been shown to increase blood fats, while frying them in butter has no adverse effect whatsoever on cholesterol level. In experiments at Tufts University

---

* Fred Rohé, *The Complete Book of Natural Foods* (Boulder: Shambala Publications, 1983), p. 75.

School of Medicine, animals were literally stuffed with a diet of butter. The butter was pure and fresh, and was well fortified with vitamins, while the rest of their diet consisted of rich, wholesome foods. The animals grew paunchy and lazy on this diet, all right. But their blood cholesterol stayed exactly the same. Variations of this same experiment have been tried many times, usually with the same outcome.

Butter fats differ chemically from other saturated fats, and some physicians feel this difference is not just quantitative. Unlike meat fats, they believe, butterfat may actually have a helping effect on the cardiovascular system. Studies indicate,* for instance, that the proper absorption of calcium depends to a sizable extent on fats in the bloodstream, especially butterfat, and that without the presence of these fats this precious mineral will be eliminated from the organism before being fully assimilated. Certain vegetable oils, at the same time, are found to *depress* calcium absorption to the body, especially oils high in some of the fatty acids we have not yet met: stearic, myristic and palmitic.

When calcium is depleted from the system, many researchers believe, cholesterol and triglyceride levels are elevated in the blood, while adequate levels of calcium stabilize cholesterol levels, due mainly to the part the calcium plays in getting rid of cholesterol through the feces. In other words, research indicates that butterfat stabilizes blood-fat levels, while vegetable oils produce the opposite reaction.

Further: Fats in butter have been found to be congenial to the growth of helpful digestive bacteria in the intestines, while polyunsaturates have no such beneficial action. In fact, there is evidence that polyunsaturates act as depressants of intestinal flora and thus of the vitamin pyridoxine— vitamin B-6—which is synthesized by these flora. A lack of vitamin B-6, some researchers believe, may in some way contribute to heart trouble.

Dr. Roger J. Williams in his landmark book *Nutrition Against Disease* has much to say on this question. He calls attention to a well-known study done on the dietary habits of people in northern and southern India. Testees from the northern Indian population, Williams relates, eat sizable amounts of butterfat and very few polyunsaturates. In the south the diet consists of large quantities of polyunsaturates (almost half of the fat consumption) and practically *no* butterfat.

Cardiovascular diseases, it then turns out, are rampant in southern India and relatively rare in the butterfat-eating country up north. The death rate from heart disease in the south is *fifteen times higher than in the north.*

* Roger J. Williams, *Nutrition Against Disease* (New York: Bantam Books, 1978), pp. 299– 302.

Williams and other scientists suggest that this disparity is due in part to the fact that the high-butterfat diet among northern Indians is more favorable to promoting internal synthesis of the B vitamins.

> It may be [he writes] that the diets of the Northern Indians are favorable in promoting intestinal synthesis of B vitamins, particularly pyridoxine, which protect against atherosclerosis, and do not create cellular (antioxidant) malnutrition from a too high consumption of polyunsaturated fats. The Southern Indian's diet may act to depress intestinal synthesis while promoting both vitamin E and B-6 deficiencies by a too high consumption of polyunsaturated fats, finally resulting in atherosclerosis. Be that as it may, no other current hypothesis, as far as we know, has been offered in explanation of these (unpopular) data.

There is something else of importance too in the butter question that you ought to know about, a little-known twist on the matter that is significant for anyone interested in natural eating.

Ghee: The Secret Alternative

Butter, it turns out, can take more than one form. If we lived in the East, and in India particularly, we would regularly cook with a food that is virtually unknown in our own country, though it is sometimes used in French cuisine: clarified butter. It is called ghee in India (rhymes with she), and its virtues in that country are legendary. As Dr. Rudolph Ballentine writes:

> When the watery part [of butter] is removed, so that only the clear fat is used, the result is an excellent cooking fat, superior to whole butter which scorches and turns black if heated above a certain point. In the East, however, many other virtues are ascribed to such clarified butter, and it is said that it has the capacity to take on and to magnify the properties of that with which it is combined. For this reason, it is said to not only make food more nutritious, but is also an important ingredient in the preparation of many natural medicines.*

Several studies have shown that ghee actually promotes within the system a kind of protective effect against hardening of the arteries. Studies published in Britain have also shown that clarified butter is more condu-

---

* Rudolph Ballentine, M.D., *Diet and Nutrition, a Holistic Approach* (Honesdale, Pa.: The Himalayan International Institute, 1982), p. 106.

cive to the proper assimilation of calcium and phosphorus in the system than are fats with high melting points, and especially hydrogenated fats.*

On the practical side, ghee, unlike other dairy products, can be preserved for long periods of time, even without refrigeration. This means it is an ideal food in countries like India where the heat makes short work of perishables. Ghee is easy to prepare, delicious, inexpensive, and very nutritionally satisfying, all qualities that would seem to make it the perfect compromise between synthetic, nonnutritious margarine and high-fat, high-cholesterol butter.

You can purchase ghee from any Indian grocery store and occasionally at health food stores. Since, however, Indian grocery stores are hard to find, especially if you live in a rural area, you may wish to make your own ghee. It's quite simple.

MAKING YOUR OWN GHEE

1. Place a stick of butter in a saucepan and simmer it slowly for 45 to 60 minutes. As it simmers a white froth will form on the surface from time to time. Remove it.

2. When the butter turns a pleasant golden-brown pour it from the pan and strain through cheesecloth.

3. Presto! You have your ghee. Keep it preserved, as people do in India, in a sealed crockery jar and store it in a dark place. It does not have to be kept cold, though refrigeration won't harm it. The ghee may tend to crystallize a bit but this will not interfere with its nutritional value.

4. You can substitute ghee in practically any common recipe that calls for ordinary butter. One heaping teaspoonful of regular butter equals about 3½ teaspoonfuls of ghee.

COOKING OILS: HOW TO CHOOSE THE RIGHT ONES

With cooking oils the controversy turns more on what is done to them commercially than what is in them. Recall Dr. Bieler's thesis that heating a vegetable oil and subjecting it to stringent refining changes the chemical integrity of its fat content, transforming an essentially benign food into a toxic one. There is much laboratory evidence to back up this thesis. To many natural-foods-oriented experts the theory makes sense.

* *British Journal of Nutrition* (1949), 3:5.

The problem, nonetheless, remains: If cardiovascular disorders are somehow linked to fat intake, if polyunsaturates are a swindle, if processing ruins an oil entirely, what's left?

Don't despair. There are several lines of action you can take.

1. Avoid Commercial Vegetable Oils

This may seem repetitious in light of all that's been said so far, but it can't hurt to be emphatic. Simply pass them by. Don't be fooled by all the jargon and implied claims on the labels. We've seen how much all these are worth.

Commercially bottled oils, the fact is, are almost invariably processed and heated at high temperatures. Heating destroys vitamins in oil in the same way that boiling depletes vitamins in vegetables, and that's just the tip of the iceberg.

> Refining oil removes waxes, resins, stearines, and phosphatides [writes Fred Rohé]. When they are eliminated, chlorophyll, lecithin, provitamin A, vitamin E, copper, iron, magnesium, calcium, and phosphorus all disappear. The industrial oil technician sees these nutrients as "impurities," largely because he doesn't think of vegetable oil as food but as grease. He doesn't want impurities in his grease because the product the public has become propagandized into accepting is bland, virtually free of color, odor and flavor.

Rohé's picturesque description of the refining process commercial vegetable oils pass through makes the hair stand on end. It is evocative enough to quote.

> Most of the oil is usually pressed out mechanically, then solvent is added to the leftover meal to extract the remaining oil. At some refineries, the mechanical step is eliminated and solvent alone is used. Hexane is the solvent used more frequently; benzene, ethyl ether, carbon disulphide, carbon tetrachloride, methylene chloride, and gasoline could also do the job. The solvent frees the oil, then the solvent and oil are boiled to drive off the solvent, leaving extracted oil. (Oil processors, when asked how much solvent residue remains in the oil, have answered, "Very little," meaning up to 100 ppm.) These solvent residues are proven or suspected carcinogens.
>
> Next comes the massive assault against impurities: color and flavor are whipped with lye first, then caustic soda, then filtration. Then all but the faintest whiff of odor is removed by heating it at temperatures in the range of 400F for twelve hours. Before bottling this bedraggled and

woebegone grease, a preservative like BHA, BHT, or propyl gallate is usually added. . . . *

Enough said.

2. Use Cold-Pressed, Nonrefined Oils

Approximately 215 degrees is the killing point for the nutrients in most oils when cooked for fifteen minutes or more. Many processed oils are heated a good deal longer at higher temperatures.

"Cold-pressed" oils, on the other hand, are drawn from the seed, fruit or vegetable by the old-fashioned method of pressure, not by chemical extraction with a caustic solvent. If this pressing method is executed properly it is done with a machine known as an expeller. The expeller does what its name implies—it mechanically forces, or expels, the liquid out of the shell.

As the expeller presses out the crude oils, some heating does take place; there is no getting around it. Cold-pressing is not really cold. Usually though, these heats remain below 180 degrees, well below the point at which molecular changes take place within the oil itself. After the oil is crushed out of the seed, fruit or vegetable it is filtered to cleanse it of the heavier sediments. And that's it. If it's the real McCoy no further processing is done.

Cold-pressed oils thus would seem the most desirable product to search for at the market. But there's a hitch. Legislation governing what cold-pressed really means varies from state to state. In most cases there are no controls over its definition at all, and so the term is used indiscriminately. The truth is that many cold-pressed oils are exposed to extremely high heats during some point in their preparation, and that some are just as worthless as the brand-name varieties.

The best clue lies in the labeling. If, for instance, the label tells you an oil is cold-pressed (the term "expeller-pressed" is even better) *and* unrefined there's a considerably better chance of its being pure. Unrefined oils, those that have not been boiled and chemically adulterated, come as close as you can get to "natural." Their stores of vitamins and nutrients will more or less weather the pressing and filtration techniques, and even though some heating does take place to prevent the vegetable fats from coagulating, most of the vital ingredients still stay put.

The only problem with unrefined oils is that in the beginning it can be a little disconcerting learning to use them, mostly because of the oils'

* Rohé, p. 74.

unique taste, and perhaps even more, their low smoking point. Smoking point is the specific temperature at which an oil will burn and emit smoke when heated. (One reason commercial oils are refined is to raise their smoking point. Then they can be used to fry those hashbrowns and onion rings without fear of smoking out the kitchen.) The more unrefined and pure an oil is the sooner it will smoke.

This, however, shouldn't deter you too much. Frying starchy foods such as potatoes or doughnuts, as Dr. Bieler has pointed out, transforms the nutritional integrity of fats into a nonfood, and much laboratory evidence backs up this notion.* If you wish to eat more sanely you should make it a general rule to avoid deep-fried foods in the first place. Period. Instead use the faster pan-frying wok method, as described on page 118. You'll get some smoke this way using an unrefined oil, but not too much, no more than when you cook an ordinary hamburger. And it will go a lot easier on your digestion if you do. Sautéing is the next best cooking method; just be sure you do it quickly and at moderate heats.

What about the taste? Unrefined oils are strong all right, but to most palates, pleasing as well. They go especially well in salads, to which they impart a zesty flavor. One of the reasons cooking oils are refined in the first place is to make them odorless and tasteless. Commercial unsaturates are basically designed to be invisible; not to flavor the food, simply to lubricate it. With unrefined oils it's the other way around. The oils add their own particular flavor to the salad, and for most people the addition is an enhancement.

If you're going to use unrefined oils house them in the refrigerator once they're opened. Unlike synthetic oils, which keep for months in the most sweltering locations, untreated oils are living fluids and quite perishable. Store them in a dark bottle too, if possible. A few years back, you'll recall, commercial cooking oils were sold mostly in darkly translucent jars. Since light is an enemy to oil, this was only as it should be. When the purity craze seized oil buyers, however, the fact that you could look through the glass and see the oil sitting there in all its refined crystal clarity became a major selling point, and so the dark bottle became obsolete. Still, it's better to keep *any* oil in a dark container, even a commercially processed one.

If the label says "no preservatives" that ups the oil's credibility even more. No preservatives means that it probably won't keep very long, however, even in the refrigerator. Try buying unrefined oils in small amounts and use them within two or three weeks after purchase.

---

* For examples, see the many references to laboratory experiments in heated oils listed in Williams, *Nutrition Against Disease,* p. 296.

EGGS: NOT AS BAD AS YOU THINK

Eggs are one of nature's gems. Nutritionwise, everything is there for the developing fetus to draw upon during its silent journey to birth. It is the veritable stuff of organic life, and anyone who brings it to table gets to partake in the spread: the best-quality protein of any food in the world, and hence an abundance of essential amino acids; also, important dietary fats, enzymes, vitamins (eggs are one of the few real dietary sources of vitamin D), iron, sulphur, and many minerals and crucial trace minerals too.

From the consumer's standpoint, the high nutritional value of eggs makes them one of the great dollar-for-dollar bargains, and as far as cuisine goes there is no food so versatile. Nor must the egg lover worry about commercial pollutants. Food processors have yet to devise a way to refine, preserve or spray the yolks and whites before they come out of their shells.

Despite all these assets, however, eggs have become perhaps *the* central target of the anticholesterol scare; ounce per ounce they hold more of this dreaded substance than practically any other food on the market. For instance, a large-sized AA-grade egg contains about 250 mgs. of cholesterol, almost all of it deposited in the yolk. By comparison, three ounces of cooked beef have approximately 80 mgs., and one glass of whole milk has around 35. In our cholesterol-crazed society, it doesn't take much figuring to understand why eggs have become the cardiac sufferer's public enemy number one.

The irony is, as we have now seen, that the link between how much cholesterol you take in and how prone this makes you to heart disease is conjectural. A person who enjoys a dozen eggs a week, researchers have found, may have an upped serum cholesterol level in his blood. Or he may not. No direct relationship can be established.

Even if a person does pile in the eggs, what's more, there is no direct evidence that the cholesterol taken in food is necessarily the same cholesterol that builds arterial lesions. As Ancel Keys, one of the early and most important researchers in this field, relates, "Cholesterol levels in humans are essentially independent of the cholesterol intake over the whole range of natural human diets." *

Sometimes people who eat many eggs even show *less* tendency toward cholesterol buildup than those who abstain. There is simply no pattern that can in any way be termed definitive, and it is for this reason that most physicians, somewhat apologetically perhaps, still recommend

* Williams, *Nutrition Against Disease*, p. 248.

at least one egg a week and perhaps two or three to their patients. Such a prescription is even advised for patients suffering from heart disease. That's how important eggs are to our nutritional well-being.

Behind all the cholesterol fracas there is another factor too in the egg story that is seldom talked about in the doctor's office and generally ignored by conventional nutritional thinking. Eggs, you see, may contain the antidote to their own cholesterol. It is called *lecithin.*

Basically lecithin is an emulsifier, and its ability to preserve substances in chemical suspension has made it popular among food manufacturers who often use it to keep candy and baked goods fresh. One of lecithin's many tasks is to dissolve excess cholesterol and to help remove it from the body. One clinical study showed that cholesterol level in twelve patients was dramatically reduced when subjects were fed an ounce of lecithin each day for a month.* Another showed that the arteries of lab animals force-fed on cholesterol remained unclogged but only as long as lecithin supplies were simultaneously added to their feed.†

To keep the record straight, certain studies have also failed to prove the value of lecithin as an anticholesterol agent while others remain inconclusive. Some have turned up contradictory or even negative findings. The hall of mirrors again—there are no sure things as far as the atherosclerosis question goes. Nor does the rush to stock up on lecithin pills seem to be the answer either, as there is no proof that commercially packaged lecithin supplements make any difference in the rise or fall of blood fats.

Perhaps then in the long run the best way to find out whether lecithin helps is to try it yourself. If you're worried about how fatty foods affect you, or if lab tests indicate that you have an abnormally high cholesterol count, try introducing lecithin-high natural foods into your diet for, say, the next two months and then measure the difference.

To start with, have your serum cholesterol level checked at a medical lab. It's a simple test and relatively inexpensive. Then go on the high-lecithin-food regime for two months. At the end of this period have your blood cholesterol level tested again, and note any changes.

For whatever mysterious reasons, lecithin, like so many of the other supplementary food substances sold at health food stores, seems to help some people and not help others. You may be one that it does help. You won't know until you try. Just be sure to stick to the regime without wavering, and make certain the lecithin-high foods you choose are fresh and nonprocessed.

* L. M. Morrison, "Serum cholesterol reduction with lecithin," *Geriatrics* (1958), 13:12.
† Williams, *Nutrition Against Disease,* p. 251.

What foods are stocked wtih lecithin? Beans and peas are loaded with it, both of which, incidentally, have been noted in several tests to lower serum cholesterol rates. Other lecithin-rich foods include nonprocessed vegetable oils and soybean cakes. But above all, the food it appears in most predominantly is the egg.

So we come the full circle. As the saying goes, "The cure is often in the ill."

Are Organic Eggs Better?

In a word: Yes.

Consider commercial eggs. They are laid by chickens raised on pesticide-soaked feed, tranquilizers to ease their blood pressure, antioxidants to color the egg yolk a deeper yellow, sodium bicarbonate to harden the shell, antibiotics to stimulate egg-laying capacity. Sometimes as many as fifty thousand chickens will be housed together in a huge, artificially vented, windowless poultry factory. Here each poor bird is confined to a tiny cage for its entire life; most will never move more than a foot away from the spot; none will ever know the barnyard.

Since chickens kept in this way are prone to psychological as well as physical diseases, the hens' beaks will be sliced off at an early age to prevent them from doing damage to themselves in a fit of madness, or to their neighbors. Since light accelerates egg production, artificial lamps glare at all hours of the day and night in the hen factory, spurring on the chickens' pituitary glands and hence their egg production. Some lay as many as three hundred eggs a year, practically one every day. This of course tends to wear out the animals and deplete their calcium supplies, so that the hens frequently suffer spontaneous fractures of the legs and wings. Many of them can no longer walk.

While the normal life span of a Leghorn hen is ordinarily several years, commercially kept chickens burn out in months and are quickly replaced by others, all born via the latest techniques in artificial insemination; a rooster in the hen house is a thing of the past. And hence none of the eggs that roll out of the hens' tiny cells and onto the ever-moving conveyor belts below are ever fertile. (Although many people don't realize it, hens can lay eggs without the assistance of a rooster. These eggs will be sterile eggs, however. They will be minus the growth hormones present in fertile eggs.)

The result of this highly efficient and thoroughly inhumane system is that the quality of the egg itself becomes inferior. Poisoned, unhealthy, unhappy chickens must necessarily produce eggs of a similar stripe. Since the calcium supplies given these creatures are meager, the shells of their eggs tend to be thin and fragile. Force-feedings of poultry at regular hours fail to make up for the lack of wholesome feeds, and so the commercial egg itself is deficient in many of the nutrients present in the organic varieties. Commercial eggs at the supermarket, though billed as "farm fresh," are usually kept in storage before reaching the market. Some are many weeks old. Others are placed in cold storage for months, a method that severely depletes the egg of its most essential vitamin stores.

In contrast to all this heartless efficiency, the so-called organic egg is produced by hens that are allowed the free run of a chicken pen and that are intentionally fed on a diet of table scraps, whatever worms and insects they catch themselves, and fresh feed. Roosters are kept in the vicinity so that the eggs will be fertile. This is a big plus as far as the eggs' nutritional value is concerned. An old advertising slogan once had it that "happy hens lay happy eggs." It was right.

Organic eggs can be purchased at any health food store, though they are often expensive. If the produce really is organic—it is easy to fake matters in this department—the extra nutritional value is worth the extra cost.

How to Tell If an Egg Is Really Organic

First, find the owner of the natural food store and ask him where he buys his eggs. If he informs you they're shipped to the store from some remote spot seven states away, be suspicious. Even if the eggs are organic they may not be fresh, and that's important. The best store-bought eggs should be local, say from three or four hundred miles away at most. (To tell if an egg is fresh, put it in a bowl of water. If it floats, it's fresh; if it sinks, it's not; if it half floats, it's only half fresh. Another method is to shake the egg. You should hear something approaching a rattle inside. If not you know it's stale.)

The white of an organic egg is more solid and compact than that of a commercial egg, the shell is harder and thicker, and the yolk doesn't break easily—when making scrambled eggs you may have to literally poke and prod the yolk to get it to disperse.

Organic eggs may look a bit "dirtier" than the commercially produced varieties, as their shells have not been bleached or dyed. Occasionally when you get one home and break it open you'll find something that resembles an embryo inside. That's exactly what it is: A chick that never hatched. But don't be put off by this. It simply means that the eggs are fertile, and that this one happened to get by the scanner. Place the rest of the eggs from this batch in the refrigerator and eat them quickly, as organic eggs spoil more rapidly than commercial. If, by the way, you have a child who is allergic to eggs, try giving him or her the fertile organic kind. Children who are allergic to commercial eggs are sometimes sensitive to things that are done to these eggs rather than to eggs themselves.

A Few Good Things to Know About Eggs

• Two eggs have about as much protein in them as three or four ounces of hamburger. The quality of this protein is better than meat. If you're not eating meat, eggs are an ideal way to get your protein supply.

• Eggs that are fried at too high a heat become rubbery and tough. It's better to fry them longer and at a simmer than at high heats for short spurts. A so-called "three-minute egg" is best boiled for seven or eight minutes over medium-to-low heat. Soft-boiled eggs can be cooked over low heat for four or five minutes.

• To prevent eggs from cracking while boiling, start them in cold water with a tablespoon of vinegar or salt added. Both the salt and vinegar will seal the calcium and harden the shell. If the eggs come directly out of the refrigerator and are chilled, place the eggs in a pot of warm water first and allow them to reach room temperature, then proceed as described above.

• To make scrambled eggs especially light add a little water to them while they are cooking. The secret of good scrambled eggs is to cook them in very, *very* little oil or butter at extremely low temperatures. Don't whip or froth them up before scrambling. Egg beaters add nothing to either the taste or the nutritional value of an egg.

• If you are going to beat or whip eggs, leave them out of the refrigerator for several hours first. Egg whites whip best at room temperature. Cold makes them sludgy and stiff.

• If your child is a finicky eater and is not getting enough protein, eggs can easily be sneaked into a number of foods without detection to supply missing nutrients. If your child is addicted to junk foods try adding eggs to malted milks, pancakes, muffins, French toast, or to cocoa. With a little cunning they can even be incorporated into such foods as hamburgers or pizza.

• Though there is still some disagreement over the matter, it seems that brown eggs contain more or less the same basic flavor and nutritional stores as white. One seems to be no better than the other, though brown eggs often sell for more.

• The notion that an egg yolk that is especially bright and yellow has more vitamin A than a dull yolk is not true. In fact, a dull yolk is often better than a bright one. Remember, commercial egg producers often feed additives to their hens designed to color the yolk a merry and inviting yellow.

• While most of the food value in an egg is located in the yolk, the white of the egg has good protein supplies (ovalbumin) and some sulphur. Unfortunately, the white also contains an enzyme called *avidin,* which interferes with the digestion of certain B vitamins. The avidin is removed in the cooking, along with any traces of Salmonella, as long as the cooking temperature is above 140 degrees. For these reasons it's best to stay away from raw eggs in foods such as eggnog or steak tartar.

• Hard-boiled eggs are especially good when included in a reducing plan. They remain longer in the digestive system and keep the dieter from feeling prematurely hungry.

• What about synthetic eggs? Hear the famous natural food champion and entrepreneur J. I. Rodale on the subject:

> I also wish to advise against food products that are supposed to contain eggs, but either don't, or have them in a chemicalized form. Take the headline that appeared in a New York paper in 1957. It said, "Chemists are helping bakers to economize on eggs." But the question is, do those chemists know what they're doing? Do they know anything about nutrition? They suggest that, in making prepared dry cake mixes, whole eggs be replaced with methyl cellulose and a little extra milk, with, they say, very palatable results. They consider that up to half the normal amount of egg whites may be omitted from prepared dry cake mixes, if these chemicals are used. Then there's the patent recently issued by the U.S. Patent Office for a process of preparing dried egg white where glucose oxidase and catalase are used. Then, an aliphatic polyhydric alcohol is used, constituting from 4 to 22 percent by weight of the finished dried egg white products. One perhaps might not mind alcohol . . . but aliphatic alcohol is a horse of a different color. It is a chemicalized alcohol and has no place in egg whites. And who wants glucose oxidase and catalase in his egg white? Do you know who? The food manufacturer who saves money by practicing these shenanigans.*

• To peel a hard-boiled egg more easily, leave it in the pan for five minutes after it has boiled. The heat and steam will circulate around the shell, helping to loosen the bond between shell and egg.

• Store uncooked eggs in a dark, airtight container. A traditional method of storage is to keep eggs in a vat of cold water to which a small amount of cooking oil has been added.

• Normally, uncooked eggs should be kept no longer than a week, even if they are the commercial variety. Two weeks is tops.

* J. I. Rodale and staff, *The Health Seeker* (Emmaus, Pa.: Rodale Books, 1972), p. 269.

● If push comes to shove and you have a large number of egg yolks left over from a recipe, they *can* be frozen. Remove any ice tray from the fridge, clean it thoroughly, and place each yolk in an individual ice cell. You can then remove the eggs all at once at a later date for cooking or pop them out one at a time. The freezing point for eggs is 28 degrees. Don't keep them frozen longer than a few months.

● Never—repeat, never—buy eggs with cracks in them. Any break in an egg is a possible breeding ground for the dangerous Salmonella bacteria.

● Natural Easter egg dyes can be made by boiling certain vegetables and fruits until their particular colored juices are extracted. For instance, carrots can be cooked until the water turns orange. Stewed blueberries will afford blue dyes. Grapes will give purple dyes. Or use concentrated grape juice. Try the juice from cooked beets for a deep-red dye. Green dyes can be extracted from spinach or kale. Let the eggs remain in the dye water overnight. The colors will come out less gaudy than with artificial dyes, but they'll be there, and the kids will have the fun of doing Easter eggs the old-fashioned way.

● Eggs are one of nature's more easily digested proteins. The fat is in an emulsified state and is digested in the stomach as well as in the intestines. For this reason egg yolks—not the whites—are often added to an infant's formula. Certainly yolks are better for their digestive tracts than meat, and some people believe that if an infant is given plenty of eggs the first year, meat may be entirely unnecessary. When starting an infant on egg, check for allergic symptoms. The white of the egg is usually the culprit.

CHAPTER FOUR

Proteins

Protein: Is a Lot Really a Lot Better?

"Get to the protein of the matter" reads the milk advertisement on a thousand billboards across America. It shows a cherubic redhead who might have doubled for Huckleberry Finn wiping a ring of milk froth from his lips and smiling gleefully. Note the use of the word "protein" as a synonym for something at the heart of the matter. The essence of things. That's the way Americans have tended to look at protein over the past several decades.

The truth is that protein is resoundingly important. It's as essential to our bodies as air. But a little goes a long way, and too much is way too much.

The problem is overkill. The lion's share of the responsibility for this is due to America's special love affair with the cow; and secondarily with the pig, the lamb, the turkey, the duck and the chicken. Beef above all is thought to be the *ne plus ultra* among proteins, with its extended family of cuts: roast beef, pot roast, prime roast, rib roast, hamburger. Animal protein has even become something of a status symbol in its own right. The poor live on bread and beans, we all know. The rich eat prime ribs. When your boss or your in-laws come to dinner it would be unthinkable to serve anything but a roast or some impressive-looking piece of carefully selected animal flesh. And were Americans not once promised, as the ultimate sign of security, "a chicken in every pot"? Indeed, in the minds of the general public the word "meat" and the word "protein" have become identical twins. There are even those who believe that meat is the *only* source of protein. Certainly, they'll tell you, it's the best!

Well, it's not quite that way. Your body needs protein, yes. But as a rule no more than 10 to 15 percent of your diet need be composed of it. To indulge in larger amounts is almost—not quite, but almost—worse than eating none at all, particularly if the protein is taken predominantly from meat and not from the other major sources: dairy foods, grains, eggs and vegetables.

What can happen if you overeat on proteins? What's so terrible? For starters, it has been established that too much protein has a nasty effect on the kidneys and the eliminative system. Unlike fats and sugars, proteins cannot be stored in the body for any length of time. A little is kept in the liver for emergency situations such as starvation, but not much. Most of the extra must be quickly eliminated.

A little surplus is easily handled. But when this extra turns into a prodigious overload, the body must work so hard to get rid of it, along with all the nitrogenous and sulphurous wastes that result, that it damages itself in the process. Both the kidneys and the liver become enlarged, and eventually disabled.

Excess animal protein has a tendency to produce acids that in turn steal vital calcium salts from the blood. Too much of this thievery can demineralize and weaken the skeletal structure and ultimately lead to spontaneous bone fractures. Large amounts of protein in the digestive tract, what's more, are assimilated at an extremely slow rate. The human body, not being exclusively carnivorous by biological design like the dog or the lion, was not built to take on *too* much of this substance at one time, so that when excess protein *is* taken in, some escapes digestive processing and is transformed into toxic substances. Some people believe that these substances are partially responsible for increased aging of the human organism and for certain degenerative diseases.

Too much protein can make you fat—a little known and not widely advertised fact. The extra calories that the body cannot use in a high-protein food are stored as adipose tissue, just like any other food substance. Anyone, by the way, who thinks that meat is a low-calorie food better double-check his calorie counter; most meats have more dietary fats in them than they have protein. Heavy meat eaters are likewise heavy additive eaters—meat is loaded with the stuff, making the dangers in certain high-protein animal foods more than just nutritive ones.

At the same time, contrary to popular misconception, protein is *not* an instant high-energy food but serves more as a long-term tissue builder rather than an immediate source of stamina. On this count both fat and carbohydrate are far more concentrated and efficient resources. In the years before sports nutrition came into its own, one often read about professional training camps where vast quantities of animal protein were shoveled into athletes for "instant strength." On game days we were told how players were "powered up" on breakfasts of beefsteak, eggs and bacon, while the trainers solemnly presided over the ritual, making sure every mighty morsel was consumed.

The irony of all this, besides the fact that protein is not a fast action food, is that meat digests in the gut so slowly that most of the energy that it does contain is not available for hours or even days after the meal, long after the game is over and the last fan has left his seat. Meanwhile, all that half-digested weight is sitting in the athlete's intestines during the game, where it bogs down his playing style a good deal more than it revs it up.

On the Positive Side

The good news is that protein is *extremely* important, absolutely vital. "Unquestionably the most important of all known substances in the organic kingdom" is the way one of its early discoverers, the Dutch chemist Mulder, described it in 1838. "Without it no life appears possible on our planet. Through its means the chief phenomena of life are produced." The word "protein" itself is from the Greek, meaning "to take the first place." Scientifically "protein" is a group name for the main nitrogen-bearing constituents of all living tissue.

Proteins then are obviously basic to human health and growth, but in a somewhat different way than most people believe. Though to a limited extent stored protein can contribute to the powering of the body's functions, its prime value is as a sort of construction and maintenance material for all body tissue. Protein is everywhere in the body, a ubiquitous presence overseeing all growth and decay. When you eat foods containing it, the materials are broken down into their various amino acids, passed into the bloodstream, and then carried to each and every one of the billions of cells in the body.

There the digested proteins go to work shaping and manufacturing new living tissue. Protein is the substance used to rebuild wounds and breaks, to construct new body protoplasm of every size and variety. When our cells are formed they are formed from proteins. Proteins assist in neutralizing and distributing body water, in keeping bodily fluids from becoming too acidic or too alkaline. Many enzymes are produced from the end products of food proteins. Secretin, the hormone that acts as intermediary between the intestine and the pancreas during digestion, is a protein derivative. Hemoglobin itself, the stuff of our blood, is protein-based. Muscle, hair, the kidneys and the liver, the tendons, the nerves, the gut, all are forged of this universal protoplasmic compound.

In all of nature protein has the largest, most complex and most convoluted of all molecular structures. A particularly large protein molecule compares in size to a typical carbohydrate molecule as the earth compares to the sun. Some protein molecules are so enormous they can almost be seen through low-level microscopes. Chemically, these long, serpentine protein chains are composed of nitrogen-containing compounds familiar to just about everyone under the name of "amino acids." The first of these was discovered almost a century and a half ago, and since then twenty-two have been identified and isolated, about a third of which have been termed "essential." It is in the form of amino acids, both the essential and nonessential kinds, that food proteins are assimilated in the digestive tract and carried off to tissue to do whatever repair and maintenance work they must.

Essential Amino Acids: The New Nutritional Heroes

Among the twenty-two different varieties of amino acids, eight are said to be essential.* What this means is that the essential amino acids:

(1) cannot be synthesized by the body itself.

(2) must be taken in from the food we eat.

(3) are vital for human health—without them a person will develop protein-deficiency-related ailments such as anemia, fatigue, low blood pressure, poor resistance to disease, indigestion and brittle bones.

An essential amino acid is thus that part of the protein that the body cannot manufacture itself, and that the system cannot be denied for long without showing signs of malnutrition. It is now possible to isolate amino acids in the laboratory and to concentrate them into separate pills or powders. These synthesized products are then ingested as dietary additions, much in the way one takes vitamin C or vitamin A. The healing claims made for such products sometimes border on the miraculous, and it would not be surprising if within the next ten years they supplant vitamins as the nutritional superstars. Certainly you should take these claims with a grain of salt until more conclusive information is in on their effectiveness. At the same time, there's no doubt that these essential acids

* Two other amino acids, arginine and histidine, are sometimes listed among the essential grouping. Both are more important for children than for adults.

are powerful body regulators, and that under certain circumstances they can be put to good use.

Supplements of the amino acid tryptophan, for instance, are frequently taken the week before one is about to embark on a long plane trip, as tryptophan is reputed to fend off jet lag. Lack of tryptophan causes the hair to fall out in laboratory animals, inspiring some scientists to theorize that poorly synthesized tryptophan is somehow related to male baldness. A relationship is also believed to exist between inadequate supplies of tryptophan and male sterility.

Refined commercial wheats are often low in an amino acid called lysine. Bread manufacturers are required to replace it artificially—perhaps you've noticed the mention of lysine on bread labels lately. Methionine, another of the essentials, is sometimes used to treat mental illness. It is known to reduce levels of a substance called histamine in the system, which in turn is responsible for the garbling of mental processes in certain cases of schizophrenia.

Of special interest for those prone to dark moods is the way the essential amino acid DL-phenylalanine (sold commercially at vitamin counters under the name DLPA) is currently being used to treat depression. We quote the *Erewhon Foods Nutrition News:*

> Studies since 1974 show it [DLPA] to be particularly beneficial in cases of endogenous depression. This is the type of depression that is characterized by a decrease in energy and interest, feelings of worthlessness, and a pervasive sense of helplessness to control the course of one's life. Significant improvement has also been achieved with people suffering from reactive depression (thought to be caused by environmental influences such as a death in the family) . . . In a recent double-blind controlled study, DLPA was found to be equally as effective as the tricyclic drug imipramine, the most commonly prescribed antidepressant. When taken along with tricyclics, DLPA may enhance their effectiveness.*

Erewhon Foods Nutrition News also claims that DLPA can help women combat premenstrual blues.

> As we go to press, there is some exciting news to relate about the treatment of premenstrual syndrome with DLPA. Evidence indicates that DLPA may be useful in the alleviation of the mood disorders associated with PMS (Pre-Menstrual Syndrome). Reports from clinical investigations

---

* *Erewhon Foods Nutrition News,* Vol. VI, No. 10, 1983.

have revealed that over 80% of all patients suffering from PMS have experienced good to complete relief.*

What Is a "Good" Protein?

There is thus no underestimating the importance of getting enough dietary essential amino acids. Just as crucial though is the *number* of essential acids contained in each specific protein-bearing food, and it's this factor that determines whether a protein is, as they call it in nutrition almanacs, "good," "fair," or "not so good." Or as commonly: "complete" or "incomplete."

A good protein, a complete protein, is a protein source that contains *all* eight essential amino acids. These include meat and milk and animal products in general: fish, meat, fowl, and dairy products.

Incomplete proteins, on the other hand—let's forget the awkward term "not so good"—are protein sources that do *not* include all eight essential amino acids. They come mostly from the plant world and include grains, legumes, seeds, vegetables and certain varieties of plant gelatins.

Since the most complete proteins in nature are found in animal products, it would therefore appear that animal foods *must* be included in everyone's daily diet. And as to the question of going vegetarian? Well, the answer seems quite unarguable. How can we avoid meat if its absence is going to make us sick?

But the matter is not so simple.

TO EAT MEAT OR NOT TO EAT MEAT

The question of whether the human organism is biologically meant to eat meat has been debated from the most ancient times. Certain civilizations have lived on meat quite nicely. Others have forbidden it, and they too have prospered. Still others, including many of the famine-ridden underdeveloped countries today, have gone without it and ended up undernourished and protein-starved.

While such information is contradictory at best, many modern nutritionists still insist that lamb, beef, pork and chicken *must* be loyally included in the weekly if not the daily diet of every able-bodied citizen, and that without it human health will fail. Up to a few years ago the idea of going meatless was practically unthinkable to millions of Americans, and

* *Ibid.*

this gospel was championed even by such natural food stalwarts as Adelle Davis and Carlton Fredericks. For many people meat was even a three-times-a-day affair: bacon at breakfast, lunch meat at noon, a roast for dinner. It was something of a dietary religion.

Whether this heavy animal-protein menu was due to an inherent dietary need on the part of hardworking Americans or to the power of the meat industry is debatable. Whatever the cause, things changed in the 1960s when nutrition-conscious writers, basing their findings on the eating patterns of older, traditional societies, discovered that human beings can in fact get along well without meat, but only if they have the knowledge of which vegetable-protein combinations to put in its place. We'll get to the details of how the ingenious diets that these individuals developed can be put into practice. But before we do let's address the meat question directly, and come up with at least a few clues as to why so many people warn against overconsumption of animal flesh when it appears to be such a hearty and nutritious staple.

There are, as we know, several arguments that have traditionally been made against meat. The moral one—that it is wrong to kill higher animals—is appealing to many, naïve to some. In either case it would be difficult to argue the point from nature's perspective: so many other creatures on God's good earth besides man kill without remorse in order to eat. Ultimately, it would seem, such a decision must be based on an ethical conviction rather than a biological necessity.

A less personal view, perhaps, is based on the fact that domestic livestock consume vast supplies of grain that could as easily be given to millions of starving people across our planet. A former dean of agriculture at Ohio State University estimates that 40 percent of the grain grown in the world goes for feeding livestock. A former official from the Department of Agriculture, Don Paarlberg, adds that by reducing the livestock production of the world by one half, 100 million tons of grain would be released for human consumption. A hundred million tons is approximately enough to feed every starving man, woman and child on the continent of Africa for several years. In an article on hunger, Lyle P. Schertz, an administrator at the Department of Agriculture, adds: ". . . the billion people in the developed countries use practically as much cereals as feed to produce animal protein as the two billion people of the developing countries use directly as food." *

An equally interesting if somewhat more abstract slap at man's meat habit is taken by Dr. Rudolph Ballentine's thesis—based on the tradi-

* Quoted in Frances Moore Lappé, *Diet for a Small Planet* (New York: Ballantine Books, 1972, p. 9)

tional Hindu view of food and its relationship to the body—that meat has an adverse effect on mental consciousness.

Ballentine points out that most people who become vegetarians, after the initial period of adjustment, feel more mentally focused and psychologically lucid than ever before. Their senses seem more acute in a subtle way, and the world appears more ethereal, less gross and dense.

According to Hindu philosophy, these sensations are due to three metaphysical forces that invisibly shape the world. In Sanskrit these forces are known as the *gunas,* the first of which is *rajas,* the active, aggressive, dynamic universal power. Rajas is what gives movement to things, what makes things go; while *tamas,* the second force, is what, conversely, makes things stop. It represents universal inertia and denial, decomposition and gravity. Where rajas builds up, tamas tears down. Where rajas expands, tamas shrinks.

In between these two dynamic agents exists a third force known as *sattva.* Sattva embodies the power of levity, harmony, equilibrium; it is eternally striving to maintain the balance between the two opposing forces of rajas and tamas, and to unite them.

As Ballentine explains, the traditional Indian view of meat is that it is a particularly tamaslike substance. It produces a sense of lethargy in the eater, a weight, a slowed mental agility. Vegetables, on the other hand are thought to be sattvalike. They help the eater become more centered and clear.

> In carnivores [writes Ballentine], the constituents of the meat which are not useful remain as wastes which must be eliminated. Such elimination requires a period during which the carnivore is rather sluggish and dull. This state of leghargy is termed *(tamasic)* in traditional Indian thinking and is contrasted with the active aggressive state involved in hunting called *(rajasic).* The classical Indian culture, which is predominantly vegetarian, puts a high value on the maintenance of a state of calm equilibrium *(sattvic)* which avoids either of these extremes. The lion is viewed as a typical example of the vacillation from one extreme to another. Ferocious and aggressive during hunting, after the kill and after feeding, the lion lapses into a long period of dormancy during which the meat is digested. It was perhaps the understanding of the effects of flesh-eating on consciousness that led so many of the ancient teachers to advise against it. Pythagoras, who was a spiritual teacher as well as a mathematician in ancient Greece, wrote persuasively about the advantages of vegetarianism, as did Buddha and others.*

---

* Rudolph Ballentine, M.D., *Diet and Nutrition, a Holistic Approach* (Honesdale, Pa.: The Himalayan International Institute, 1982), p. 123.

Next, there are the various physiological arguments that can be brought against heavy meat eating. These have been touched upon already: See "Protein: Is a Lot Really a Lot Better?" (page 175). And there are more.

There is, for instance, absolutely no fiber in meat, which may be one reason why people who live on a heavy meat diet are often constipated. Most meats are heavily marbled with large oily pockets of fat. If cholesterol *is* indeed related to atherosclerosis, then such foods would clearly take the booby prize. Even the so-called lean meats such as steak have heavy concentrations of adipose gristle in their most tender parts. And if you are going to eat chicken instead, be sure to remove the skin first. It's loaded with fat.

It is often claimed, moreover, that you must eat meat in order to obtain certain crucial vitamins. These vitamins are, you may be told, simply not available in any other foods. But this is downright wrong. The only vitamin you'll have trouble finding elsewhere is vitamin B-12. It's one of the rarer nutrients, ordinarily required by the body in minuscule doses. And B-12 *is* available in certain nonanimal foods, in forms of Japanese seaweed, for instance (see section on sea vegetables, page 109), or in some fermented soybean concoctions like miso (see page 113) and Indonesian tempeh (see page 112). You can also get it in tablet form, or in food supplements like desiccated liver. B-12 is most easily available, moreover, in dairy products and especially in milk, which means that if you are a vegetarian and if you take some milk or yogurt or a bit of fresh organic cheese now and then as well, your vitamin B-12 requirements will be more than fully met.

As for all the rest of the crucial nutrients we've been admonished so sternly by the meat interests to get in our steaks and chops—iron, zinc, the B vitamins, thiamine, phosphorus and potassium—all are readily available, in different proportion, from our favorite fruits, vegetables and grains. Check the individual vitamin and mineral listings in the carbohydrate section for more on this.

All of these strikes against meat, however, pale next to the one last big one.

The Reason Why You Should Be Wary of Meat

In 1906 Upton Sinclair wrote a ground-breaking book called *The Jungle*. The muckrakers were in their heyday then, and Sinclair's novel led the pack. With wit and gusto he lit into the Chicago meat industry, profiling its repulsive packing and slaughtering methods in the most vivid terms and calling loudly for reform. The book made an enormous impression in its time. But the terrible abuses that the packers and manufacturers were guilty of at the turn of the century have turned out to be mere peccadilloes compared to what's being done to meat today.

It's true, the stockyards have been cleaned up a bit since then. The blood is disposed of in a more hygienic way, and slaughtering methods have been made "humane" thanks to the insistence of outraged animal lovers. But meanwhile a whole new area of sophistication has arisen among modern meat vendors, so that today almost *all* the meat you get —whether from the butcher shop or the supermarket—all of it is so remarkably laced with dangerous compounds of one sort or another that once you get the details you may never want to eat meat again. In the long run, we might add, it is probably not a bad thing to eat a little lean meat now and then. The problem is not so much with meat per se. It is with what is put *into the meat.* That's the real reason for being wary.

A Pound of Meat, a Pound and a Quarter of Poison

To begin, consider what the animal is fed before being led to slaughter. Since speed and quantity of production are all-important in the feed business (the grains and grasses, after all, will be given to animals, not human beings, the manufacturers tell us), massive amounts of chemical pesticides, fertilizers, herbicides (including many made with Dioxin) and fungicides are used during cultivation. These substances pass into the cow or pig or chicken at feeding time, where they lodge mainly in the creature's fatty parts. After being slaughtered and packaged for market, the animals' toxin-ridden flesh is then passed directly back to the meat-eating species that fed it to them in the first place: man. The circle is complete.

All this presuming, of course, that the livestock in question is fed plant matter to begin with and not laboratory substitutes. Over the past years the FDA has allowed farmers to mix inorganic ingredients into their animal foods, sometimes to give the feed "body"—read: as filler to cut down on costs—occasionally as a substitute for *all* organic pasturage. Featured on the menu are plastic food pellets mixed with grain, a mucilage made out of ground newspaper and molasses, bone meal, sawdust, wood chips, and even chopped feathers. Chemicals like sodium chlorite have occasionally been added to low-roughage feeds to make them more digestible.

Even fodder that does somehow originate from seeds in the earth is then saturated with additives of every imaginable kind. These include arsenic in poultry feed, chemical defleecing compounds for sheep (to help the wool come off more easily at clipping time), an array of vaccines and antibacterial drugs, copper sulphate to make animals grow faster, charcoal, ground bones, artificial hormones, synthetic vitamins, tenderizing enzymes, thyroid-blocking drugs to make animals put on weight, tranquilizers, aspirin and literally dozens of other compounds.

All this is simply the overture. Once the animal is slaughtered, the meat is treated further. The natural color of meat is dark brown and sometimes even ash-gray, not blood-red, as it appears in the ads. This is the case with even the best pieces of steak. To compensate for nature's drab palette, meat companies give their product the red-blooded look by injecting it full of sodium nicotinate, a known poison. Or by using several other equally harmful food dyes. Approximately three-fourths of the meat you buy has been dyed this way. The redder it is the more dyes it contains.

By law, meat must be aged. There is no law, however, against speeding up the process with enzymatic curing agents. The days of hanging meat in the stock house and allowing it to age for several weeks according to nature's time schedule is a thing of the past. It's all done now lickety-split with chemicals.

Meanwhile, as time is accelerated in the curing room, any suspicious-looking tumors, boils or odd growths are quickly carved off the animal's carcass by specially trained knife handlers, without any questions asked about how such growths may have gotten there in the first place. If we're in a chicken processing plant we might also see a bit of water being surreptitiously injected into the carcasses of the roasters, increasing their weight and consequently their price by as much as 20 percent—8 percent is the amount allowed by law. Wonder why chickens are often so soggy? And why so much water squirts out of them when they're cut?

Most animals raised for butchering are given injections of antibiotics as a matter of routine, while substances like Aureomycin are regularly added to cattle feed. These medications raise the animal's immunity to disease and help them grow more quickly. Sometimes, however, so many antibiotics are fed to livestock that the traces later show up in the intestinal tract of people who have eaten the animal. Antibiotics are, of course, notorious for destroying friendly as well as harmful bacterial flora in the intestinal tract, and for causing constipation. This suspicious bit of circumstantial fact has caused many people to speculate on the relationship between the dramatic rise of gastrointestinal problems in this country and the increased amounts of antibiotics in our meat.

But that's not all as far as antibiotics are concerned. Later, when the butchered meat is prepared for sale at the packers, more of the same is added, in this case as a preservative. Many of the chickens that stay so fresh in your refrigerator for so long do so because they are literally embalmed with these medications. By the time meat preserved in this way finally reaches the consumer's stomach these medicinal residues have been cooked out—or so say the meat companies. Many think differently. Laboratory tests have shown frequent traces of antibiotics lodged in commercial ham, feed, chicken and lamb, even after the meat has been cooked at high temperatures for several hours at a stretch. Antibiotic residues are also known to reside in from 5 to 12 percent of all the milk samples tested by the government.

Many people—perhaps hundreds of thousands—are allergic to antibiotics, even in small doses. A slow but constant stream of these drugs introduced each day into the diet via animal fats simply can't be too healthy for their condition. A person overexposed in this way, moreover, even via the minimal doses present in meat, tends to gradually lose sensitivity to the drug. When this person becomes really sick, and an antibiotic is the only thing that can fend off the disease, the drug's potency has by now been seriously reduced. The person has, in a sense, been immunizing himself all this time against the antibiotic's positive germicidal effects by eating meat.

Still another questionable item regularly added to meats is an artificial hormone known as diethylstilbestrol—stilbestrol or DES for short. Though there has been much outcry through the years concerning the effects of this hormone on both animals and human beings, and despite the fact that the FDA itself, along with numerous doctors and nutritionists, have decried its use, the meat manufacturers still place it in their product with apparent impunity. All attempts to ban it from the meat industry have failed.

The effect of this controversial substance on cattle is to increase their weight and to make them literally more beefy in the especially marketable parts of their anatomy such as the loins. This process takes place, curiously, at the expense of the steer's very gender. Stilbestrol, being a powerful sex hormone, causes the male animal's gonads to shrink, its muscle quality to soften, and its entire body to take on female characteristics. The animal does, nonetheless, put on weight quickly, which makes stilbestrol feedings a highly profitable venture from the standpoint of the cattle raisers. Its use is said to account for more than 700,000 extra pounds of beef sold at market a year.

All well and good—if this process stopped with the bull. But there is strong evidence that the hormone passes directly from the animal to the person who eats it; and that being a form of estrogen, its effects, which admittedly are not well understood, may cause the development of feminine characteristics in male human beings as well. There may, for instance, be a tendency for male muscle to soften; for the voice to rise; for sexual identity to become confused; for the general level of sexual interest and arousal to decline. A particularly potent side effect is a parallel tendency toward male impotency. Some believe that male sterility may likewise be traced to overstimulation by stilbestrol.

> Endocrinologists point out that the balance between male and female hormones in the body is extremely delicate [writes William Longwood], and sex hormones, among other factors, determine and affect certain sex characteristics; the quantity and proportion may affect sex drive, development of sex organs, breast development, quality of facial and body hair, height, voice pitch and similar characteristics. A similar imbalance between male and female sex hormones in the body is said to result in the individual's acquiring some physical characteristics of the opposite sex.
>
> Among the hormone experts who have warned about the possible sexual repercussions stilbestrol-treated meat may have on human beings is Dr. Christian Hamburger of Copenhagen . . . In 1957, Dr. Hamburger said that men who ate hormone-treated fowl may develop feminine characteristics. He said Danish health authorities prohibited the use of hormones for capons. After breeders inserted female hormones into the muscles of the fowl, some men who ate the treated capons became temporarily impotent. The hormones were not destroyed in cooking, he said.*

As if all this wasn't enough cause for alarm, stilbestrol has also been identified as being a prominent carcinogenic. In many experiments the substance has caused cancer in test animals; practically no interested parties, with the exception of the meat industry, now deny that its safety is in question. The National Cancer Institute, in fact, has made it quite clear that the amount of stilbestrol added to steer meat, the 10 milligrams or so per pound, is about fourteen times the amount required to give cancer to mice, while since the time of the Delaney hearings, held before Congress almost thirty years ago, experts have insisted that stilbestrol is quite directly implicated in the development of several kinds of cancer, breast cancer being paramount among them, and that it may also be the cause of sudden menstrual hemorrhaging in women.† The indictments could fill a volume. And yet the substance is added to our commercial meat by growers about as casually as if it were ordinary table salt.

---

* William Longwood, *The Poisons in Your Food* (New York: Simon and Schuster, 1968), p. 137.
   † *Ibid*, p. 148.

Now most of what we have discussed is what's done to the meat *before* it reaches the packager. During the course of preparation and processing, a whole new attack begins, with chemical after chemical coming into play. The names of some of these materials are on the labels of sausage or bacon or hot dogs. Most are not. Here are a few:

• Benzoic acid—Used to preserve smoked fish. It is known to cause extensive nerve damage in laboratory animals. Its use is forbidden in many countries.

• Butylated hydroxyanisole, or BHA—A petroleum-based antioxidant used to preserve flavor and retard rancidity in sausage and bacon, among other foods. This additive interferes with digestion as well as with muscular coordination. It can cause serious allergic reactions.

• Butylated hydroxytoluene, or BHT—A recently banned substance that for years was widely used in frozen meats and shortening. Its list of harmful effects reads like a textbook on pathology. Some of the agonies it is believed to cause include dermatitis, severe allergic reaction, asthmatic attack, water retention, swelling of the joints. respiratory imbalance, glaucoma, and extreme physical enervation. It is also suspected of being a carcinogen.

• Calcium disodium EDTA—Used as a flavoring and coloring for shrimp and certain other seafoods. Known to cause indigestion, muscle cramps and kidney damage. It interferes with the normal clotting of blood and with the metabolism of iron.

• Calcium propionate—A preservative placed in poultry stuffing, among many other food substances. Many people have violent allergic reactions to it; its high sodium content makes it particularly insidious for people with hypertension. Despite its potentially damaging effect, it is often hidden in meats without any written warning.

• Monosodium glutamate, MSG—The immediate effects of MSG are well known to patrons of Chinese restaurants: headache, diarrhea, dizziness, palpitations. Used primarily to bring out the flavor in meats, its long-term harmful effects include chronic indigestion, muscular numbness, bone and nerve damage.

• Nordihydroguaiaretic acid, or NDGA—An antioxidant banned in most countries but still used in most American meats. Known to cause severe damage to the digestive and circulatory systems of laboratory animals.

• Sodium nicotinate—Used as a coloring agent. It is so dangerous that it is banned in many states. It is a deadly poison and when placed too liberally in cooked meat has been known to be a direct cause of death.

• Sodium nitrite—Used to flavor and preserve hot dogs. sausage, bacon and many other packaged meats. It's more toxic than its twin— and the substance it is often mistaken for—*sodium nitrate,* which in its own right is believed to bring on epileptic reactions in borderline epileptics, and to be a carcinogen. During digestion, sodium nitrate is transformed into sodium nitrite.

Sodium nitrite is known to diminish vitamin stores in the body, especially vitamin A, and to exacerbate arthritic conditions in the elderly. People allergic to it frequently die if they receive too great a dose. In some cases it can result in respiratory failure, especially in young children. Both nitrites and nitrates, moreover, when they combine with protein during cooking or digestion form compounds known as nitrosamines, which are recognized carcinogens. Nitrites, by the way, are present not only in meat and in a majority of the rest of our foods, but in much of our drinking water as well.

• Sodium sulphite—Used as a preservative. Can cause permanent damage to the digestive system and rob the system of B vitamin supplies.

The above is just a sampling, of course. We might mention the "edible" plastic used on sausage casings; the toxic soaps used to wash meat down and disinfect it; the enzymes employed to tenderize meat; these and a host of other laboratory substances that are added to our meat as it passes along the technological assembly line from stockyard to consumer. The end result is a product that is—there is no other way to say it —dangerous for human consumption.

This means that we must more or less forget the traditional arguments pro or con eating meat. It is an entirely different ball game now in the late twentieth century, a desperate situation due principally to the unconscionable things that are being done to commercial livestock from the day it is born to the day it is eaten. Whether or not meat itself—wholesome, untreated, fresh-killed meat—is good for you or not is thus no longer really the issue. The likelihood is that it is good for certain people, not so good for others. But this concern has little meaning in light of the fact that wholesome, untreated, fresh meat is simply not available to the ordinary shopper, and that most of us have become the captive audience of food suppliers who no longer offer us options in the matter.

The real question then is this: Should you as a concerned consumer take the chance of feeding yourself and your family large quantities of a substance that is known to contain materials that may impair your immediate health, and that over the long run may contribute to your premature death? This is a tough question. But it is based on fact, and it should be faced fairly and squarely.

The natural response to it is, of course: What are my options? The answer is: There are two.

1. Organic Meat

Eating organic meat is the first. Organic meat comes from animals that have been pastured most of their lives in unsprayed fields, and that have been allowed the free run of field or pen or barnyard. Such animals have been fed wholesome feed—grasses, grains, table scraps, and in some cases organic feeds. They have been given no hormones, no growth accelerators, no smell retarders or chemical fatteners or synthetic vitamins or anything else from science's arsenal of nature "improvers."

Once these animals have been slaughtered, their meat is not tampered with. It is aged naturally, if aging is required, then sold fresh. It is, in other words, like so many other natural foods, meat as it was once raised and prepared before economic pressures mandated that it be mass-produced like car fenders or plastic parts.

There is a problem with organic meat, however: finding it. The state or government controls that do exist over this market are poor, and just about anyone can claim anything he wants concerning a meat's "organicness." What exactly does it mean, anyway? That the meat is untreated but nonetheless taken from animals given synthetic feeds? That "natural" vegetable dyes have been used to color the meat rather than synthetic ones? That only *some* of the preservatives, dyes, flavorings, antioxidants, plasticizers, and so forth normally put into meat have been added to this particular product? Like so many items for sale among natural food purveyors, definitions are hazy and confusion is rife.

Still, even if your meat is only somewhat organic, that's better than nothing. Health food stores usually have a stock of it on hand in their freezer cases. Some, as mentioned, may be of dubious quality. If you intend to regularly spend the 30 to 100 percent extra dollars you'll be charged for organic meat, you'd do well to quiz the owner of the store about where the meat comes from and how it was raised. Inquire if any official authentication is available.

Another way to obtain organic meat is through a natural food co-op. There are many such organizations around these days—inquire among your friends, or among people who are involved with natural eating. Libraries often maintain listings of such groups. Since co-ops are in a position to buy in relatively large volume they can procure organic meats at something approaching wholesale prices.

Still another possibility is to raise the livestock yourself. This, no doubt, is impractical for some and impossible for most. Still, those who are interested can start small. If a quarter acre is available either on your own land or in the backyard of a willing friend you can board chickens as a starter. After the initial investment for a hen house, feed, fencing wire, livestock and sundries these animals are relatively easy to care for. And you get the added bonus of eggs every morning. Some people also keep a single sheep or a single cow on their property and let them graze wild. If you are not adept at butchering animals yourself, or if you are too soft-hearted, most local butchers will be happy to do the job when the time arrives.

Along the same lines, you might also consider, either alone or with friends, purchasing a cow, pig or lamb carcass directly from a farmer, especially one who raises his animals the organic way. Before you do, make arrangements with a local butcher to pick up the carcass from the farmer, slice it into parts, package it, and keep it frozen in his (or your) cold locker until you need it. In rural areas many people save hundreds of dollars a year on their meat bill this way, and they have many months' supply of unprocessed meat in the deal.

If you're going to buy commercial beef, at least know what's best. The top beef in this country is known as USDA Prime. It will be so marked somewhere on its flank. Next in quality is USDA Choice. You'll find this variety mostly in the supermarkets (Prime is ordinarily sold in good butcher shops). Usually Choice meats are tender and have a lot of the natural juices still left in them. Last on the scale is USDA Good. This meat tends to be drier and less tasty—Good is a kind of euphemism for not so good. On the other hand, USDA Good meat also has less fat in it—it is the fat that imparts a good deal of the taste to meats—and is thus better for dieters and for those trying to avoid fatty foods.

2. Eat Vegetarian

The second way to beat the poisoned-meat game is to avoid animal flesh entirely. Or at least to cut back on it to the point where you're having meat, let's say, once or twice a week at most. The rest of the time you're living on a low-fat, high-natural-carbohydrate diet.

The conventional objection to a meatless diet, of course, is that vegetarians won't receive adequate nourishment. And the main question that must then be addressed is: How do you get the equivalent of a complete protein into your diet, with all the eight essential amino acids that go with it, without eating meat?

The solution is not as simple as just giving up meat for the rest of your life and substituting fruit and vegetables in its place. Many well-meaning people have placed themselves on a spare vegetarian regime, only to discover that the diet has made them weak and undernourished within a matter of months. Through the years there have even been isolated cases of people dying from malnutrition while practicing various all-grain or all-fruit diets. Nutritionally speaking, it is not how much food you eat—these undernourished victims probably ate several hearty meals a day—but *how well the foods that you do eat balance and supplement one another.*

The point is that if you are considering going vegetarian, you'd do best to approach this venture from a systematic and educated point of view. Becoming a vegetarian is not simply a matter of eating raw vegetables at random. It means readjusting your fat-carbohydrate-protein triangle from a meat-oriented balance to a nonmeat-oriented balance and making sure that you maintain your nutritional equilibrium in the process.

To do all this it's necessary to be familiar with the things we've already talked about concerning complete proteins. And as an adjunct, to have a clear picture of two further points. We can call them the principles of compensation and combination.

Compensation works like this. Let's say, for the sake of argument, you're now a vegetarian. You remember that wheat has lots of protein in it, so you decide to eat plenty of bread each day to satisfy your daily protein requirement. Wheat, however, even the best of varieties, is an incomplete protein. Some of the essential amino acids are there, some are not, and your body must get *all the essential amino acids at once* if it is to synthesize protein correctly.

So, instead you determine to eat several big bowls of kidney beans every day, another good protein bet. The protein in beans, however, is not complete either. Beans contain some of the essential amino acids that bread is missing, but they are missing others that bread contains. What's worse, in order to make a complete protein, the amino acids in a food must be included in a certain ratio, as they are in meat—just this amount of tryptophan must be included, just that amount of lysine, so much of valine, leucine, threonine, on through the list of aminos, all in fixed proportion to one another. The beans don't match up on this score. They won't do either. Is the problem unsolvable? How are you supposed to get one complete protein from so many incompletes?

Combination, of course, is the simple answer. You combine them. You combine one, two or three *incomplete plant proteins* to make *one complete protein.* In this way the absence of specific essential amino acids in one incomplete protein is compensated for by their presence in another incomplete protein. The two incompletes add up to a complete. The resulting protein is more than enough to satisfy minimum protein requirements.

The easiest and most pleasurable way of putting the principles of protein compensation and combination to work is to serve vegetarian dishes that include both *grains and legumes* in the same meal. The essential amino acids that are missing in grains are provided by the legumes—and vice versa. It is perfect protein complement. This kind of combination has traditionally been a part of standard cuisine in countries throughout the world. We've referred to such combinations elsewhere: rice (grain), lentils (legume) and flat bread (grain) in India; pasta (grain) and beans (legume) in Italy; grits (grain) and black-eyed peas (legume) in the South; baked beans (legume) and brown bread (grain) in New England; black beans (legume) and rice (grain) in Cuba; tortillas (grain) and beans (legume) in Mexico; corn (grain) and peas (legume) in American succotash; bean curd (legume), rice (grain) and soy sauce (legume) in China and Japan.

While the simple grain-legume balance by itself is a totally adequate way to keep the body in sufficient protein, there are also numerous ways they can be combined, especially if you add other protein sources like nuts and dairy products. In Thailand cooks frequently put peanuts (a legume) in rice dishes. The same in Iran. Cashews can be combined with kidney beans and chick-peas in a cold salad. Pecans can be added to spinach salads. Rice can be cooked with pignoli nuts. Fresh green beans and peanut slivers go together wonderfully. Sesame seeds can be sprinkled over cold bean curd or dropped into vegetable stews. Almonds are cooked with couscous. Sunflower seeds, which are especially high in protein, are delicious mixed with regular nuts, sprinkled over rice, used on whole-grain breakfast cereals, or mixed in a summer salad. The possibilities are endless.

Then, lastly, comes the *coup de grâce*. Any lingering notion that human beings must have meat to prosper is expunged with the final entries to the vegetarian menu. Unless you have given up animal foods entirely, add to the already wide and nutritious range of complete protein possibilities two more: dairy products and eggs. Both are *complete proteins*—eggs are the best of all complete proteins—and both make an ideal meat substitute. Together they comprise a powerful protein bulwark. With a diet ample in dairy products and eggs, meat is not only unnecessary but superfluous. Too much protein becomes a stress to the body, and we return once again to our list of dangers that result from excess dietary protein.

SEITAN: A MACROBIOTIC MEAT SUBSTITUTE

People serious about their vegetarianism but who yearn for the full taste of meat will find this recipe, courtesy of the macrobiotic cooking system, amazingly like the real thing. Place 3 cups of whole-wheat flour in a mixing bowl with 6 to 7 cups of warm water. Knead the dough mass until it reaches a batterlike consistency, then cover with an inch or so of warm water and let it sit for 30 minutes. Knead the dough again for several minutes while it remains in the water, remove, and place it in a large strainer (the kind you ordinarily use for spaghetti), and place the strainer in the large bowl. Pour a stream of cold water over the dough and knead it once again while in the strainer, continuing until you have a solid, sticky ball of gluten with all the bran removed. Continue to knead, letting hot and cold water run over the dough as you do, pouring off the water when it becomes too cloudy. When dough is ready, rinse it a final time with very cold water for 5 minutes, divide it into 6 or 7 pieces, and let pieces sit in boiling water for about 5 minutes, or until they rise on their own to the top. Pour approximately ¼ cup Tamari sauce into the water and continue to boil for 5 minutes, then simmer for 45 minutes. You can add a strip or two of kombu sea vegetable to the pot (see page 111) for added flavoring. Serve seitan with rice, in a stew, sautéed with vegetables, anywhere that meat is ordinarily found.

A holistic picture now emerges. We have six basic groups of nonmeat protein foods. Two are complete proteins: dairy products and eggs. Four are incomplete: legumes, grains, seeds/nuts, and vegetables. (Some fruits also contain protein too, but in such negligible amounts that they can't be counted on as a dependable source.)

Within each of these groups there is, moreover, a wonderfully wide spectrum of individual protein-rich foods to choose from, enough so that one's palate will never get bored. Just a sampling includes:

GROUP ONE: Legumes (1 cup gives approximately 12 grams of protein)

navy beans	kidney-bean salad
hummus	black-eyed peas
adzuki beans	peas
lentils	mung beans
tofu	sprouted mung beans
black beans	string beans
peanuts	lima beans

miso	tempeh
soybeans	Yankee beans

GROUP TWO: Dairy products (1 cup liquid or ½ cup solid gives approximately 10 grams of protein)

yogurt	milk
cottage cheese	buttermilk
hard cheese	soft cheese
butter	ghee
kefir	acidophilus milk

GROUP THREE: eggs (1 medium-sized raw or boiled egg gives approximately 6.5 grams of protein)

GROUP FOUR: Seeds and nuts (1 cup gives approximately 25 grams of protein)

cashews	almonds
pumpkin seeds	sunflower seeds
chia seeds	walnuts
pecans	sesame seeds
poppy seeds	chestnuts

GROUP FIVE: Grains (1 slice of bread gives approximately 2 grams of protein; 1 cup of cereal or cooked grains gives approximately 3 grams of protein)

oatmeal	whole-wheat bread
barley	cooked millet
granola	flat breads
rye bread	couscous
kasha	polenta
grits	rice
buckwheat	whole-wheat pasta

GROUP SIX: Vegetables (varying amounts of proteins)

kale	lettuce
cabbage	watercress
cucumbers	turnips
squash	onions
potatoes	celery

There are dozens of excellent vegetarian cookbooks on the market today featuring outstanding nonmeat dishes. Some of these are listed in Books for Further Reading. Certainly one of the classics—and the one on which much of the above material is based—is a work we have mentioned before, *Diet for a Small Planet,* by Frances Moore Lappé. It comes highly recommended, not only for really sound, tested recipes but for a detailed explanation of how protein substitution works.

THE MILK DILEMMA

Many of us were brought up on the notion that milk is the perfect food. Skip the greens, the fruit, even the meat if you must, but *not* that sip of protein heaven in a glass. Perhaps because of its association with infancy and motherhood, perhaps because of the extraordinarily effective PR used to promote it, milk has come to take on an aura of sanctimony for many people and is even spoken of not only as a food but as *the* food, a mannalike substance containing each and every nutrient necessary for human survival.

But milk is decidedly not a perfect food, despite what the dairy lobby once told us, and human beings would quite definitely wither if forced to live on dairy products alone. Many people, especially black Americans, Semites and Asians, have an intolerance to lactose, the predominant milk sugar, and are incapable of digesting milk and many milk products. Lactose intolerance, in fact, with the bloating and diarrhea it produces, has been named the "familiar poisoner" by those who warn that the symptoms of this disorder go too frequently undiagnosed.

There is little doubt that mother's milk is the best food infants can receive and that, as many studies substantiate, little ones fed on this precious substance are as a rule more healthy than those "nursed" on formulas. Milk in this instance, however, means *mother's* milk, not cow's milk; there is a substantial difference between the two. It has been pointed out that human beings are the only animals that drink milk after infancy. Children who drink too much milk, in fact, according to the American Academy of Pediatrics,* can easily become anemic, both because such a diet tends to exclude other iron-yielding foods (milk has very little) and because the process of digesting milk can instigate small leakages of blood throughout the gastrointestinal tract. According to the American Academy

---

* Mentioned in Jane Brody, *Jane Brody's Nutrition Book* (New York: Norton & Co., 1981), p. 255.

of Pediatrics, children who are anemic, who become easily constipated, or who are picky eaters should have their intake of this drink substantially reduced.

We know, furthermore, that the sugar in cow's milk is especially hard on babies' teeth, rotting them with special efficiency if the child has the habit of taking a bottle to bed at night; also, that in both children and adults milk allergy is more common than most people realize. Milk is not an easy substance for the body to assimilate, and it is often the last straw for those with weak stomachs, producing bouts of cramps and indigestion. Indeed, if we are to believe macrobiotic theory (see page 216), the excess fat content of dairy products and their tendency to produce mucus are two of the principal reasons why we milk-imbibing Westerners are so toxified and disease-ridden.

All this said, we can now return to the middle of the road, somewhere between the positive and negative extremes. Dairy products are, by and large, a useful food, and some believe an extraordinarily good food. For centuries they have been a mainstay of the human diet, especially in Northern Europe, Africa and India. Their excellent nutritive virtues cannot be denied. They are storehouses of calcium, vitamin A and riboflavin, and vegetarians will discover them to be one of the rare nonmeat sources of vitamin B-12. Though liquid, milk contains more solids than many "solid" foods (more than one hundred separate solid components have been identified in milk), and it is an exemplary source of protein, second only to eggs in the quality of its amino acids. Indeed, as a supplement to cereal proteins, milk is perfection, supplying the amino acids lysine and tryptophan, both of which are limited in grains.

Thiamine, vitamin C, and, when artificially added, vitamin D are all liberally available in milk, as are potassium, phosphorus, iodine and copper. Plenty of rich butterfat is present too; while once considered as anathema in the cholesterol department, this substance has come to be considered by many nutritionists an active *anticholesterol* agent and a possible boon to human hearts (see the sections on butterfat, page 159, and cholesterol, page 146). While milk is not the perfect food, it is clearly a thoroughly good food and one that deserves a place on the natural-eating menu.

The issue of whether dairy products are good or bad is further complicated by matters of commercial processing. Over the past fifty years the quality of dairy-counter milk has declined considerably. The cows themselves are, of course, raised on hormones, antibiotics, growth accelerators, synthetic foods et al., much of which finds its way directly into the milk. This milk is then further altered from its original state via pasteurization, homogenization and sterilization. Additives and preservatives are put in and the milk is then packaged, stored, shipped, placed on a market shelf, sometimes for days, then stored again in the home refrigerator. By the time it is finally consumed the substance scarcely resembles that warm, white nectar that once gushed so freely from the mother cow.

It also happens that many of the nutrients in the milk are volatile ingredients that must be ingested *immediately* to derive their full food value. Milk that sits for more than a day or so out of the mother's body, be it the milk of a cow or of a human being, quickly loses many of its finest qualities. Add to this the heating process to which commercial milk is subjected during sterilization and pasteurization (a process that kills most of its enzymes and many of its vitamins, reduces its protein content by 20 percent and depletes its calcium by 8 percent) and you have a commercial product that is truly a shadow of its former self.

Before you either race out to find the nearest cow or swear off milk entirely, however, remember that health measures such as pasteurization are exactly that—health measures. Tuberculosis, typhoid fever, streptococcal sore throat and undulant fever, among many others, can all be transmitted through milk. Despite the stringent inspection laws governing dairy farms, diseased herds are still reported with some frequency throughout the United States. The truth is that raw milk *can* be dangerous.

What then to do? Suffer with the commercial pasteurized varieties? Take a chance on drinking a neighboring farmer's fresh, raw supply? Avoid milk entirely? The answers—there are several—lie somewhere in between.

1. First, after the age of twelve you should probably keep your milk consumption relatively low, three to four glasses a week at absolute most. Hold to this rule even if you drink milk that is fresh and unpasteurized. Due to its diminished ability to produce lactase (the enzyme that breaks down milk sugar), the adult stomach is simply not built to process a great deal of this substance. A little, yes. But too much taxes the digestion and does indeed produce mucus throughout the system. Keep milk intake low.

2. If raw milk is available from a nearby farm, make certain the barn and milking equipment are immaculate and that the cows are kept clean and healthy. If there is the *slightest* suspicion concerning sanitation it is better not to chance it. If you're satisfied, though, take the raw milk home, and:

3. Boil it. But only for a few minutes. Flash-boiling is fairly gentle on the nutrients in milk and leaves its chemical structure more or less intact.

It sterilizes the milk in the process, makes it a bit more digestible and, for some palates at any rate, makes it a bit better-tasting too.

4. Some states, California for one, allow the sale of certified raw milk. The farms that produce this milk work so hard to attain their certification and are monitored so stringently, far more than regular dairy farms, it might be added, that you are probably on safe ground drinking it. Still, some people prefer to boil even the certified store-bought variety as a double precaution. The fact is that in the states where it is allowed there has been a minimum number of sanitation problems connected with the sale and distribution of certified raw milk.

5. If you have trouble digesting cow's milk try goat's milk instead. Goat's milk is, as a rule, easier to digest and consequently is prescribed for infants by many pediatricians. It also makes less mucus than ordinary cow's milk, especially when watered down by about 20 percent before drinking. Goat's milk is expensive though, and not always easy to find. Some natural food stores carry it, but usually in a can. The fresh, refrigerated varieties are better. If you live in a rural area you might consider keeping a goat yourself or purchasing milk from a nearby farm. If you do so, make certain you flash-boil the milk before drinking it.

WHOLE MILK, LOW-FAT MILK, SKIM MILK: THE DIFFERENCES

WHOLE MILK contains approximately 3.5 percent butterfat. A single cup contains around 160 calories.

LOW-FAT MILK contains approximately 2 percent butterfat, with around 150 calories per cup.

NONFAT OR SKIM MILK contains less than .4 percent butterfat, with less than 90 calories per cup.

NONFAT DRY MILK is a powdered form of nonfat milk that has approximately the same nutritive and calorie count as the liquid but is somewhat less expensive.

Other Dairy Products

Cheese

In many ways cheese is simply coagulated milk, so much of what was said concerning the nutritive value of milk holds true for this ancient dairy food too. The fine points concerning what makes one cheese different from the next and what causes one cheese to be better for you than another include innumerable variables: how long the cheese is aged; how much cream is added to it; its butterfat content; what breed of cow the milk is taken from; and, for that matter, whether it is made from the milk of a cow, goat or sheep. Also, what variety of coagulator is used (today it is usually rennin; in an earlier age it might have been vinegar, fig juice, or even decoctions of thistle tops and artichoke flowers). Of importance too is the type of coloring agent added, the age of the milk, whether the milk is fermented and for how long, whether the milk is raw or pasteurized, and of course the kinds of spices, sweeteners, herbs, seasonings and preservatives that are added.

Try to buy fresh, noncommercially produced cheese whenever you can. There are still local manufacturers around, and you'll quickly come to appreciate the taste difference. The best cheeses are made from slightly soured milk, which renders the cheese somewhat more digestible. Better too is cheese that is entirely uncolored (cheese's natural color is a kind of dirty white—American cheese, most commercial Cheddars, and the other golden slabs you see on display at the dairy counter are all dyed).

If you are on a diet, and if you *must,* you can also purchase various nonfat or low-fat cheeses. But is it really necessary to throw the baby out with the bath water? The very essence of cheese is the fat, the butterfat to be exact; a cheese that has been stripped of this all-important ingredient is really a cheese in name only. Go out and taste a slice if you don't believe us. Remember too that the butterfat in dairy products, not just in the cheese but in the milk and yogurt too, aids in the digestion of calcium. Remove this fat and you reduce a powerful metabolic aid.

Be wary though of the so-called raw cheeses. As Fred Rohé points out,* due to certain technicalities in the legal definition of the word "raw," many "natural" cheese manufacturers are peddling their product under dubious pretenses, and much of what passes as raw cheese is really just the pasteurized stuff in disguise. According to Rohé, there are no more than five or six manufacturers in the entire country making genuine raw-milk cheese.

Note also that while the sophisticated imported cheeses such as Brie, Boursin, Gouda, Tilsit, etc. are difficult to make at home, simple ones such as cottage cheese are a breeze. Here's the recipe:

COTTAGE CHEESE

2 quarts milk	**Caraway seeds or chives**
Sea salt	**(optional)**

---

* Fred Rohé, *The Complete Book of Natural Foods* (Boulder: Shambala Publications, 1983), p. 65.

1. Heat the milk until it becomes lukewarm. Cover the pot, place it in an unlighted oven and let it remain there for about two days, occasionally heating the oven for a minute or two at a low temperature to keep the temperature hovering around 85 degrees. (Instead of using the oven method you can also, if you prefer, place the pot of warm milk directly in the sun and let it sit there for the same period of time. Just make sure the pot is tightly sealed and that it is away from sources of contamination such as insects.)

2. After two days remove the lid. As you will see, the curd has risen to the top of the pot and the whey has sunk to the bottom. Skim off the curd, place it in a colander lined with cheesecloth, and allow the liquids to drain off. Now add a little sea salt and some caraway seeds or chives to taste, if desired. Keep the cheese refrigerated after draining.

Yogurt

If milk is so difficult to digest, why is it that yogurt, a milk-derived product, is touted as such a wonderful digestive aid? The answer lies in the fact that the milk used in yogurt is soured first, that is, fermented for varying periods of time via the use of a so-called yogurt starter made up of living bacteria. During this fermentation process, the lactose that is so difficult for many people to assimilate breaks down into the more digestively beneficial lactic acid. The souring procedure also makes the yogurt immune to harmful bacteria and friendly toward the growth of digestively helpful bacteria, both the bacteria that are already in the gastrointestinal tract and those that are contained in the yogurt itself.

These different strains of friendly bacteria attach themselves to the inside of the colon where they cooperate with various enzymes and digestive juices, helping dissolve food substances and speeding up the elimination of putrefying wastes. The process is really a kind of wondrous alchemy where a food that was once a digestive liability becomes transformed into a digestive aid.

Besides all this, yogurt boasts all the vitamins, calcium and minerals that dairy products in general contain. It is a decidedly good food. But once again the familiar warning must be issued: Watch out for the commercial brands. The key to making healthy yogurt is that the bacteria used in its starter must be, and must remain, *alive*. A majority of the store-bought varieties have their milk pasteurized *after* this living starter has been added to the yogurt. The result: The bacteria are boiled to death in the pasteurization process, and the yogurt that reaches the supermarket shelf is also dead; it will offer no help whatsoever to the digestion. In fact, it will probably hurt, as many of the commercial yogurt brands are laced with jelling agents, stabilizers, coloring, artificial flavorings, preservatives and above all, lots of sugar. The fruit-flavored brands are especially culpable in this department; some will contain as much as *two teaspoonfuls* of fructose. When purchasing yogurt from the store, be it the supermarket or natural food store, check the label and make sure it tells you the yogurt is made from *living bacterial cultures.*

Or, as an alternative, assure yourself that your yogurt will always (1) be made of a living culture; (2) be absolutely fresh; (3) contain no additives. How? By making it at home.

HOMEMADE YOGURT

1 quart milk	**Yogurt starter culture**
3 tablespoons noninstant dry	**(available at natural food**
milk (optional)	**stores)**

1. Pour the milk into a pot and warm on low heat. Add the optional dry milk if you wish to give the yogurt extra body, and stir. Scald the milk but do not let it boil. Remove and allow the milk to cool down to 110 degrees.

2. Add the starter culture, making sure the culture is thoroughly mixed and dissolved into the milk (no lumps). Pour the mixture into clean jars and cap. Place the jars in 110 degree heat for 3 to 8 hours. You can control this heat by arranging the jars in a pot of lukewarm water, placing the pot on the stove, controlling the heat beneath it, and periodically checking the heat with a cooking thermometer to make sure that the temperature is correct.

Buttermilk

Originally, buttermilk was derived from the liquid that separated out from the cream while butter was being churned. (If you look at old butter churns you'll see a plug in the bottom; when opened, the buttermilk would drain out of this hole into a waiting bowl.) Today store-bought buttermilk has little to do with this ancient process. It is manufactured by placing a bacterial culture, not unlike that used for yogurt, in skim milk, pasteurizing the liquid at a somewhat higher temperature than is used for milk, and allowing the mixture to sour.

A liking for the strong, pungent taste of buttermilk is a somewhat cultivated taste. In a few natural food stores the original butter-churned substance can still be purchased, though for some this mixture is too tart to take. In general, modern buttermilk is most popular when mixed into pancake batter or when used to give tang to sourdough bread. Because of its high vitamin B content, it is often recommended for nursing and pregnant mothers. Dieters should not, however, be fooled by the word "butter" in its name; being made from skim milk, buttermilk is an exceptionally low calorie drink, which makes it ideal for those who are watching their waists.

Kefir

A drink that has become so popular over the past several years that it is starting to appear in supermarkets, kefir is a tangy milk product produced by adding strains of a particular bacteria and yeast to milk as fermenting agents and allowing the milk to stand and sour. Most commercial kefirs have fructose added as a flavoring agent, and indeed, kefir's natural tartness augmented by fructose's extreme sweetness makes a drink delicious enough to substitute for a milk shake.

On the other hand, the tangy, pungent taste of kefir also stands quite nicely on its own without added flavorings, and it can be produced at home with less trouble than it takes to make yogurt. Here's the recipe.

KEFIR

Kefir culture   **1 quart milk**

1. Purchase a package of kefir culture from your local natural food store or send away for it from:

Rosell Institute, Inc.
Chambly, Quebec J3L 3H9, Canada

2. Scald milk, pour into sterilized jars and allow it to cool. Add the kefir culture (instructions and amounts will be included on the package) and let the mixture stand unrefrigerated for a day. Then refrigerate for 6 hours and serve.

Acidophilus Milk

Acidophilus is a strain of bacteria employed in the production of certain of the better yogurts. It is used as well in the production of a low-fat fermented dairy drink, acidophilus milk by name. For some this drink is pleasingly tart and flavorful. Others declare it to be sour and unpalatable. Generally speaking, if you like the taste of unflavored yogurt you'll probably like acidophilus milk too. Try it and see. It's available at most natural food stores.

Acidophilus milk's major health asset is that most of its milk sugar has been predigested, making it an excellent drink for anyone with lactose intolerance. Like yogurt, the bacteria in acidophilus adhere to the intestinal walls and are said to help in the digestion process, though this claim has not been entirely substantiated in laboratory tests. Acidophilus cannot —repeat, cannot—be used in cooking, as heating destroys its useful bacteria and renders it useless as a health-giving potion. When you have it at home, keep it cool if not refrigerated at all times and drink it within several days after purchase: It spoils easily, even when kept cold.

Soy Milk

Not a dairy product at all, not a milk product at all. Derived directly from soybeans, soy milk has approximately as much protein in it as regular milk, a good deal more iron (though a lot less calcium), and less than a third the calories and fat. Some people enjoy its vegetable taste *au naturel,* others add flavorings to it. The fact that it contains none of the digestive drawbacks of dairy milk makes it an excellent supplemental food for infants, providing, of course, the infant can tolerate it—not all can. Soy milk is available at natural food stores in both powder and fresh form. Always buy the fresh, unadulterated varieties if you can, and stay away from the canned brands.

SOURCES OF PROTEIN, AND HOW MUCH YOU REALLY NEED

Let's have a closer look at the amounts of protein that are included in different foods. This can be of help to anyone who wishes to keep track of how much protein they are getting each day in their regular diet, and to see how this amount compares with standard dietary recommendations.

Calculations for how much protein our bodies actually need every day, and hence how many protein foods we should eat, can only provide approximate figures. Each person has decidedly different requirements: One person will do well on a diet entirely lacking in animal foods of any kind; another follows the same diet and withers away. One educated estimate among many, this one based on figures issued by the National Academy of Sciences, suggests that an adult's Recommended Daily Allowance (RDA) should include at least .36 grams a day of protein per pound of body weight. This figure is probably somewhere in the right ball park, though some will argue for more and others for less.

Don't be put off by the decimals in such numbers as .36 grams a day, or by the mention of metric grams. The calculation required to find your protein RDA in ounces is easy. If, for example, I weigh 180 pounds, I start by multiplying my weight—180—times .36, which, as mentioned, is a typical adult RDA for protein per pound of body weight. So I get: 180 × .36 = 64.8 grams. There are roughly 28 grams in an ounce. So divide 64.8 (or whatever number you get by multiplying your own weight times .36) by 28: 64.8 ÷ 28 = 2.31. The final figure tells me that I should eat 2.31 ounces of protein a day.

Our protein needs, furthermore, vary from day to day and from one state of health to another. If a person is in crisis, for instance, his or her protein needs will increase dramatically, sometimes as much as 100 percent. Those experiencing the death of a loved one, a job loss, a divorce, a sickness, an accident or a move frequently develop conditions of malnutrition without even realizing it—in the midst of their confusion and angst they become more careless than usual about what they eat at a moment in life when, ironically, they should be most cautious. Anyone experiencing extra stress is well advised to maintain adequate protein nourishment, not only because of this tendency toward nutritional neglect but because the nutritional benefits that come from adequate protein supply can help one deal more effectively with whatever stress is at hand.

Children, by the same token, since their bodies are in the formative stages, require especially large daily helpings of protein. According to the National Research Council's Food and Nutrition Board, children's daily protein supply should include the following:

1–3 years old	.81 grams a day per pound body weight
4–6 years	.68 grams per pound body weight
7–9 years	.55 grams per pound body weight
10–14 years	.45 grams per pound body weight
15–18 years	.45 grams per pound body weight
19 years to adult	.36 grams per pound body weight

Pregnant and lactating mothers have especially high protein needs. There is conclusive evidence that the children of women who receive insufficient protein nourishment during pregnancy are less healthy than those born from mothers who were adequately nourished. The National Research Council suggests that women in the first trimester of pregnancy take in around 80 protein grams a day, and that women who are nursing receive around 100.

These recommendations are not to be interpreted too literally, by the way, and you shouldn't worry if you don't get exactly the prescribed amount each and every day. They are general guidelines, and a certain amount of flexibility is understood. As said, protein requirements are very much an individual matter, and Americans tend to go overboard in their frenzy to get enough. If the American protein RDA errs it surely errs on the high side.

On the other hand, being too cavalier or careless about protein intake is a mistake as well, especially if you are a vegetarian. Since the body does not store protein like fats, fresh provisions are constantly required. Without adequate supplies the body is incapable of repairing itself and it quickly starts to lose strength. The fact is that our bodies can more or less be deprived of dietary fats entirely and not get into serious trouble for a while. They can go without carbohydrates for lesser periods of time; nonetheless they will manage. But protein does not wait. The diet should include adequate supplies of it *every day*. Anything less and you're asking for trouble.

As to the question of how much protein you can get from various common foods, the following table provides the basic facts. Though this table is by no means exhaustive, it gives a wide sampling of the important and the not-so-important protein sources you're most likely to find on your daily dinner table. To make practical use of the table, determine your own daily protein requirements, then match it up to various foods on the list.

You may learn, for example, that you need around 60 grams of protein a day to stay well nourished. You find from the table that ¼ cup of dried kidney beans gives you 10 grams of protein a day. That a cup of buttermilk contributes around 7, while several dollops of peanut butter on a slice of whole-wheat bread provides another 10. Add the figures: 10 + 7 + 10 = 27. You're just about halfway there.

Next, ¼ cup of cashew nuts as a snack provides 7 grams. Two bananas make another 2. Some cooked haddock for dinner adds 19, along with a cup of yogurt, worth 8 grams. Add the 7 + 2 + 19 + 8 and you get 36. The 27 + 36 = 61. You're just about on target as far as your daily requirement is concerned. A little over even.

Protein Content of Selected Foods

Food	Approximate Serving Size	Amount of protein (grams)
Almonds	1 cup	25
Asparagus	10 stalks	2
Avocados	½	2
Bacon	3 medium-sized slices	7
Bananas	1	1
Beans, Dry	1 cup	42
Beans, Lima	1 cup	14
Beef, Cooked	3 average-sized slices	35
Beef, Hamburger	1 large patty	18
Bread, Rye	1 slice	2
Bread, White	1 slice	2
Bread, Whole Wheat	1 slice	3
Chard	⅓ cup after cooking	1
Cheese, Cheddar	1 cup grated	27
Cheese, Cottage	1 cup	30
Chestnuts	1 cup	9
Chicken	3 average-sized slices	28
Codfish	1 average-sized serving	17
Coleslaw	2 cups	3
Corn	1 medium-sized ear	4
Cornmeal	⅔ cup	8
Cream (Heavy)	½ cup	3
Dandelion Greens	½ cup after cooking	3
Dates	14 fresh	2
Eggs	2 medium-sized	13
Farina	⅔ cup	4
Figs	3 average-sized	1
Filbert Nuts	½ cup	16
Flounder	1 average-sized serving	15
Flour, White Enriched	¾ cup	11
Flour, Whole Wheat	¾ cup	13
Frankfurters	2	14
Grapes	20 average-sized	1
Haddock	1 average-sized serving	19
Halibut	1 average-sized serving	18
Ham	3 cooked pieces	23
Herring	1 cup	22
Kale	½ cup cooked	4
Kohlrabi	½ cup fresh	2

Protein Content of Selected Foods (*cont.*)

Food	Approximate Serving Size	Amount of protein (grams)
Lamb	2 average-sized slices	24
Lettuce	6 large leaves	1
Liver, Beef	1 average-sized serving	20
Lobster	⅔ cup meat	18
Mackerel	1 average-sized piece	19
Milk, Buttermilk	1 cup	7
Milk, Condensed	1 cup	24
Milk, Dried, Skimmed	1 cup	36
Milk, Evaporated	1 cup	14
Milk, Nonfat	1 cup	8
Milk, Whole	1 cup	9
Mushrooms	10 small	3
Oatmeal, Cooked	1 cup	5
Oysters	5 to 8 medium-sized	10
Parsnips	½ cup sliced	2
Peanut Butter	6 tablespoons	26
Peanuts, Roasted	¾ cup shelled	27
Pears, Fresh	1 large	1
Peas, Dried, Split	½ cup	25
Peas, Fresh	¾ cup shelled	7
Pecans	¾ cup	9
Pork, Cooked	1 average-sized serving	23
Potato Chips	50 pieces	7
Potatoes, Baked	1 medium-sized	3
Potatoes, French-fried	20 medium-sized pieces	5
Potatoes, Mashed with Milk and Butter	½ cup	2
Radishes	10 medium-sized	2
Raisins	½ cup	2
Rice, Brown, Cooked	1 cup	5
Rice, White, Cooked	1 cup	4
Salmon, Canned	1 average-sized serving	20
Sardines, in Oil	¼ tin	26
Sauerkraut	1 cup	2
Scallops	½ cup	15
Sesame Seeds	1 teaspoon	2
Shad	1 average-sized serving	19
Shrimp	12	28
Tuna, Canned	3 ounces	24

Protein Content of Selected Foods (*cont.*)

Food	Approximate Serving Size	Amount of protein (grams)
Turkey	3 average-sized slices	25
Walnuts	10 medium-sized	7
Yogurt	1 cup	8

A Few Last Thoughts on Protein

• Pound for pound, dollar for dollar, it makes a lot more sense to get most of your protein from vegetables and dairy foods. Meat is traditionally the most expensive item on the shopping list. Imagine how much less you'd spend weekly if you just *halved* the amount of meat you consume.

• If you are going to depend on meat as a source of protein, organ meats such as beef liver, pancreas and kidney are top sources. All are still relatively inexpensive as far as meats go, and all are rich in nutrients, especially vitamin B. Liver is delicious cooked alone, while kidney and pancreas go well in meat pies. All represent the most complete protein you can get in meat. Proteins from the so-called muscle meats such as steak, lamb chops and pot roast are complete proteins but contain lesser amounts of the essential amino acids.

• If you are a supplement taker, a wonderful source of protein is brewer's yeast. Besides being a complete protein—it has nineteen amino acids in total—it contains eighteen different important minerals and trace minerals and has all the major B vitamins except vitamin B-12. You can buy brewer's yeast in powder form and sprinkle it over cereal, into stews, or drink it in milk. It also comes in tablets, available at any good vitamin counter. It is recommended that if you take regular amounts of brewer's yeast you take calcium lactate with it—yeast is high in phosphorus, which in large doses tends to deplete the body's calcium supplies.

• Lack of protein in the diet has been claimed by some nutritionists, Adelle Davis, in particular, to be responsible for premature aging. Our bodies, she explains, are primarily composed of protein, and they constantly require this vital nutrient to heal and strengthen. If insufficiently supplied, the body must plunder certain cellular tissues to free amino acids that normally should be supplied through the diet. Such a process may go on year after year, says Davis, without apparently affecting health. But meanwhile: "Unseen abnormalities set in because blood proteins, hormones, enzymes, and antibodies can no longer be formed in amounts needed. Muscles lose tone; wrinkles appear; aging creeps on; and you, my dear, are going to pot." *

• Contrary to popular belief, hard labor does *not* increase a person's need for protein. Calories, yes, but the protein needs of an office worker and a construction engineer are approximately the same.

• It is considered probable that increased protein in the diet of a sick patient speeds convalescence. Certainly it aids a person to regain his or her strength after a prolonged illness, and its regenerative effects are especially good for one who has endured severe physical trauma such as an accident or surgery.

• There is some indication that people in cold climates require more protein than those in temperate locales. During the cold months, it seems, the body must work especially hard to produce inner body heat. This process is largely dependent on a constant supply of adequate dietary protein, just as greater amounts of wood are needed to increase the heat of a fire. If you are going to eat meat, wintertime is when it's most needed.

* Adelle Davis, *Let's Eat Right to Keep Fit* (New York: Signet Books, 1970), p. 35.

CHAPTER FIVE

Finding a Natural Diet That's Right for You

Biochemical Individuality

Roger J. Williams, co-founder of the Clayton Foundation Biochemical Institute at the University of Texas, has spent much of his professional life crusading for the acceptance of a single scientific point. In capsule form it is this: Physiologically we are more different from one another than is ordinarily supposed. He writes:

> The existence in every human being of a vast array of attributes which are potentially measurable (whether by present methods or not) makes quite tenable the hypothesis that *practically every human being is a deviate in some respects.* Some deviations are, of course, more marked and some more important than others. . . . In the majority, the "abnormalities" may be well enough concealed so that they are not revealed by clinical examination, though they may easily have an important bearing upon the susceptibility of the individual child to disease later in life.*

Throughout his well-documented book *Biochemical Individuality,* Williams continually drives home the point that both the anatomy and

---

* Roger J. Williams, *Biochemical Individuality* (Austin: University of Texas Press, 1973), p. 3.

the bodily processes of each person are wholly unique to that one individual being, that, physiologically speaking, there is no "average" or "normal" person. We are all unique. The way one child breathes is different from the way another child breathes. The way this woman digests starch is different from the way that man digests starch. A healthy blood pressure for this man over fifty is different from a healthy blood pressure for that man over fifty.

Look, for instance, at the way different people metabolize minerals. In a study of the subject Williams found that there is a sixfold variation in the amounts of calcium normally urinated by various test subjects. Also, that there is a 30 percent difference in the sodium content of blood cells among subjects, a fourfold difference in salivary sodium, a fivefold difference in amounts of magnesium in the saliva. In one study, samples of blood were taken from eleven different men and women. The samples were separately analyzed for sugar level, urea, inorganic phosphorus, lipase, lactic acid and many other substances. Results showed that subjects routinely yielded values considerably above or below the commonly accepted normal range: One subject was above average in uric-acid content, another was below in enzymatic production, a third was way above "normal" in alkaline phosphatase values. Almost nobody *was* average. Despite this wide range of discrepancy all individuals were apparently healthy.

Studies of particular organs reveal dramatic differences in size, shape and even position. Looking at the widely varied dimensions and contours of a number of stomachs illustrated in Williams' book, it's difficult to believe they are all the same human organ. Even a relatively simple part of the body such as the aortic arch, a major grouping of arteries, can show extraordinary variation from one cardiac system to the next.

Williams spent many laboratory hours compiling his own research and studying the work of others concerning deviations in endocrine activity, genetics, nerve and bone structure, vitamin and mineral requirements, musculature, hair composition, body weight, skin chemistry, dental development, excretion patterns, sensitivity to pain, basal metabolism, sex drive, blood composition and many other crucial physiological functions and activities. Even people's different reactions to external stimuli such as electric currents or nicotine were considered. Correlating these findings, he concluded that *variation in the biological workings of the human body is the norm, and that exact agreement with preestablished norms is the exception.*

Of tantalizing interest are Williams' studies on human nutrition. As with other parts of the body, he learned, both the shape and the workings of individual human digestive systems vary. He observed that different individuals metabolize foods at divergent speeds, that people require vastly different quantities and qualities of food to remain well nourished, that the amounts of vitamins, minerals, enzymes and nutrients required to stay healthy vary enormously from one individual to another.

For example, individual calcium requirements, perhaps the most important of all mineral needs, are far more difficult to establish than is ordinarily supposed. In a study of nineteen males, Williams tells us, one man maintained his calcium balance quite nicely on 225 milligrams a day, while another was given 256 milligrams per day and became dangerously calcium deficient. The total requirement for calcium balance among all nineteen men varied between subjects by as much as 1,018 milligrams per person per day.

Amino-acid metabolism also vacillated. Ordinarily we've been told that the "average" person needs X number of grams of protein a day to stay healthy—.36 per pound of body weight, you will recall, is one common estimate—and that without getting an amount approximate to this figure a person will automatically become protein starved.

Then in laboratory tests it was learned not only that different subjects have different total amino-acid requirements, based on their individual physiologies, but that they have different specific needs for specific amino acids as well. The range of tryptophan requirement, for instance, varied from .15 grams to .25 grams in different subjects. Lysine needs varied from .4 grams to .8 grams; threonine, from .3 grams to .5 grams. Even more surprising, findings showed that the so-called "nonessential" amino acids, those that can be synthesized within the body, are in fact essential for certain people.

A good case in point is the amino glutamic acid. While tests show it is extremely important to some individuals, it proves entirely unimportant to others; in some people the self-manufactured supply is adequate, in others it is not.

Williams goes down the list: vitamins A, B, C, D; minerals; trace minerals; enzymes; proteins; fats; carbohydrates. The requirements for each are quite specific to the individual, and every person needs them in different proportions. The reasons for these discrepancies, while not always apparent, he claims, are not unknowable either. In explanation of why vitamin needs contrast so dramatically between individuals, Williams writes:

> The augmented need which an individual has for a particular nutrient may invoke not only his own internal metabolism, but also that of the intestinal or other bacteria which he harbors. For example, if an individual furnishes a "climate" which is highly favorable to the presence of ribofla-

vin-producing bacteria, he may not need any of the vitamin at all in his diet. On the other hand, assuming for the moment that most people get a substantial part of their riboflavin from intestinal bacteria, an individual whose internal climate is highly unfavorable to these organisms may have a need for this reason alone which is far above average. The production of a "climate" suitable or unsuitable for specific kinds of microorganisms is doubtless related to natural immunities and to peculiarities in metabolism, both of which are genetic in origin.*

According to the viewpoint adopted by Williams and his colleagues at the Clayton Foundation Biological Institute, it is therefore difficult if not impossible to set absolute guidelines for how much of any particular nutrient we really need. Generalizations are about the best we can come up with, and these should always be tested against a person's own nutritional needs and experience.

Williams' suggestion for dealing with these biochemical variations in nutritional needs, moreover, is interesting and largely uncharacteristic of the orthodox nutritional approach. He terms it the "self-selection of foods"; in essence, he means body wisdom.

He cites the example of a middle-aged man who through the years has shown little or no tendency to put on weight. This man's food consumption will be well balanced against his metabolic needs, Williams maintains, since his weight remains so stable. If he ate more than he needed he would become overweight. If he ate less he would be underweight. Something within this man's instinctive body intelligence knows just how much he needs, and that something guides him.

> The ability to strike this kind of balance [Williams remarks] is a wisdom *of the body;* superior knowledge about calories or food values is not at all necessary, since this feat has doubtless been accomplished millions of times quite unconsciously by people who had no basic nutritional knowledge at all or even the ability or machinery to weigh themselves. What is it that makes it possible to perform this feat? We know little about the delicate mechanisms involved; we do know definitely that some people have the necessary wisdom of the body to perform the feat and others do not.

It's More Up to You Than You Might Think

Williams' book is one of many researched and written by a well-equipped professional yet considered by other professionals to be of fringe interest

---

* Williams, *Biochemical Individuality,* p. 158.

at best, primarily because it dares take a stand against the mechanistic approach to health care that is so firmly entrenched in our society, and because, if what it says—and more important, what it implies—is accurate, a healthy rethinking of both medical and nutritional practice would be in order.

If what Williams tells us about human variability is true, especially his findings concerning the individualization of nutritional needs, then health-care professionals would be forced to question the value of all generalized diets geared to treat the "average" person. They would have to reassess the worth of official "minimum daily requirements" calculated to fulfill "normal" human needs, of vitamin and mineral quotas published by local governments for worldwide populations, and of a scientific method that is founded on statistical rather than individual results.

If, furthermore, we contemplate the implications of this thesis, several more unorthodox conclusions force their way to attention:

1. In order to come up with an eating plan that maximizes nutritional balance, one must first understand the nutritional needs *of one's own body*. Forget what's good for the other guy. You're the one—and the only one—responsible for the state of your physical well-being. To randomly adopt this high-carbohydrate diet, that megavitamin supplement program, these vitamin regimes, without knowing what your actual nutritional needs are in these areas, is putting the cart way before the horse. And it can be dangerous.

2. Beware of automatically assuming that any food, no matter what good things are officially claimed for it, is right for your own particular nourishment. Even such natural favorites as brown rice or honey or yogurt or whole-wheat bread should be viewed through the lens of personal experience—How well do they sit in *my* stomach? How successfully do they really nourish *me?*

3. In the long run, it's up to each person to determine his or her own personal way of eating. This must be done by the process of experience, by trial and error, by accumulation of knowledge, and by a sincere attempt to hear the voice of one's body wisdom. Individual food-tolerance levels, nutritional deficiencies, state of health, physiological eccentricities, allergies, weight, metabolism, taste perceptions, excretion habits, digestion, enzymatic patterns, blood, bone and sinew composition, anatomy, body type, appetite, energy needs, all vary from person to person. One man's meat is truly another man's poison. You must learn for yourself what your meat really is.

Choosing Your Own Diet

With all this in mind, we move now to the question at hand: choosing one's own eating plan. In the field of natural foods there are, of course, as many diets and as many holistic approaches to nutrition as there are numbers of people confused by it all. Among schools of natural nutrition almost no one agrees, even on the most basic matters. And perhaps this is as it should be, for the rightness or the wrongness of a diet should depend less on universal rules, more on individual needs.

This chapter therefore presents several of the most interesting and popular approaches to natural eating. Since each of these varies considerably from the others, you'd be well advised to contemplate each, sample one or all as the spirit moves you, and then come to your own decisions. You may also wish to take the most attractive features from several of these diets and integrate them into a plan that fits your own particular style. Many people do. Then again, if you find that none of these diets adequately fills the bill, go ahead and search farther afield.

The first diet we'll look at closely is called macrobiotics. It's been around for some time now, has a number of followers, yet is surrounded by many misconceptions that should be cut away from the start.

DIET ONE: MACROBIOTICS

It's difficult to sum up macrobiotics in a few pages, mainly because this system is as much a way of life as it is a diet, and most of its practitioners approach it in this spirit. Founded in the 1930s by a Japanese businessman named Georges Ohsawa, macrobiotics is based on a combination of traditional Japanese cuisine, the daily diet of Zen Buddhist monks, and Ohsawa's own learned intuitions concerning sickness, health and food.

Primary to Ohsawa's approach—"philosophy" is a better term—is the notion that all things in nature are striving toward balance, and that behind this striving is the interplay of two primal, universal forces, the active male force—yang—and the passive female force—yin. Practitioners of macrobiotics, along with a good part of the Asian world, see the relationship between these two cosmic forces as responsible for the manifestation and maintenance of all phenomena, from the dynamism of human metabolism to the making of a star.

To keep the human body in harmony with these two forces, Ohsawa and his best-known disciple, Michio Kushi, developed a diet based on the attainment of a yin-yang equilibrium. From a scientific standpoint, yang foods are alkaline, yin foods acidic. When the two are eaten in the proper ratio the macrobiotic diet is said to be successful. In fact, if practiced properly, macrobiotic followers believe, this method will not only keep the body entirely free of disease, it will cure diseases that are already there. Macrobiotics looks upon itself as much as a system of medicine as a way of eating.

The Ohsawa/Kushi technique of balance and counterbalance in diet is a complex one and requires much study of macrobiotic theory. Followers of the method are usually urged to attend classes and to learn cooking methods directly. Some literally devote their lives to it. The following précis, though limited to essentials, gives a fairly broad indication of how this philosophy translates into practical terms in the kitchen, and how it reaches out to an approach to living in general.

The Macrobiotic Approach at a Glance

1. Approximately 50 Percent of the Macrobiotic Diet Consists of Grains

Whole-wheat bread (prepared without yeast) and brown rice are the staples in this department. Millet cakes, whole-grain cereals, whole-wheat pastas, corn, oats, grits, buckwheat, rye bread, and buckwheat noodles are all recommended.

2. Macrobiotics Do Not Eat Meat

Meat of any kind, be it beef, pork, turkey, lamb, chicken, is forbidden. Nonoily fish like flounder or sole is eaten approximately once a week by some macrobiotics, depending on which of their specifically prescribed diets they are following.

3. Approximately 10 to 15 Percent of the Diet Should Consist of Legumes

Adzuki beans are a special favorite of macrobiotics, though chickpeas, lentils, soybeans, black beans et al. are all standard. Legumes are never taken alone but always in the company of grains.

4. About 20 to 30 Percent of the Diet Should Consist of Fresh Vegetables

These range from the green leafy kind to yellow squash (which macrobiotics particularly approve of) to turnips, Brussels sprouts, cabbage, radishes, broccoli; also, certain Oriental vegetables such as daikon radishes, burdock root, shiitake mushrooms, bean curd and lotus root.

5. Only Small Amounts of Fruit Should Be Eaten

The diet should include no more than 5 percent at most. Apples, pears and the sour, salted umeboshi plums are the standards.

6. Only Varieties of Foods That Are Native to One's Climatic Zone Should Be Eaten

This is a fundamental tenet of macrobiotics and one on which practitioners are quite insistent. It sounds easy enough until you realize that tomatoes, asparagus, yams, cucumbers, beets, zucchini and many more of our standard vegetables are of tropical origin and hence forbidden to anyone who lives in a temperate zone. The same is true for fruits: Bananas, oranges, grapefruits, papayas, guavas, pineapples, kiwis and avocados are all limited to those who live in the warmer climates.

7. Sugar of Any Kind Must Be Avoided

Another strict part of the doctrine. Barley malt and rice syrup are allowed. All others—table sugar, honey, molasses, fructose—are disallowed. Macrobiotic cooks use the natural sugars that occur in various fruits and vegetables to sweeten main dishes and desserts. Learning to use these natural sugars is a basic part of macrobiotic cooking technique.

8. The Diet Should Contain at Least 5 to 10 Percent Sea Vegetables Every Day

Sea vegetables—wakame, arami, hijiki, kombu, dulse, nori (see page 109)—are all a fundamental part of the macrobiotic eating experience. Usually they are flavored with Tamari, an aged form of soy sauce, and served with brown rice.

9. Do Not Drink Too Many Liquids

To preserve the integrity of the kidneys (which macrobiotics feel are sorely overworked by our habit of drinking too many liquids with our food), fluid intake should be kept to a minimum, especially at meals. The best drinks are Japanese teas such as bancha-twig tea, kukicha tea, Mu tea, plus various grain and vegetable mixtures. Apple juice is okay in small quantities, though people in temperate or cold climates should avoid most other juices, especially orange juice and grapefruit juice, both of which are tropical.

10. The Macrobiotic Practitioner Must Learn Which Foods Are Yin, Which Foods Are Yang, and Always Eat with an Eye Toward Keeping Them in Balance

This is the fundamental teaching of macrobiotics. Meat, as a case in point, is very yang. Sugar is extremely yin. Foods with such a strong bias in either direction are considered dangerous, as they throw the body's internal chemistry intensely out of balance.

In general, yin foods are grown in warm climates and have a sour, bitter, sweet or hot taste. Yin vegetables grow above the ground, contain much internal water, and mostly take the form of leaves and fruits plus the end products of fruits, like sugar. Yang foods come from cold or temperate climates, are salty, pungent, bland or slightly sweet. They tend to be less watery than yin foods. Yang vegetables grow below the ground, like onions or carrots. Yang foods in general include stems, roots, seeds and animal foods.

Yin foods tend to expand—like sugar on the tongue; yang foods tend to contract—like salt on the tongue. Yin is acidic; yang is alkaline. Vegetables tend to be yin, animal foods yang. Eggs, meat, poultry and fish are yang. Dairy products, fruit, spices and sugars are yin. Legumes are somewhat in between the two poles, and grains are even more balanced. Indeed, grains are the most perfectly balanced of all foods, say the macrobiotics; and among these the best is rice. It contains most of the important nutrients our body needs, and contains them in perfect equilibrium. Man cannot live on bread alone, a macrobiotic would claim, but he'd come pretty close with rice.

A breakdown of the different functions and values of yin and yang can be traced from the following table devised by Michio Kushi: *

Quality	Yin	Yang
Tendency	Expansion	Contraction
Function	Diffusion	Fusion
	Separation	Gathering
	Decomposition	Organization
Movement	Inactive, slower	Active, faster

* Michio Kushi with Alex Jack, *The Cancer Prevention Diet* (New York: St. Martin's Press, 1983), pp. 61, 62.

Quality	Yin	Yang
Vibration	Shortwave, high frequency	Longwave, low frequency
Direction	Vertical	Horizontal
Position	Outward, peripheral	Inward, central
Weight	Lighter	Heavier
Temperature	Colder	Hotter
Light	Darker	Lighter
Humidity	Wetter	Drier
Density	Thinner	Thicker
Size	Larger	Smaller
Shape	Expansive, fragile	Contractive, harder
Form	Longer	Shorter
Texture	Softer	Harder
Atomic Particle	Electron	Proton
Elements	N, O, P, Ca, etc.	H, C, Na, As, Mg, etc.
Environment	Vibration, air	Water, earth
Climatic Effects	Tropical climate	Colder climate
Biological	More vegetable quality	More animal quality
Sex	Female	Male
Organ Structure	Hollow, expansive	Compacted, condensed
Nerves	Peripheral, orthosympathetic	Central, parasympathetic
Attitude, Emotion	Gentle, negative	Active, positive, aggressive
Work	Psychological, mental	Physical, social
Consciousness	More universal	More specific
Mental Function	Deals with future	Deals with past
Culture	More spiritual	More material

11. There Are Strongly Yang and Strongly Yin Substances That Must Always Be Avoided

These include coffee, black tea, tobacco, foods with chemical additives in them, sedatives and tranquilizers, highly processed foods, fluoridated water, liquor, soft drinks, artificially carbonated drinks, and all narcotic drugs.

12. There Are Several Specific Macrobiotic Diets, Each Designed to Suit Individual Needs

Beginners may find themselves fitted to one of several different diets, depending on their personal nutritional requirements and their present state of health. The standard seven, as formulated by Ohsawa and prescribed according to a person's needs, are as follows:

Diet No.	Cereals	Vegetables	Soups	Fish	Fruits	Desserts	Liquids
7	100%						Sparingly
6	90%	10%					Sparingly
5	80%	20%					Sparingly
4	70%	20%	10%				Sparingly
3	60%	30%	10%				Sparingly
2	50%	30%	10%	10%			Sparingly
1	40%	30%	10%	20%			Sparingly
−1	30%	30%	10%	20%	10%		Sparingly
−2	20%	30%	10%	25%	10%	5%	Sparingly
−3	10%	30%	10%	30%	15%	5%	Sparingly

There are also specific diets designed for particular diseases. A macrobiotic "specialty" is the dietary approach to cancer. In this area Michio Kushi has done much research and has devised a number of eating plans for cancer sufferers, some leaning toward yin foods, others toward yang foods, all in relation to the kind of cancer a person is afflicted with.

In his book *The Cancer Prevention Diet,* Kushi deals with a list of different cancer types. Brain cancer, according to Kushi, results from the overconsumption of protein and fat, especially animal protein. He stresses that all eggs, meat, poultry, dairy foods, and oily fish be eliminated. He also suggests an eating regime that includes 50 to 60 percent whole-cereal grains, 5 to 10 percent miso and vegetable soup, 20 to 30 percent cooked vegetables, 5 percent beans and sea vegetables.

Lung cancer, according to Kushi, is due to a different set of problems, specifically an excessive intake of acid, mucus-forming, fatty foods that accumulate slowly in the lungs and serve as a kind of "glue" for pollutants, keeping them trapped in toxic suspension for long periods of time. After a while the lungs become so congested with these foreign substances they can no longer police themselves of carcinogens. Eventually this toxic state poisons the lung cells and turns them toward cancer.

Kushi suggests that since lung cancer results from a condition of both extreme yang and extreme yin, yang foods such as meat, eggs, and dairy products must be eliminated, and yin foods such as sugar, sweets, fruits and juices, spices, and refined foods should generally be avoided. He then prescribes a diet in line with the lung-cancer sufferer's particular nutritional needs.

13. The Way a Food Is Cooked Is Almost as Important as the Food Itself

Students of macrobiotics are taught special ways of handling kitchen chores—cutting vegetables, washing food, grinding grains, boiling, chopping, sautéing, pressure-cooking, serving. Many of these techniques are believed to improve the taste, nutrition and even the spiritual quality of the food. Every aspect of food must be taken into consideration, they believe, from the planting of the seed to the serving on the plate.

14. A Diet Should Vary with the Seasons

Macrobiotics adjust their diet and their cooking methods to stay in harmony with the transitions from season to season. Since the winter is yin (cold) and the summer yang (hot), a predominance of yang foods are eaten in winter to counterbalance the yin force of cold, and, vice versa, yin foods are eaten in the steamy months of summer. In the winter, foods are cooked and heated more thoroughly than in the summer because the hot yang element is missing in cold weather and is needed to complement the cold yin; in the summer, raw, uncooked yang foods are best.

15. Food Should Be Eaten Slowly and Chewed Thoroughly

Macrobiotics suggest that a person chew each bite at least fifty times and preferably one hundred before swallowing. This method forces the eater to slow down. Tranquil eating, they insist, is conducive to good digestion and peace of mind.

16. Food Grown Locally Is Better Than Food Imported over Long Distances

A backyard garden is the best source, though any produce grown in one's neighborhood is acceptable.

17. Kitchen Tools Should Be Simple and Made of Natural Materials

Electric mixers, food processors, blenders and the like are discouraged. Wood, stainless-steel and bamboo kitchen instruments are encouraged.

18. Followers of Macrobiotics Are Encouraged to Lead a Natural Life and Pursue a Spiritual Path

Since macrobiotics is a holistic approach not only to food but to life, the balance and harmony of the diet are meant to carry over into all branches of daily activity. Practitioners are urged to wear clothes made of natural materials and to avoid synthetics of any kind; to get plenty of fresh air and exercise; to shun drugs, liquor and tobacco; to drink pure water; to bathe regularly; to maintain an open and loving attitude toward other people; to work hard, in the spirit of unselfish cooperation; and to participate in whatever spiritual discipline most attracts them.

Macrobiotics: Pros and Cons

Is macrobiotics for you? It depends. The assets are there all right. Many practitioners will tell you they never felt better, that their thinking is clearer, their health better, their lives more meaningful than ever before. There are, as well, literally thousands of testimonials supporting the Ohsawa-Kushi thesis that proper diet can not only prevent cancer—and most other degenerative diseases too—but in some cases cure it as well. Kushi's book on the cancer prevention diet is filled with authenticated case histories.

On the deficit side, there is the monotony of the diet. No matter what macrobiotics may tell you, the limited number of foods you are allowed, many of which are exotic and difficult to get used to, as well as the old habits you must break in order to follow the diet, are all sizable obstacles. So are the withdrawal symptoms you may have to go through when beginning this diet: headache, malaise, lack of energy, excessive discharge of mucus, severe weight loss and intense cravings. Such withdrawal symptoms are to be expected, you will be told; your body is readjusting and purifying itself from years of toxicity. True enough. But this does not make them any easier to endure.

All in all, the macrobiotic approach demands commitment, study and effort. It is not something to be entered into lightly. If the rewards are really as great as they are claimed to be by followers of this method—

good health, mental clarity, increased vigor, expanded spiritual knowledge, and freedom from disease—then the returns would clearly seem worth the effort.

DIET TWO: FOOD COMBINING

A considerably different approach to nutrition and diet is taken by followers of the food-combining method. Though most partisans of this system are wholly in favor of eating fresh, wholesome, unrefined and unprocessed foods, the quality and even the quantity of foods ingested take something of a backseat to the *ways in which these foods are combined with one another.*

If this blending is done correctly, they believe, all other nutritive and metabolic concerns will then take care of themselves in turn.

In essence, the food-combining method is based on four working principles. These are:

1. Modern eating habits are haphazard in regard to the kinds of foods that should be eaten together at the same meal. The only thought given to food combinations is whether foods *taste* good together, not whether they are chemically compatible in the digestive system.

2. Our digestive system was not constructed to deal with extremely complex mixtures of food. Man was not meant to eat a wide variety of foods all at the same time.

3. Within the stomach and intestines certain kinds of proteins, carbohydrates and fats are compatible with one another, certain kinds are not. If incompatible nutrients are mixed, the foods will not digest properly.

4. Enzymes are protein substances, the chief catalytic agents of digestion. Their function is to speed up the chemical process of fermentation and to expedite the breakdown of food. While enzymes do their job with wonderful efficiency, they are also relatively inflexible, programmed to perform certain tasks, and these tasks only.

When an overabundance of different carbohydrates, fats and proteins are eaten at a meal, and no thought is given to which of these foods are compatible, too many chemical messages are sent to the enzymes, and things get garbled. For example: An enzyme such as lipase, which works exclusively on the breakdown of fats, cannot function properly in the company of, say, too many protein-digesting enzymes. Another example: Certain sugars resemble one another chemically but actually require entirely different enzymes to break them down. When too many of these different sugars are eaten together they broadcast many conflicting messages, causing one sugar-digesting enzyme to attempt to do the work of another, with only chaos to show for it.

The final result of this confusion is that important enzymes become neutralized or even canceled out, others do their job only partially, and still others do not work at all. The food is not assimilated properly and a variety of difficulties may result. Indigestion problems will be the short-term effects. Malaise, malnourishment, chronic gastrointestinal problems and eventually disease will be the long-term results.

These four principles are based on the concept that digestion is the number-one factor in good nutrition. A follower of the combining method would say that unless food digests properly and the nutrients from it reach the right parts of the organism, there's no sense worrying about whether it is natural, unnatural or anything else. In the food-combining system, the philosophy is: First make sure that the nutrition-extracting mechanisms are working at their best. Then, after you're certain everything's perfect in that department, go ahead and tend to the quality of the food. If you care enough about the first concern, you'll no doubt care about the second too.

How to Combine Foods Properly

In order to put this plan into practice you must know which foods contain which food values—that is, which food is a protein, which a starch, and so forth—and, also, which are complementary and which are antagonistic.

The broad division between proteins, fats and carbohydrates is probably familiar to you by now. But food combiners carry the categorization one step further, breaking down the protein-fat-carbohydrate classifications into subgroups to make combining methods clear. If you intend to try this method, the following table of these subgroups is a must. It was devised by H. M. Shelton, one of the pioneers in the field of food combining. Much of the information presented here is based on his work.

Classification Table for Food Combining

PROTEINS

Nuts	Fish	Meat
Cheese	Olives	Peanuts
Dried beans	Peas	Dried peas
Milk	Yogurt	Butter
Fowl	Grains	Kefir
Eggs	Gelatin	Seeds and nuts

Classification Table for Food Combining (*cont.*)

STARCHES

Grains	Pastries	Pastas
Breads	Chestnuts	Peanuts
Jerusalem artichokes	Squash	Dried beans
Dried peas	Potatoes	Cakes, pies, etc.

MILDLY STARCHY

Rutabagas	Beets	Carrots
	Salsify	

SYRUPS AND SUGARS

White table sugar	Lactose	Cane syrup
Corn syrup	Molasses	Honey
Barley malt	Rice syrup	Fructose
Maple syrup		

SWEET FRUITS

Raisins	Dates	Grapes
Dried pears	Dried apricots	Persimmons
Figs	Prunes	Bananas

FATS

Olive oil	Sesame oil	Safflower oil
Sunflower oil	Cream	Pecans
Almonds	Tallow	Lard
Fatty meats	Avocados	Nut oils
Butter	Cottonseed oil	Corn oil
Margarine	Almonds	Walnuts
Olives		

ACID FRUITS

Oranges	Pineapples	Pomegranates
Crab apples	Limes	Lemons
Grapefruits	Sour grapes	Tomatoes
Sour plums	Sour peaches	Sour cherries

SUBACID FRUITS

Fresh figs	Sweet cherries	Apricots
Huckleberries	Blueberries	Raspberries
Strawberries	Sweet peaches	Sweet plums
Sweet apples	Mangoes	Pears
Guavas	Papayas	

NONSTARCHY AND GREEN CARBOHYDRATES

Lettuce	Rhubarb	Celery
Cabbage	Watercress	Chives

Onions	Chicory	Mustard greens
Leeks	Turnips	Garlic
Broccoli	Kale	Asparagus
Parsley	Green peppers	Red peppers
Sorrel	Okra	Chard
Spinach	Kohlrabi	Zucchini
Brussels sprouts	Escarole	Radishes
Bamboo shoots	Eggplant	Collards

MELONS

Watermelons	Persian melons	Honeydews
Crenshaws	Cantaloupes	Muskmelons

Chart based on information taken from H. M. Shelton, *Food Combining Made Easy* (San Antonio: Willow Publishing, 1982), pp. 9, 10.

Next consideration: How are these foods properly integrated? There are, according to Shelton, a number of possible ways in which the major food groups can be combined. A few of these combinations, he believes, will promote good digestion. Most won't. Here's the basic list:

1. Acid-Starch

Acids destroy the starch-digesting enzyme ptyalin in the saliva. This means you shouldn't mix acidic fruits such as oranges or pineapples with starches like breads or beans or potatoes. Tomatoes are also basically acidic. Avoid using them on whole-grain sandwiches or blended with starchy vegetables like potatoes or squash.

2. Protein-Starch

Starch requires an alkaline medium to digest; protein, an acidic one. The two don't mix. The old meat-and-potatoes combination is not the faithful standby we've been led to believe, according to food combiners. Same with meat and bread. Meat sandwiches, or sandwiches with cheese or egg on them, don't digest well together either. Same with that age-old standard, cereal and milk.

If both these foods, protein and starch, happen to be unavoidably included on the same menu there *is* a way to get around the incompatibility problem. Eat the protein first, allow a little time for it to digest, *then* take the starch. In this way the two substances will be separated by time and space in the digestive tract and will not cancel each other out.

3. Protein-Protein

Not all proteins are the same. One may be broken down by a different enzyme than another, and at varying rates. Meat and eggs are a good example. You can mix any two or three kinds of meats you wish in the same meal; and milk and flesh, while not ideal, more or less go together. Unacceptable, however, are eggs and meat, eggs and milk, eggs and nuts, nuts and milk.

4. Protein-Nonstarchy Green Carbohydrate

This is an ideal combination. Meats, dairy products, nuts and eggs go especially well with cabbage, broccoli, Brussels sprouts, watercress, kohlrabi, onions and salad greens. The tradition followed by many American steak houses of serving a large salad with a meat entrée is based on sound food-combining wisdom.

5. Starchy-Nonstarchy Green Carbohydrate

Also good. Starchy vegetables like potatoes, squash, turnips, carrots, cauliflower and legumes of all kinds go well with vegetables like broccoli, greens, leeks, scallions, eggplant, radishes plus the nonstarchy vegetables mentioned on the list.

6. Acid-Protein

Avoid using acidic fruit juices with meats or dairy products. Milk and pineapple, for example, is a bad combination. So is a vinegar- or lemon-based dressing poured over salads and then eaten with meat. Many people drink orange juice with their meals, and this, it is believed here, is basically gastrointestinal suicide. Acidic juices like orange juice, pineapple juice and grapefruit juice should be sipped alone.

7. Fat-Protein

Fats have an inhibiting influence on the protein-digesting gastric juices. They should be eaten separately. This means that the fat on meat should not be mixed with the meat itself. Dairy cream used with foods like grain or legumes is not a good combination. If, moreover, fat and protein are taken together at the same meal, which is not unusual—most meats are served with salads, for instance, and most salads are anointed with oil—then the addition of plenty of nonstarchy foods to the menu will help the two incompatibles blend better.

8. Sugar-Protein

Sugars should always be taken alone. Don't mix them with any other foods, especially proteins.

9. Sugar-Starch

Again, sugar should be taken by itself and not mixed. The hallowed American tradition of sugaring breakfast cereal, or for that matter grapefruit or lemonade, is productive of overfermentation in the stomach, and can result in severe heartburn and indigestion.

So What Can You Eat?

Most of these food combinations, as you've no doubt noticed, are negatives. Besides the few acceptables on the list, what then constitutes proper food combining? According to Shelton, you can do any of the following:

1. Mix acidic foods like fruits with nonstarches, especially green vegetables.

2. Mix acidic fruits and nonacid fruits.

3. Mix proteins with acids when the protein has a high fat content and the acid is a fruit. Cheese, nuts and avocados, all high-fat proteins, go well with acidic fruits. Desserts like fruit compote or fruit cocktail with walnuts are recommended. You might also take buttermilk with fruits, or pour cream over them.

4. Mix animal flesh, dairy, nuts with nonstarchy foods and some mildly starchy vegetables.

5. Mix various starches with each other: rice and beans; corn and squash; millet and lentils. The grain-legume mixture is an especially good one.

6. Mix fats with other fats.

7. Take fruits, vegetables, starches, grains, dairy products, meats, sugars, fats by themselves—within moderation—at any time.

8. Shelton has devised several sample diet menus, one for the spring and summer seasons, one for the fall and winter.* A perusal of these makes it clear just how an ideal food-combining diet would work from day to day.

*Shelton, pp. 53, 54.

Spring and Summer Menus

Breakfast	Lunch	Dinner

SUNDAY

Watermelon	Vegetable salad	Vegetable salad
	Yellow squash	String beans
	Potatoes	Okra
	Chard	Nuts

MONDAY

Peaches	Vegetable salad	Vegetable salad
Cherries	Beet greens	Spinach
Apricots	Carrots	Cabbage
	Baked beans	Cottage cheese

TUESDAY

Cantaloupes	Vegetable salad	Vegetable salad
	Okra	Broccoli
	Green squash	Fresh corn
	Jerusalem artichokes	Avocados

WEDNESDAY

Berries with cream	Vegetable salad	Vegetable salad
	Cauliflower	Green squash
	Okra	Turnip greens
	Brown rice	Lamb chops

THURSDAY

Nectarines	Vegetable salad	Vegetable salad
Apricots	Green cabbage	Beet greens
Plums	Carrots	String beans
	Sweet potatoes	Nuts

FRIDAY

Watermelon	Vegetable salad	Vegetable salad
	Baked eggplant	Yellow squash
	Chard	Spinach
	Whole-wheat bread	Eggs

SATURDAY

Bananas	Vegetable salad	Vegetable salad
Cherries	Green beans	Kale
Glass of sour milk	Okra	Broccoli
	Irish potatoes	Soy sprouts

Fall and Winter Menus

Breakfast	*Lunch*	*Dinner*
	SUNDAY	
Grapes	Vegetable salad	Vegetable salad
Bananas	Chinese cabbage	Spinach
Dates	Asparagus	Yellow squash
	Baked caladium roots	Baked beans
	MONDAY	
Persimmons	Vegetable salad	Vegetable salad
Pears	Kale	Brussels sprouts
Grapes	Cauliflower	String beans
	Yams	Pecans
	TUESDAY	
Apples	Vegetable salad	Vegetable salad
Grapes	Turnip greens	Kale
Dried figs	Okra	Yellow squash
	Brown rice	Avocados
	WEDNESDAY	
Pears	Vegetable salad	Vegetable salad
Persimmons	Broccoli	Okra
Bananas	String beans	Spinach
Glass of sour milk	Irish potatoes	Pignoli nuts
	THURSDAY	
Papayas	Vegetable salad	Vegetable salad
Oranges	Carrots	Chard
	Spinach	Yellow squash
	Steamed caladium roots	Unprocessed cheese
	FRIDAY	
Persimmons	Vegetable salad	Vegetable salad
Grapes	Green squash	Red cabbage
Dates	Parsnips	String beans
	Whole-grain bread	Sunflower seeds
	SATURDAY	
Grapefruit	Vegetable salad	Vegetable salad
	Fresh peas	Spinach
	Kale	Steamed onions
	Coconut	Lamb chops

SUNDAY

Honeydew melon	Vegetable salad	Vegetable salad
	String beans	Baked eggplant
	Vegetable soup	Kale
	Yams	Eggs

Food Combining: Pros and Cons

While the food-combining system does allow some meat on the menu, it emphasizes the fruits-grains-vegetables trio, and plays down animal products in general. This is probably good, if what we have discovered so far about meat is correct. If you want to eliminate animal flesh entirely from this diet it can easily be done by combining a grain and a legume in the place of meat.

The biggest drawbacks of food combining are: (1) the diet tends to be restricted and monotonous; (2) it stresses food combinations at the expense of the quality of the food itself; (3) it has almost no margin of tolerance for many of the traditional food mixtures that our taste buds have accustomed themselves to, and that for may people are what make eating worthwhile; (4) it requires a dramatic change in eating habits, one that requires more than a little dedication and power of will.

On the positive side—and this is a very big positive—there's the way you'll feel when you follow this regime for a while. Or amendment: the way *many* people feel. Occasionally some find the monotony of it too overbearing, or worse, the particular combinations of foods don't seem to offer enough for a person's particular energy needs. Clearly different diets suit different physical types.

People who do find this diet agreeable, however, and there are many, make impressive claims for increased energy level, better health and an overall sense of well-being. Those who profit most from the combining technique, it might be added, often tend to suffer from weak stomachs or digestion problems. Food combining really does work to help relieve the classic gastric symptoms that occur when foods are mixed too carelessly: bloat, gas, heartburn and sour tummy.

If you're prone to gastrointestinal problems, or if you simply want to go on a more simple, wholesome eating regime, give the combining method a try and see what happens. If you stick to it carefully you should see results in less than a week. If you don't see positive results in a month —or if you're feeling logy and out of sorts after two or three weeks of eating this way—food combining is not for you. Shelve it and go on to Diet Three.

DIET THREE: METABOLIC TYPES

In the field of natural nutrition a curious enigma continues to present itself: Diets that make one person feel great have no effect—or the reverse effect—on another. Certainly Williams' biochemical-individuality theory goes a long way toward explaining this phenomenon in broad terms. It took, however, the work of a Texas scientist by the name of William Donald Kelly to refine this notion into practical nutritional terms.

William Donald Kelly had long been a teacher and researcher at Baylor University in Texas. The thrust of his studies over the past several decades had been to establish exactly why diet A is good for person A but not for person B and vice versa, and then to devise a nutritional system *based* on these differences, yet still inclusive of everyone within the spectrum of normal human metabolism.

The method he devised is based on the theory that mankind is not one but many—ten to be exact—basic *metabolic types*. Each type interacts with the world according to a particular set of biochemical needs and characteristics; nutritionwise, each requires a somewhat different eating regime to get well and stay well. Kelly set himself the task of determining exactly what it is each of these types really needs, and then of supplying it to them.

Before discussing how these types can be identified, and how you can determine your own metabolic type, let's illustrate some of Kelly's basic principles, using a simple lesson in neurology as a starting point.

The Body's Two Nervous Systems

Though we speak of it in the singular, the human nervous system is a two-part mechanism: the voluntary and the autonomic nervous systems.

The voluntary nervous system is under the control of our conscious will. It's what allows us to mail a letter, dig a ditch, solve a subtraction problem, give a speech or run a mile, all with consistency and—more or less—rationality. The autonomic nervous system, on the other hand, is located in a different part of the brain. It behaves, as it were, on its own, without conscious participation or awareness. Its responsibilities include the regulation of breathing, circulation, glandular secretions, heartbeat, digestion and a number of other functions that, thank heaven, we don't have to keep track of with our conscious minds.

The autonomic nervous system is divided into two further parts, the *sympathetic* and the *parasympathetic*. The job of the sympathetic nervous system is to convey messages to the body that tell it to speed things up, to make things go, to run, work, plow full steam ahead. The parasympathetic has the opposite effect: It says: "Whoa! Wait a minute! Slow down!"

For example, it is the sympathetic nervous system that increases the heartbeat in time of danger; it is the parasympathetic that returns body functions to normal. It's the sympathetic that causes the pupils of the eyes to grow large when we see something we like. It's the parasympathetic that makes them small again.

One part of the autonomic nervous system, in other words, represents force, the other inertia. Working together they police the body's delicate balance between activity and rest, its metabolism.

The balance of every man's, woman's and child's metabolism, according to Kelly, is under the primary management of either (1) the sympathetic nervous system; (2) the parasympathetic nervous system; (3) both the sympathetic and parasympathetic to an equal degree.

Therefore, when we speak of a "sympathetic type" or a "parasympathetic" or a "balanced sympathetic-parasympathetic," we speak of the three major metabolic categories to which all human beings, regardless of size, sex, race or politics, belong. Each group has its own particular needs and its own distinguishing characteristics. It is these differences that make each person nutritionally unique and that explain why certain foods are good for one person and not for another.

What are these characteristics? Let's start with the first type, the sympathetic.

The Sympathetic Type

According to Kelly, sympathetic types are volatile, quick-thinking, fast-moving people who oxidize food at an extremely slow rate. Traits you can use to identify them include:

- A tendency to make rapid decisions.
- Dislike of fatty foods and meat; preference for fruits and vegetables.
- A tendency toward dry skin and hair, insomnia and frequent indigestion.
- A strong sex drive, rapid heartbeat and sensitivity to the cold.
- A tendency toward pale skin coloring, constipation and thin, wiry builds.
- Quick temper; impatient and easily irritated; a nervous and high-strung temperament; a love of physical activity and exercise; strong startle reaction.
- Cheerfulness and absence of an inclination toward depression.

• Good powers of concentration; a tendency to have a small appetite, crave sweets and fruits, and to be underweight.

• Thin, flat chests; rapid breathing patterns; gums are a pale light color; thick eyebrows; tendency to dream rarely and to not recall dreams.

Sympathetic types receive more nerve stimulation in their energy-producing glands than in their organs of digestion, according to Kelly. Their constitution does not need—and usually does not crave—meat. For this reason he terms them "vegetarian" types. This, in contrast to the parasympathetic types, who love meat, and whom Kelly dubs "carnivores."

The Parasympathetic Type

Parasympathetics experience more nerve stimulation in their digestive organs than in their energy-producing glands, and they are rapid oxidizers. Their center of gravity is, as it were, in their stomachs. They *must* eat at least some meat *every* week, and in some cases, *every* day. Without it they will languish. Characteristics identifying parasympathetic types include:

• Extreme sluggishness; caution; a slow, steady, firm and positive attitude toward life.

• Low energy, high appetite, lack of energy after eating sweets; a confirmed habit of eating between meals.

• Tendency to sleep deeply with some difficulty rising in the morning.

• A temperament that is slow to anger and will endure many irritations.

• Tendency toward dejection and depression; a reluctance to exercise.

• Craves fatty, salty foods; has good digestion and several bowel movements a day; likes meat.

• Oily skin and hair; rounded chest; ruddy complexion; thin eyebrows; gums bluish color or dark pink; urinates frequently.

The Sympathetic-Parasympathetic Type

Finally there is the so-called balanced metabolizer, or sympathetic-parasympathetic. People in this category have an autonomic nervous system whose dual parts work in a balance of glandular function and metabolic activity. Of the three main metabolic groups, the balanced metabolizer is least bounded by dietary considerations and can safely enjoy the widest variety of foods. Distinguishing traits include:

- Does not tend to extremes; tendency toward occasional anger that rarely becomes excessive; copes well with stress.
- Has normal amount of drive and aggressiveness—nothing in extremes.
- Occasional dreams; sleeps fairly well; has normal sex drive.
- Enjoys a wide variety of food; not a picky eater.
- Does not tend to suffer from stomach problems; enjoys both fruit and meat; has no strong opinions on whether or not he likes to exercise.
- Normal bowel movements; seldom uses laxatives; normal-sized bowel movements; may belch occasionally.
- Skin and hair not too oily, not too dry; average-sized chest; normal coloring, not too red or too pale; gums have normal pink color.
- Normal appetite; doesn't get hungry between meals; gets started in morning without too much difficulty.
- Enjoys exercise when there is time, but is not fanatically dedicated to it; has occasional periods of fatigue; can endure pain well.

Finding Your Own Metabolic Types

Sympathetic—parasympathetic—sympathetic-parasympathetic: these, as Kelly sees it, are the three types that make the world go round. But that's not all. Within each major group there are subdivisions, ten in all, in which individual traits are further broken down.

Among the sympathetic group, for instance, there are three subtypes. The first is a pure vegetarian; he or she oxidizes carbohydrates slowly and is able to maintain a stabilized blood-sugar level with little trouble. Such people do well on a 100 percent raw vegetable and grain diet. The second sympathetic type burns carbohydrates faster, and can eat moderate amounts of fowl and fish without trouble, along with a little beef and eggs. Contrast both these types with the metabolic type II in the parasympathetic group. Being almost pure carnivores, and having a tendency toward unbalanced blood-sugar level, the type II parasympathetic *must* have meat, preferably fatty, heavy meat, to slow their carbohydrate/sugar metabolism and maintain a balanced blood-sugar level.

While a complete examination of each subgroup is of value only to the person who is deeply involved with the Kelly method—and involvement can be both time-consuming and expensive—it will no doubt be of interest to learn how to establish which of the major groups you belong to—sympathetic, parasympathetic and balanced—and what kind of diet is recommended for your type.

Natural food expert Fred Rohé has devised a self-administered written test designed to help his pupils determine which metabolic class they belong to. He calls the test the Autonomic Nervous System (ANS) Equilibrium Self Test. It is easily taken in a matter of a few minutes, and will help you quickly determine which category you belong to. The only instruction is that you answer all questions as well as you can, according to how things are with you *at the present time.* If you have been a vegetarian for many years, answer as a vegetarian. If you have recently gone on a nonmeat diet, answer according to your *old* eating patterns.

Autonomic Nervous System (ANS) Equilibrium Self Test

Answer each question:
   (a) always or often
   (b) sometimes
   (c) rarely or never

---

1. I could eat a steak for breakfast. (a b c)
2. I prefer a light breakfast. (a b c)
3. I like butter on my soft-boiled eggs. (a b c)
4. I can skip breakfast without feeling hungry or tired. (a b c)
5. I feel better when I have bacon and eggs for breakfast. (a b c)
6. I feel hungry between meals and satisfy it with something sweet. (a b c)
7. I feel a bit weak if I go without food for two or three hours. (a b c)
8. I drink a lot of water. (a b c)
9. I could eat beef *every* day, even twice a day. (a b c)
10. I like raw onions. (a b c)
11. I get hungry between meals and like to snack on salty nuts, cheese and crackers, maybe *even* a hot dog. (a b c)
12. I crave sweets. (a b c)
13. I like olive oil. (a b c)
14. I find the vegetables that go with a steak or roast more interesting than the meat. (a b c)
15. I prefer liver with bacon to liver with onions. (a b c)
16. I prefer liver with onions to liver with bacon. (a b c)
17. I like a lot of salt on my food. (a b c)
18. I like salads and raw vegetables and they agree with me. (a b c)
19. I don't like cooking smells, even though the foods taste okay at the table. (a b c)
20. I like lettuce, cottage cheese, and fruit for lunch. (a b c)
21. I like a lot of lean salt pork in baked beans. (a b c)
22. I eat something sweet like fruit, pastry, or candy, and it picks me right up when my energy gets low. (a b c)

23. I like steak and lobster together for dinner. (a b c)
24. I like soft drinks. (a b c)
25. I feel tired during the day but snap out of it after eating a big portion of meat for dinner. (a b c)
26. I like to drink a large glass of fruit juice. (a b c)
27. I find candy or cake too sweet. (a b c)
28. I would prefer carrot and celery sticks to olives and sardines for appetizers. (a b c)
29. I want something like cheese or nuts after dinner. (a b c)
30. I prefer to eat hamburgers with a lot of ketchup and/or tomatoes. (a b c)
31. I get hunger pains. (a b c)
32. I look forward to fresh fruit season and like to make a whole meal of fresh fruit. (a b c)
33. I like pickles. (a b c)
34. I like meatless meals. (a b c)
35. I like fatty meats like ham and pork chops. (a b c)
36. I eat small portions. (a b c)
37. I like potatoes. (a b c)
38. I forget to eat meals, or would if someone didn't remind me. (a b c)
39. I would choose some nuts over an apple for a snack. (a b c)
40. I prefer wine over beer. (a b c)

Count the number of "a" answers to odd-numbered questions _____
Count the number of "c" answers to even-numbered questions _____
Add them together for your "P" (parasympathetic) score: P: _____
Count the number of "a" answers to even-numbered questions _____
Count the number of "c" answers to odd-numbered questions _____
Add them together for your "S" (sympathetic) score: S: _____
Count the number of "b" answers for your "B" (balanced) score: B: ___

Your ANS (Autonomic Nervous System) Equilibrium profile is:

PARASYMPATHETIC if your highest score is P.
SYMPATHETIC if your highest score is S.
BALANCED if your highest score is B.
Enter your ANS Equilibrium profile here _____

Here are two further confirmation tests that complement the above findings.

1. Take 50 milligrams of niacin on an empty stomach. Wait a half hour. If your skin becomes hot, red and itchy, you are a parasympathetic type. If you feel nothing after this time, you are a sympathetic type. If

you feel warm and the color in your face improves, you are a balanced type.

2. Take 8 grams of ascorbic acid for three straight days. If you are a woman and experience irritation in your vaginal area, or if you are either male or female and become depressed, fatigued, anxious and impatient, you are a parasympathetic type. If you feel *more* energy and if you experience a glow of well-being, you are a sympathetic type. If nothing happens you are a balanced metabolizer.

How Should Each Metabolic Type Eat?

Now, thanks to Rohé's and Kelly's self-administered tests, you know your metabolic type. The next question is: What should you eat as a member of one of these metabolic groups?

While it's impossible here to go into the intricate dietary specifics that participants in Kelly's system follow, some general guidelines can be given.

The Sympathetic

You're probably not that much of a food person to begin with. All your life you may have been told that you *must* eat more, that you're too thin, that you've got to pay more attention to your diet. The problem is that your appetite is not that hearty, and food is not that important to you. Better for you to disregard all this well-meaning advice and just eat until you feel satisfied, even if the size of the servings doesn't amount to a hill of beans. Food may feel like a lead weight in your stomach, which is one reason why you aren't a big eater. One of the solutions to this annoyance is to go with the natural inclination of your metabolic type and eat less meat, or even none at all. You will do quite nicely on a balanced vegetarian diet, and some of the ailments you may chronically suffer from, such as heartburn, gas, halitosis, constipation, restlessness and an overall feeling of toxicity, will be helped. The best foods for you are the alkaline types, fruits and vegetables especially. The best vitamin and mineral supplements are vitamins D, C, B-1, B-2, B-6, niacin, potassium, magnesium and zinc.

The Parasympathetic

Parasympathetics are the big eaters of the three metabolic groups, and the meat eaters par excellence. Vegetables and fruits are of secondary nutritional importance, which is no great problem, as parasympathetic types often have little fondness for such foods (too many leafy green vegetables may actually make them sick). Grains are a bit more acceptable, but meat is always number one. Without it the parasympathetic becomes restless, weak and unsatisfied. While sympathetics have skimpy appetites due to their slow oxidization of sugar, parasympathetics require large portions and frequent feedings. Where the sympathetic sleeps better on an empty stomach, parasympathetics require food in their systems to get them comfortably through the night. Parasympathetics tolerate more protein and dietary fat in general than sympathetics, whereas eating too much fruit may give a parasympathetic an uneasy or jumpy feeling. The main nutritional supplements they ordinarily require are vitamin E, zinc, calcium, phosphorus, pantothenic acid. Parasympathetics should be wary of all B vitamin supplements except vitamin B-12.

The Balanced Metabolizer

The diet of the balanced metabolizer should include fair helpings from both the meat and vegetable/fruit groupings. It is not wise to go strictly vegetarian, nor to eat too much meat and dairy; a balanced, well-distributed choice made from a wide variety of foods is ideal—balanced metabolizers are the only true omnivores among the three groups. The balanced metabolizer must concentrate carefully on choosing high-quality foods and making certain his food is prepared in a wholesome, natural manner; these types may be especially sensitive to carelessly cooked meals or low-quality foods, especially highly processed junk foods; of the three types, balanced metabolizers are most apt to get sick from such inferior rations. As far as nutritional supplements go, the balanced metabolizer usually requires vitamins A, E, B-1, B-2, B-6 and B-12, calcium, magnesium, phosphorus and folic acid. Of all the metabolic types they are the ones most likely to require a regular course of daily dietary supplements.

The Kelly Diet: Pros and Cons

Involvement in the Kelly diet is a full-time affair, and expensive. To do it right you must contact the Nutritional Counseling Service, P.O. Box 402607, Dallas, Texas 75240 (phone: 800-527-0453). They will tell you the location of the nearest metabolic-style counseling service in your area. After filling out forms and taking tests, you will be given a computer printout "metabolic profile" that expounds on the details of your particular metabolic type and tells you what you should and should not eat. The tests are not cheap to begin with, but even more expensive are the huge numbers of nutritional supplements that participants are urged to take along with the prescribed diet. For some people these various minerals, vitamins and megavitamins may cost as much as several hundred dollars a month. Moreover, the question of whether or not megavitamin doses are good for you—or bad for you—is far from resolved. While certain people make great claims for their effectiveness, there is some rather persuasive evidence that vitamin/mineral megadoses are sometimes useless and even occasionally harmful.

On the positive side is the important fact that this diet is tailor-made for *you*. Nobody else. It is based on how you as an individual digest and assimilate your food. Providing that Kelly's method and philosophy are correct—and remember, no one can say for sure that Kelly or any other diet maker is 100 percent right—there is probably no other diet you will ever find that is so personalized, so intimately tailored for your individual nutritional needs as this one. For more detailed information on how this method can be applied on a day-to-day basis see Fred Rohé's book, *The Complete Book of Natural Foods,* especially the section he calls "The New American Diet."

DIET FOUR: THE BIRCHER-BENNER DIET

For many years the first thing people pictured when they heard the dreaded term "health foods" was a relentless, tasteless torture regime of uncooked vegetables. No meat, no sweets, no dairy products, no nothing. Just a few measly grains and lots and lots of carrots.

A good deal of work has been done since then to dispel the raw-carrot myth, and to show that natural eating, even raw natural eating, can be good eating too. The trick to making the vegetarian diet palatable, in a word, is to use inventive recipes. One of the most successful attempts comes from the European-based Bircher-Benner method.

The Bircher-Benner clinic is in Zurich, Switzerland. It was founded some years ago by Dr. Max Bircher-Benner specifically to help invalids regain their health and to provide natural cures for a host of chronic diseases. Visitors to his clinic were carefully nourished on a vegetable/ grain diet specially devised by Dr. Bircher-Benner while they availed themselves of various forms of exercise, relaxation, fresh air and massage. The clinic was one of the early attempts in Europe to create a holistic health environment.

So successful was Bircher-Benner in healing the most chronic cases that his diet gradually became a staple at a number of European sanitariums. Slower to catch on in the United States, the Bircher-Benner diet has gained some notice in various health circles, primarily because of the popularity of Bircher muesli, a commercial breakfast cereal that is based —in part, at least—on Bircher-Benner's original recipe. Two cookbooks were published in the early part of this century presenting the Bircher-Benner philosophy but neither of these made much of a splash in the United States. In 1972 Penguin Books published a revised translation of the 1926 edition edited by several members of the Bircher-Benner family and this book has done a good deal better. It is called *Eating Your Way to Health* and in it are many of the original Bircher-Benner recipes.

The Bircher-Benner Philosophy

1. Pure Natural Food Is a Medicine

Dr. Max Bircher-Benner, like other physicians of his time, practiced medicine for some years with only a varying rate of success. After continued disappointment using conventional remedies he concluded that something was missing from the standard medical approach. This notion was substantiated when one day a woman came to his office suffering from an inability to digest her food. Nothing Bircher-Benner could do would bring her any relief. She was dying.

Discussing the case one night with a friend who happened to have an active interest in the writings of the ancients, Bircher-Benner was astonished when the friend suggested he try a remedy that the Greek philosopher Pythagoras had once recommended for extreme digestive problems: a diet of raw fruits mixed with fresh goat's milk and honey. At first the doctor dismissed the idea out of hand. But the friend pressed his point— What had they to lose?—and so eventually Bircher-Benner agreed. Almost as soon as the woman was put on this strange raw-food diet, to Bircher-Benner's amazement, she improved. Before too long her symptoms disappeared entirely.

Bircher-Benner now began to treat patients exclusively with diet and nutritional counseling. The more rapidly his cure rate escalated the more convinced he became that proper nutrition was the answer to many of humanity's incurable ailments. But precisely what was there about food and diet that helped so many seemingly hopeless cases? His conclusion was that it is the *freshness* of the food, the *rawness* of it, and its *purity* that matter most; that in their natural states foods contain all the vitamins and enzymes necessary not only to maintain health but to restore it as well.

When a food is stale, processed, or overcooked, Bircher-Benner likewise concluded, its dietary effectiveness is reduced and at times even reversed, so that what was once a healthy food becomes a dietary menace. This weakened food now not only fails to nourish the person properly, it actively disrupts his or her state of health. Foods must, as a result, be eaten in a state as close as possible to the uncontaminated living state, he decided, in order to have the effect on human beings that nature intended.

From our perspective today, of course, there's nothing original or earthshaking about these simple observations. But see it from the vantage point of the late 1880s and 1890s, when technology was heralded as the panacea for all mankind's problems, and when almost no one was aware of what ill effects air pollution, artificial chemicals, industrial wastes and food processing have on our food and drink. Bircher-Benner, from this standpoint, was one of the early pioneers to sound the warning whistle against environmental defilers. He was one of the first in his time to call attention to the fact that the quality of human food was declining so rapidly that it was already making people sick.

2. The Greatest Single Influence on Human Health Is Nutrition

From the standpoint of the Bircher-Benner system, health is a matter of seeing the whole picture: hygiene, exercise, heredity, personal psychology. But most important is the way one eats. So important is this concern, followers believe, that even if a person has a strong constitution, a right mental outlook, and a congenial home environment, if he or she eats poorly, his or her health will inevitably deteriorate. Inevitably. Nothing can prevent it. Of all human health concerns, the Bircher-Benner advocates claim, diet comes first.

Raw Foods Have Healing Power

Fresh, uncooked plant foods grown in uncontaminated soils will, as the authors of *Eating Your Way to Health* tell us, "restore the conditions essential to life, and will relieve and regenerate the regulative systems and that of the endocrine glands. This nutrition at the source, where as yet no contamination or devitalization can have taken place, preserves the natural wholeness of foods and their rare qualities."

Prolonged cooking is particularly hard on the enzymes that occur naturally in plant tissue, the authors inform us:

Heating also destroys the numerous enzymes present in the plant cells. As has recently been found, these enzymes perform two functions that offer a further explanation for the curative effect of raw foods. To start with, they produce, as it were, a self-digestion of the raw food within the intestinal tract, thus relieving the digestive glands. Previously it was doubted whether the enzymes reached the colon in an efficient state. It has now been shown that 60 to 80 percent of them arrive there unimpaired and—by oxygen fixation—establish anaerobic conditions in the intestinal tract, the medium in which the beneficial coli bacteria grow and multiply, and thus drive away the pathogenic ones.*

4. Half of the Daily Diet Should Include Raw Foods

The Bircher-Benner system does not require that all vegetables be uncooked. At least half can be lightly steamed—never boiled for prolonged periods of time—or quickly sautéed. Of the raw foods, all should be garden fresh. Take plenty of carrots, turnips, cabbage, peppers, tomatoes and fresh fruits. Bread should be freshly baked and made from whole grains. Grains, preferably raw grains, are, in fact, an essential part of the Bircher-Benner diet. Take them in cereals, especially in Bircher-Benner's own famous recipe for muesli:

BIRCHER MUESLI

2 tablespoons rolled oats	2 tablespoons wheat germ
2 tablespoons chopped almonds	2 tablespoons honey
2 tablespoons milk	Juice from ½ lemon
2 apples, chopped	

Soak oats overnight. Next day add the remaining ingredients, mix together, and serve at once.

Most important, however, are leafy green vegetables. "No day without green leaves" goes a Bircher-Benner slogan, and indeed, at the Zurich clinic a fresh green salad accompanies all meals.

5. Take All Raw Foods at the Start of the Meal

Special aromatic substances in raw foods, it has been found, seem to play a part in preventing a condition known as "digestive leucocytosis," unavoidable when food is cooked before it is eaten. Leucocytosis is a concentration of white blood cells in the walls of the intestines that interferes with the internal processing of foods. According to the Bircher-

* Ruth Kunz-Bircher, et al., *Eating Your Way to Health* (Baltimore: Penguin Books, 1972), pp. 4, 5.

Benner followers, raw foods taken at the start of a meal prevent this condition.

Even if cooked food is eaten afterwards this leucocytosis fails to materialize, provided a sufficient portion of raw food was eaten at the beginning of the meal. The absence of leucocytosis frees the white blood corpuscles for other tasks, saves the body the effort of a defensive action and therefore strengthens the powers of resistance to disease. Hence the Bircher-Benner maxim: Begin each meal with raw food. Raw food before, not after, the cooked food.*

6. Avoid All Meat

The Bircher-Benner diet tolerates no meat and is opposed to high-protein diets. Adequate protein is received, advocates claim, through a proper balance of whole grains, green-leaf vegetables and dairy products. Meat has a deleterious effect on the health over a prolonged period of time, Dr. Bircher-Benner believed, not only because of the biological nature of meat itself but because of the processing that almost all commercial meat is put through before it reaches the store. In weight-loss diets it actually stimulates appetite rather than satiates it, thus working against the diet's primary purpose.

Meats are also high in dietary fats, and these too must be held to a minimum. Long before it was a public issue, Dr. Bircher-Benner was loud in his pleas for a cutback in daily consumption of fats and for a reduction in the amount of oils used in cooking. As a general rule, the Bircher-Benner diet asks its adherents (1) to be sparing in their use of vegetable oils; (2) that when vegetable oils are used they be of the pure, cold-pressed, virgin variety; (3) that oils be heated as little as possible during food preparation. Adequate amounts of dietary fats will be received, they maintain, by purposefully including plenty of nuts and whole grains in the regular cuisine.

7. Take Dairy Foods Sparingly

Dairy is secondary at the table of the Bircher-Benner clinic to grains, fruits and vegetables. Milk, cream, yogurt and butter are looked upon as a necessary protein addition rather than a main food. Any dairy products that are eaten must be scrupulously pure—raw milk obtained from cows pastured on unsprayed grazing lands.

*Kunz-Bircher, et al., *Eating Your Way to Health*, p. 6.

8. All Foods Must Be Organic

This is a strict rule among all the European clinics that feature the Bircher-Benner menu, and it is followed with fastidious care. If the food is not toxin-free the whole premise of the system is endangered. Purity of food, along with freshness, is the first tenet here.

9. Beware of Overeating

Meals should consist of well-balanced foods that keep one wholesomely sated from meal to meal—foods such as rice, beans, whole-wheat dishes in general, uncooked fruit and vegetables. A person should always leave the table feeling pleasantly full. Bloated or leaden feelings in the stomach are a danger sign.

Breakfast should be sparse; lunch can be the largest meal of the day; dinner is light, with raw foods predominating. By and large, the Bircher-Benner people believe that modern man eats too much food at each sitting. Meals should be smaller in size and calories, they insist, with emphasis put on quality. Between-meal snacking is discouraged.

> The art of cooking, therefore, should not consist, as is customary today, of offering dishes containing too many concentrated foods that pass as rapidly as possible into the bloodstream. People should not be induced to eat and drink too much, but rather in the reverse. All foods should and must be rich in natural fluids, in fibrous bulk, vitamins and mineral salts, but not particularly rich in calories. A pleasant sensation of satiety should follow as soon as the limit of capacity is reached.

10. Eat Plenty of Fermented Enzyme-type Foods

These include fresh pickles, homemade sauerkraut (see recipe page 96), miso (see page 113), tempeh (see page 112), soured milk, yogurt, and tangy cottage or farmer cheese. The enzymes in fermented food are a special aid for the digestive process, adding plenty of bacterial flora into the intestines.

Some Typical Bircher-Benner Meals

Next comes the matter of putting these principles together into a cohesive day-to-day menu. As with some of the other dietary systems we've met, the Bircher-Benner clinics adapt their eating plans to the seasons. Here's a sample menu, taken from the Bircher-Benner archives.* It provides some idea of how a relatively limited vegetarian regime can be expanded into a workable and good-tasting daily meal planner. The actual recipes for many of the dishes mentioned are in *Eating Your Way to Health* and are highly recommended. Remember, all these foods must be freshly picked and organic.

MAY

EVERYDAY MENUS
Fruit
Raw Salad:
   radishes, lettuce
Cooked Dishes:
   spinach soup
   zucchini with tomatoes
   risotto

Fruit
Raw Salad:
   radishes, cauliflower, lettuce
Cooked Dishes:
   sugar peas
   potato salad
Dessert:
   rhubarb tart

Fruit
Raw Salad:
   beetroot, zucchini, lettuce
Cooked Dishes:
   broth with caraway
   cauliflower with sauce
   potatoes with chives

Fruit
Raw Salad:
   carrots, cabbage, lettuce
Cooked Dishes:
   barley soup
   broccoli with sauce
   French-fried potatoes

ECONOMICAL MENUS
Fruit
Raw Salad:
   tomatoes stuffed with celeriac
     or turnips, lettuce
Cooked Dish:
   onion tart

Fruit
Salad:
   salad Niçoise (radishes,
     tomatoes, lettuce, potatoes,
     egg)
Cooked Dish:
   pea soup

Fruit
Raw Salad:
   beetroot, zucchini or tomatoes,
     lettuce
Cooked Dishes:
   spring soup
   Lyons potatoes

Fruit
Raw Salad:
   fennel or chicory, carrots,
     lettuce
Cooked Dish:
   tomatoes with rice

* Kunz-Bircher, et al., pp. 241–244.

Fruit
Raw Salad:
   cress garnished with radishes,
     lettuce
Cooked Dishes:
   stuffed tomatoes
   noodles
   strawberries and cream

Fruit
Raw Salad:
   beetroot, cauliflower, lettuce
Cooked Dishes:
   potato-and-leek soup
   lettuce as a vegetable
   cheese croûtes

Fruit
Raw Salad:
   carrots, cress, lettuce
Cooked Dishes:
   carrots and peas
   filbert potatoes
Dessert:
   farina pudding with strawberry
     or black-currant sauce

Fruit
Raw Salad:
   radishes, spinach, lettuce
Cooked Dishes:
   herb soup
   red or white cabbage
   spaetzle fried with bread
     crumbs

Fruit
Raw Salad:
   tomatoes and lettuce
Cooked Dish:
   millotto
Dessert:
   fruit salad and cream

Fruit
Raw Salad:
   black radishes, turnips
   carrots or lettuce
Cooked Dish:
   macaroni soufflé

Fruit
Raw Salad:
   stuffed tomatoes, with
     cauliflower, cress, lettuce
Cooked Dishes:
   ravioli
   peas
   castle potatoes
Dessert:
   lemon whip and wafers

Fruit
Raw Salad:
   beetroot garnished with olives,
     sauerkraut or white cabbage,
     lettuce
Cooked Dishes:
   asparagus with hollandaise
   cauliflower polonaise
   parsley potatoes
Dessert:
   apple strudel

The Bircher-Benner Diet: Pros and Cons

The Bircher-Benner diet is a classic vegetarian cuisine with all the yeas and nays that go along with such an eating regime. Despite the fact that their menu planning is diversified, and that some of the Bircher-Benner recipes are really delicious, like any vegetarian menu it takes an addicted meat eater a good deal of time to get used to it all. For some people the menu is just plain bland. For others it gets to be, well, just plain boring.

The great stress the Bircher-Benner people put on organic foods makes things doubly difficult. Organic produce is expensive and not always easy to find. Rip-offs at health food stores are not unknown, and you can wind up spending a good deal of precious time and money simply shopping for food and preparing it, only to discover you are not getting what you shopped for in the first place.

At the same time the Bircher-Benner clinics' records speak for themselves. They have helped restore countless convalescents to good health, and several of their special restorative diets have track records that are hard to argue with. The Bircher-Benner recipes have been developed and refined now for almost a hundred years, and these people know what they're doing as far as getting the most taste mileage out of food and at the same time maximizing its therapeutic clout. We dare say that of all vegetarian diets this one *tastes* the best, and that's no small recommendation.

If this diet interests you we strongly suggest you get a copy of *Eating Your Way to Health* and try some of the recipes yourself. The section on feeding children is worth the investment alone. A visit to one of the Bircher-Benner clinics would be, of course, premature at this point, but later on you may wish to experience their traditional holistic methods firsthand. If you have a taste for vegetables, and at the same time like your vegetarian diet to include some zip, this diet may suit you best of all.

DIET FIVE: THE ALL-ROUND, EASY-TO-FOLLOW NATURAL DIET

The last diet is in many ways the least demanding and the most flexible of all the eating plans presented so far. It is designed for those who wish to take the middle road in their dietary travels, navigating between the Scylla of processed junk and the Charybdis of a natural diet that demands too much time, attention and expense. It is founded on a collection of holistic eating principles, and it also serves as one of the most sensible and practical natural-eating plans available today.

Unlike several of the other diets we've looked at, the all-round natural diet is not vegetarian. Meat intake is kept at a minimum, it is true, but it *is* included. And so are eggs. This view is based on the notion that animal flesh is generally good for a person's health and nourishment as long as it is (1) organic; (2) lean; (3) taken in small amounts. If you happen to have a distaste for meat, or if you are avoiding it on vegetarian grounds, simply skip the meat dishes offered in the menu below and compensate by eating more vegetable and dairy protein.

Here are the general ground rules for the all-round natural diet.

1. The Diet Should Include at Least 50 Percent Grains

Grains are the mainstay of the all-round natural diet. This means whole grains, of course: brown rice, whole-wheat breads, millet, rye, barley. Two, and preferably all three, meals should include at least one dish of grains.

2. At Least 20 Percent of the Diet Should Include Vegetables and Fruits

By this we mean *fresh* vegetables and fruits, many of which are eaten raw. The kinds of vegetables and fruits recommended most enthusiastically are profiled on pages 88–115 and 120–131. Of this 20 percent, three-quarters should be garden vegetables, one-quarter fruits. Fruits should be chosen, if possible, from varieties native to your climate, and should preferably be freshly grown in nearby locales.

Included in this category too are sea vegetables—hijiki, wakame, arami, nori (see pages 109–111). These, we firmly believe, should be included in *everyone's* daily food supply. Next to grains they are perhaps the most substantial and nutritious food available.

3. Fifteen Percent of the Diet Should Include Legumes

Mostly the dried varieties—peas, beans, lentils, etc. (see page 99). Legumes are among the most versatile, healthy and hearty of all foods. Though they have so much protein and so many vitamins that they are often grouped in the same food category with meat, they are many times cheaper than meat and, when mixed together with a grain, equally, if not more, nutritious.

4. Five Percent of the Diet Should Include Meat and Eggs

Once a week, and at most twice a week, meat may be eaten on this diet. Lean varieties are best—chicken, fish, turkey, veal. Beef and pork are better avoided completely. Liver is okay if eaten sparingly, but only if it is organic. Eggs should be fresh, local, and, if possible, taken from chickens that were given the run of a pen and fed on grains, table scraps, insects and such. Eat no more than four eggs a week.

It should be noted that these percentages are guidelines and are not to be taken as irrevocable dictums. If you find that eating meat twice a week is leaving you listless and unfilled, the quota can be adjusted upward until it reaches a satisfactory level. The primary goal is to eat the right kinds of meats, and to purchase only the nonprocessed varieties. Stay away from heavily treated commercial types. The combination of high fat content and high chemical toxicity makes them perhaps the single most dangerous item in the supermarket today.

5   Five Percent of the Diet Should Include Dairy Products

The quality of protein is so outstanding in dairy products that we include them as a basic, if minimal part, of this diet. Fresh yogurt is especially recommended. Fresh butter can be taken in small quantities, along with milk, though cream is better left alone. Investigate the use of ghee (see page 164), and if possible purchase certified raw milk rather than the processed supermarket varieties.

If you are worried about the possible bacterial dangers of raw milk, try bringing the milk quickly to a boil before serving it—fifteen seconds is adequate—then allow it to cool at room temperature. This method will serve the same purpose as pasteurization but will accomplish the process faster and without sacrificing as many nutrients. Some people also flash-boil their pasteurized milk, believing that the rapid boiling helps improve milk's digestibility, especially for children.

6.   Five Percent of the Diet Should Include Other Dietary Fats; Certain Natural Sweeteners Can Be Used Occasionally

You'll probably get enough dietary fats in dairy products and meat anyway, but we're giving it a small percent of the pie because fats are one of the three basic food nutrients. Take both your saturated and unsaturated oils v-e-r-y sparingly, and avoid cooking with oils whenever you can (see page 164). One of the best natural sources for dietary fats are seeds and nuts.

As far as adding a bit of sweetness to your meal, honey, maple syrup, molasses, malt syrup and all other natural sweeteners mentioned in the sugar section (see page 65) are acceptable on an occasional basis.

7. Certain Foods Should Always Be Avoided

No surprises here. If you want to stay healthy you'd better kick the white-sugar habit right away. To this list also add sugared gum, saccharin, and other artificial sweeteners, sugared desserts and confections, chocolate, etc.

8. Certain Foods Should Be Eaten Infrequently and Then Only in Moderation

Coffee should be taken with utmost temperance. One cup a day at most, and preferably less than that. None is best. Black tea, while not as overstimulating as coffee, should also be measured out in short spoonfuls.

If you must use salt then use sea salt, but use it sparingly. (Sea salt contains more minerals than the commercial kind, and most brands are unprocessed.) If you automatically reach for the saltshaker and sprinkle it over your food before even tasting it, it's time to change your ways. Follow any good natural diet and all your salt needs will be taken care of via the food itself.

Pepper is a needless garnish and has little nutritional value. Add a little now and then if you must, but sparingly, sparingly. It's better to use fresh peppercorns and grind them directly onto the food with a hand pepper grinder than to buy the tired and sometimes adulterated pre-ground commercial varieties.

Sausages, hot dogs, salami, bologna, headcheese, knackwurst, pepperoni and the like are frequently made from the most undesirable parts of the animal. Some hot-dog manufacturers randomly toss all leftover cattle viscera into the grinding vat, small bones and all, and crush it to a pulp (which is one reason you often find those tiny fragments of bone in the cheaper varieties of franks). This mash is packed in sausage casings and sold for public consumption, crowned with the proud label "100% pure beef." It's all beef, all right—heads, tails, bones, innards and all!

Try to avoid the commercial mayonnaise habit. Use butter instead, or even nicer, tofu mayonnaise (see page 114). If you're hooked on the stuff, buy the varieties sold at most natural food stores. They're generally made of purer materials and are not as processed or adulterated. Be especially careful to refrigerate mayonnaise, as it can be a principal cause of ptomaine poisoning, especially in the warm months.

Salted snacks like peanuts, potato chips, and crackers are vat-fried in low-quality oils. They wreak havoc on the digestion and are filled with unwanted dyes and preservatives. Again, there are many natural crunchy-style seed and nut snacks being marketed at health food stores that will fill you up just as well, and treat your stomach a lot better.

9. Special Foods Deserve Special Attention

No food we know of is universally acknowledged by everyone as being good for you. Some foods, however, are generally considered so nutritious by so many that they deserve an extra-special place in the eating schedule. Included is a list of special foods that should find their way into everyone's fare at one time or another.

bean sprouts	miso
bean curd	kefir
tahini	homemade sauerkraut
burdock root	lotus root
dandelion greens	couscous
buckwheat	whole-wheat kasha
sesame seeds	sunflower seeds
pumpkin seeds	almonds
garlic	cabbage
tempeh	ginger
acidophilus milk	alfalfa sprouts
Tamari sauce	lentils
yams	Jerusalem artichokes
chick-peas	collards
daikon radish	hummus
adzuki beans	mustard greens
pumpkin	rose-hip tea
alfalfa tea	sea salt
soy milk	Japanese soba noodles
wheatgrass juice	wheat germ
brewer's yeast	bulgar
buttermilk	chia seeds
bancha-twig tea	bok choy
mochi	rice syrup
clarified butter (ghee)	nonsweetened granola
shiitake mushrooms	papayas
whole-wheat pita bread	kale

10. Whenever Possible, Eat Foods That Are Unprocessed and Organic

It's not always possible to follow this rule. But you can try. Growing your own organic garden, purchasing organic produce at the health food stores, using fresh, high-quality natural foods instead of preserved and processed commercial brands, preparing food with the principles of natural eating in mind, staying away from artificial colorings and additives while you're cooking—all these little acts of mercy help. Little by little, they help.

If, for instance, you include only one variety of organic food in your larder, organic grains, let's say, and if you follow the all-round natural diet given here, already 50 percent of your food is unprocessed. The hard fact is that refining and processing *do* make a difference in food quality, and a very negative one. Evidence for this is convincing, and it is mounting every day. Because we cannot see the poisons, or taste them, we think they are not there. But they are there. And they are hurting all of us.

11. Substitute Natural Foods for Unnatural

Use honey or maple syrup for sugar. Whole grains for refined grains. Fresh fruits and vegetables for canned. Milk instead of nondairy creamer. Butter instead of margarine. Unprocessed virgin oils in place of processed commercial oils. Country-fresh eggs rather than "chicken factory" eggs. Fresh-squeezed juices for the commercial canned varieties. Herb teas for coffee. Naturally carbonated mineral water for soft drinks. Tofu or miso spreads for mayonnaise.

12. Make As Many of Your Foods as You Can

Bake your own bread, don't buy it. Put up your own pickles, using fresh cucumbers and real whole spices. Try churning your own butter— it's not as hard as you think. And while you're at it, try your hand at cheese too. Buy some culture and start your own yogurt. Slice up cabbage for sauerkraut—it's easy. Forget using store-bought soup stock; use vegetable stock, or water left over from cooking chicken or lamb. Dry your own fruits. Preserve your own vegetables. Try your hand at homemade soups—borscht, pea, tomato. Squeeze your own juices, or extract them with a juicer. Shun store-bought salad dressings and concoct your own. Mix your own muesli and granola combinations. Toss off your own applesauce. Grind your own peanut butter. Try making sour cream, soy milk, buttermilk, kefir, vinegar—they can all be done at home in much less time than you'd imagine. The more you oversee the preparation of the food you eat, the more assurance you'll have that it's the sort of wholesome food you want to be eating.

Menu Planning for the All-round Natural Diet

If the approach of the all-round natural diet appeals to you so far and if you want to try it out for a few weeks, follow the menu below. Nothing in this diet is absolute; it is made up of a series of principles that are to be followed carefully but not slavishly. If you stick to this eating plan most of the time, the advantages will be worth the trouble. If you follow it occasionally, you will still benefit, even from the small changes, omissions and additions. Do, however, give the diet at least two weeks to work its benevolent effects; and do carefully follow the three basic parts of the dietary approach, which are:

1. Your diet should consist of approximately:
   50 percent grains
   20 percent vegetables and fruits
   15 percent legumes
   5 percent meat and eggs
   5 percent dairy foods
   5 percent other dietary fats
   Occasional use: natural sweeteners like honey or maple syrup
2. Avoid white table sugar entirely.
3. Eat as many fresh, natural, unrefined, nonprocessed foods as you can find and afford.

Here's the daily menu:

THE ALL-ROUND NATURAL DIET

DAY ONE

Breakfast

Whole-wheat buckwheat pancakes
with small amount of
pure maple syrup
Rose-hip tea

Lunch

Fresh garden salad: greens,
celery, scallions, tomatoes,
Italian olives, chunks
of feta cheese
One or two slices of
whole-wheat bread with
miso spread (see page 153)
Apple cider or apple juice

Dinner

Fresh halibut steak
Brown rice
Boiled mung, adzuki or kidney beans

Dinner (*cont.*)

Green salad with unrefined oil and
apple-cider-vinegar dressing

DAY TWO

Breakfast

Fresh apple slices on unsweetened
granola cereal (add half as much
milk to the cereal as you
normally would)
Mint tea

Lunch

Miso soup (see page 114) with
shredded kombu, lotus root slices
and diced carrots and onions added
One or two slices
whole-wheat bread

Dinner

Black bean soup
Turnips, carrot slices, onion and bean curd
sautéed and mixed with brown rice
Green garden salad including a sea vegetable
Fresh melon

DAY THREE

Breakfast

Fresh-squeezed orange or
grapefruit juice
Two pieces whole-wheat toast with
small amount of butter
One hard-boiled egg
Herb tea

Lunch

Large fresh fruit salad: apples,
strawberries, cantaloupe slices,
bananas, pears and watermelon
Small serving of cottage or farmer
cheese with sunflower seeds
Slice of whole-wheat bread
Bancha-twig tea

Dinner

Crudité of raw carrots, celery, radishes and olives
Whole-wheat spaghetti with homemade tomato sauce
Mixed white bean/black bean/chick-pea salad with
small amount of unrefined oil added
(don't use the oil the beans come in
if you use canned beans)
Honey rice cookies (see page 53)

DAY FOUR

Breakfast

Slow-cooked oatmeal with fresh
apples and raisins (add only a small
amount of milk, or none at all if
possible)
Bancha-twig tea

Lunch

Vegetable soup (see page 58)
Fresh-ground peanut butter and
honey on whole-wheat bread
Apple cider or apple juice

Dinner

Miso soup (see page 114) with daikon radish,
wakame, Tamari sauce and bean curd added
Brown rice and adzuki beans
Fresh garden salad
Mixed walnuts and raisins

DAY FIVE

Breakfast	**Lunch**
Fresh apples and cherries (in season)	Melted Swiss cheese on slices of whole-wheat bread
Rice flour coffee cake (see page 53)	Fresh garden vegetable salad with sea vegetable
Mint tea	Handful of sunflower seeds

Dinner

Liver and onions sautéed in unrefined oil
Wild rice (see page 56)
Fresh corn on the cob (if in season—
otherwise fresh tomato slices with
oregano sprinkled on top)
Dandelion-green salad
Honey rice cookies (see page 53)

DAY SIX

Breakfast	**Lunch**
Cooked millet cereal (see page 60)	Hummus (see page 102) on whole-wheat pita bread
Soft-boiled egg	Tabooley salad (see page 49)
Herb tea	Cold lemonade (made with freshly squeezed juice)

Dinner

Homemade mushroom soup (see page 106)
Cauliflower-carrot delight (see page 90)
Brown rice with sautéed bean-curd pieces
Fresh garden salad
Bancha-twig tea

DAY SEVEN

Breakfast	**Lunch**
Homemade Bircher muesli cereal (see page 244)	Fresh green garden salad with tofu mayonnaise (see page 114)
Spoon bread (see page 46) with small pat of butter	Chopped egg, cooked arami, and lettuce sandwich on whole-wheat bread
Rose-hip tea	Fresh apple

Dinner

Miso soup (see page 114) with barley
Brown rice cooked with kidney beans
Steamed fresh spinach
Bancha-twig tea

DAY EIGHT

Breakfast	**Lunch**
Slow-cooked oatmeal with raisins and sunflower seeds	Salad of cold bean-curd slices with grated ginger, scallion tips, sesame
Slice of homemade rye bread (page 62)	seeds and Tamari sauce on top Slice of whole-wheat bread
Mint tea	Fresh pineapple chunks

Dinner

Miso soup (see page 114) with
chick-peas, carrots and barley
Cold hijiki-and-carrot salad
Brown rice cooked with wheat berries
Steamed kale
Slice of honey carob fudge (see page 82)

DAY NINE

Breakfast	**Lunch**
Yogurt with nuts, raisins, apple slices	Homemade sauerkraut (see page 96)
	Whole-wheat bread with miso spread (see page 153)
	Sliced tomatoes served with a slab of feta cheese and sprouts
	Bancha-twig tea

Dinner

Appetizer of fresh snow peas
Roast chicken
Baked potato
Fresh lima beans
Baked apple

DAY TEN

Breakfast	**Lunch**
Granola cereal (see page 65) with fruit topping	Fresh vegetable soup (see page 58)
	Date-nut whole-wheat bread (see page 44) with cream-cheese spread
	Apple and carrot slices

Dinner
Brown rice
Boiled kidney, adzuki, navy or black beans
Steamed zucchini
Fresh green salad
Honey rice cookies (see page 53)

DAY ELEVEN

Breakfast

Grapefruit half
Soft-boiled egg
Whole-wheat toast

Lunch

Cold gazpacho soup (see page 93)
Steamed corn bread (see page 59)
with black-bean spread
(see page 102)
Fresh olives and dill pickles

Dinner
Indian vegetable curry (see page 100)
over brown rice
Cold yogurt
Cooked lentils
Honey chutney (see page 82)
Indian chapati (see page 46)

DAY TWELVE

Breakfast

Millet cereal (see page 60) with
sunflower seeds
Fresh-squeezed fruit juice

Lunch

Bean curd and sea vegetable
cold salad
Whole-wheat bread
Handful dried pumpkin seeds
Japanese green tea

Dinner
Marinated green-bean salad (see page 104)
Cooked bulgar (see page 48) with
sautéed vegetables and chicken slices
Fresh green salad
Millet dessert (see page 60)

DAY THIRTEEN

Breakfast

Fresh-squeezed orange juice
Whole-wheat French toast with
small amount of honey
Rose-hip tea

Lunch

Fresh homemade coleslaw with
carrots and raisins
Puréed bean curd, with a dash of
curry, on whole-wheat bread
Apple juice

Dinner

Polenta with grated Parmesan cheese
(see page 58)
Steamed broccoli
Boiled kidney beans
Watercress salad with raw onions
Mint tea

DAY FOURTEEN

Breakfast	**Lunch**
Stewed prunes	Raw vegetable salad with carrots,
Slow-cooked oatmeal	greens, bean curd, sprouts, cashew
	nuts, sesame seeds and mashed
	avocado dressing
	Whole-wheat bread
	Hard-boiled egg

Dinner

Mushroom omelet with chives and
slices of Cheddar cheese
Steamed green beans and cauliflower
Whole-wheat bread
Green salad
Fruitcake (see page 81)

The All-round Natural Diet: Pros and Cons

This diet is a middle-of-the-road eating plan. It may not appeal to those who like their diet purist and stringent. It does allow dairy foods and meat, two rather controversial items in the natural food world, and at times it tends to be a bit rich and even lavish in its allowances.

The question, moreover, of whether or not nuts, eggs, butter, liver and certain other high-fat foods included in this diet—to limited degrees, mind you—do contribute to the buildup of cholesterol in the arteries is still unsolved. If you are already worried about your serum cholesterol count and if you feel uneasy about eating foods that are on the controversial list, this diet may not sit comfortably with your needs. In general it is not meant to be a "healing" diet, as is, say, macrobiotics. It is designed for the person who is already in reasonably good physical shape; it is meant to maintain and even improve a person's health, but not to restore it.

On the pro side, the all-round diet is filled with good foods in really tasteful combinations. Although it does allow certain questionable entrées on its menu, it qualifies these allowances: dairy products should come from raw milk if possible, meat must be unprocessed, and so forth. This is the kind of diet best suited for the person just beginning to swing in the direction of natural eating. It is far less demanding than most of the other diets profiled here, yet the quality of the foods is extremely high. The choice is yours. . . .

APPENDIX

SUPPLIERS OF GRAIN MILLS

Bell #2 Grist Mill (hand mill)
C. S. Bell Company
P.O. Box 291
Tiffin, Ohio 44883

The Lee Mill (electric)
Lee Engineering
2023 W. Wisconsin Avenue
Milwaukee, Wis. 53201

All Grain (electric)
All Grain Distribution Company
3333 S. 900 East
Salt Lake City, Utah 84106

Golden Grain Grinder (electric)
Kuest Enterprises
Box 110
Filer, Idaho 83328

Samap (hand mill)
Miracle Exclusives
16 W. 40th Street
New York, N.Y. 10018

Diamant Domestic Mill & Atlas Mill
(hand mill)
In-Tec Equipment Company
Box 123, D.V. Station
Dayton, Ohio 45406

Great Northern Electric Stone Mill
(electric)
Great Northern District Company
325 W. Pierpont Avenue
Salt Lake City, Utah 84101

Corona King Convertible (hand
mill)
R & R Mill Company
45 W. First North
Smithfield, Utah 84335

Country Living Grain Mill (hand
mill)
B & J Industries, Inc.
514 State Avenue
Marysville, Wash. 98270

SUPPLIERS OF UNREFINED BARLEY

Great Valley Mills
101 S. West End Boulevard
Quakertown, Pa. 18951

Homestead Flour
911 W. Camden Road
Montgomery, Maine 49255

Walnut Acres
Penns Creek, Pa. 17862

Butte Creek Mills
402 Avenue N
Eagle Point, Ore. 97524

Lamb's Grist Mill
Route 1
Box 66
Hillsboro, Tex. 76645

Anderson's Organic Grains
Box 186
Lowe Farm, Manitoba
Canada

Arrowhead Mills
Box 866
Hereford, Tex. 79045

Stone-Burh Milling Company
4052 28th Avenue S.W.
Seattle, Wash. 98126

Golden Acres
Route 2
Box 115
Brentwood, Calif. 94513

El Molino Mills
345 Baldwin Park
City of Industry, Calif. 91746

BIBLIOGRAPHY

Abraham, S., and M. Nordsieck "Relationship of excess weight in children and adults." *Public Health Rep.* (March 1960) 75:263.

Baker, Eleanor, and D. S. Lepkovsky. *Bread & the War Food Problem.* Riverside, Calif.: College of Agriculture, University of California, 1943.

Ballentine, Rudolph, M.D. *Diet and Nutrition, a Holistic Approach.* Honesdale, Pa.: The Himalayan International Institute, 1982.

Bieler, Henry G., M.D. *Food Is Your Best Medicine.* New York: Random House, 1965.

British Journal of Nutrition (1949), 3:5.

Brody, Jane. *Jane Brody's Nutrition Book.* New York: Norton & Co., 1981.

Bronfen, Nan. *Nutrition for a Better Life.* Santa Barbara: Capra Press, 1980.

Carroll, David. *The Complete Book of Natural Medicines.* New York: Summit Books, 1980.

Davis, Adelle. *Let's Cook It Right.* New York: Signet Classics, 1970.

———. *Let's Eat Right to Keep Fit.* New York: Signet Books, 1970.

Deutsch, Ronald M. *The Family Guide to Better Food and Better Health.* Des Moines, Iowa: Creative Home Library, 1971.

Fredericks, Carlton. *Food Facts and Fallacies.* New York: Arc Books, 1969.

Gattereau, A., and H. Delisle. "The unsettled question: butter or margarine?" *Canadian Medical Association Journal* (1970), pp. 268–271.

Goeltz, Judy. *Natural Food Guide and Cookbook.* Salt Lake City: Hawkes Publishing Co., 1981.

Hunter, Beatrice Trum. *Consumer Beware!* New York: Simon and Schuster, 1971.

———. *Fact Book on Food Additives and Your Health.* New Canaan, Conn.: Keats Publishing Co., 1972.

Kunz-Bircher, Ruth, Ralph Bircher, Alfred Kunz-Bircher, Dagmar Liechti-Von Brasch. *Eating Your Way to Health.* Baltimore: Penguin Books, 1972.

Kushi, Michio (with Alex Jack). *The Cancer Prevention Diet.* New York: St. Martin's Press, 1983.

Lappé, Frances Moore. *Diet for a Small Planet.* New York: Ballantine Books, 1972.

Longwood, William. *The Poisons in Your Food.* New York: Simon and Schuster, 1968.

Mayer, J. "Obesity: physiologic considerations." *American Journal of Clinical Nutrition* (Sept.–Oct. 1961) 9:530.

Morrison, L. M. "Serum cholesterol reduction with lecithin." *Geriatrics* (1958), 13:12.

Nutrition News, Vol. VI, No. 10, 1983.

Reuben, David, M.D. *Everything You Always Wanted to Know About Nutrition.* New York: Avon Books, 1978.

Rigiser, U. D., and L. M. Sonnenberg. "The Vegetarian Diet." Quoted in Scarpa and Kiefer (q.v.).

Rodale, J. I., and staff. *The Health Seeker.* Emmaus, Pa.: Rodale Books, 1972.

Rohé, Fred. *The Complete Book of Natural Foods.* Boulder: Shambhala Publications, 1983.

Scarpa, Dr. Ioannis S., and Dr. Helen Chilton Kiefer. *Sourcebook on Food and Nutrition.* Chicago: Marquis Academic Media, 1978.

Schroeder, Henry. *The Trace Elements and Man.* Old Greenwich, Conn. Adair Publishing Co., 1973.

"Science News Letter," April 29, 1961.

Scott, Cyril. *Crude Black Molasses.* Simi Valley, California: Benedict Lust Publications, n.d.

Shelton, H. M. *Food Combining Made Easy.* San Antonio: Willow Publishing, 1982.

Stuart, R. B. "Behavioral control of overeating." *Behavioral Research and Therapy* (1971), 9.

Williams, Roger J. *Biochemical Individuality.* Austin: University of Texas Press, 1973.

————. *Nutrition Against Disease.* New York: Bantam Books, 1978.

BOOKS FOR FURTHER READING

COOKING WITH SEA VEGETABLES:

Abehsera, Michael. *Zen Macrobiotic Cooking.* New York: Avon Publishers, 1971.

Aihara, Cornellia. *The Do of Cooking.* Chico, Calif.: Georges Ohsawa Macrobiotic Foundation, 1972.

Esko, Wendy. *Macrobiotic Cooking for Everyone.* New York: Japan Publications, 1978.

Kushi, Michio. *The Book of Macrobiotics.* New York: Japan Publications, 1977.

Madlener, Judith Cooper. *The Sea Vegetable Book.* New York: Clarkson Potter, 1977.

Zorn, John W. *Seaweed and Vitality.* New York: Popular Library, 1974.

VEGETARIAN AND SEMIVEGETARIAN COOKBOOKS:

Abehsera, Michael. *Zen Macrobiotic Cooking.* New York: Avon Press, 1968.

Brown, Edward Espe. *Tassajara Cooking.* Boulder: Shambhala Publications, 1970.

Bumgarner, Marlene Anne. *The Book of Whole Grains.* New York: St. Martin's Press, 1976.

Colbin, Annemarie. *The Book of Whole Meals.* Brookline, Mass.: Autumn Press, 1979.

Ewald, Ellen B. *Recipes for a Small Planet.* New York: Ballantine Books, 1973.

Ford, Marjorie Winn, Susan Hillyard and Mary Koock, *Deaf Smith Country Cookbook.* New York: Macmillan, 1973.

Hewitt, Jean. *The New York Times Natural Foods Cookbook.* New York: Avon Books, 1971.

Hurd, Frank J. and Rosalie. *Ten Talents Cookbook.* Chisholm, Minn.: Ten Talents Press, 1968.

Katzen, Molly. *Moosewood Cookbook.* Berkeley: Ten Speed Press, 1977.

Kunz-Bircher, Ruth, Ralph Bircher, Alfred Kunz-Bircher, Dagmar Liechti-Von Brasch. *Eating Your Way to Health.* Baltimore: Penguin Books, 1972.

Robertson, Laurel. *Laurel's Kitchen.* Petaluma, Calif.: Nilgiri Press, 1976.

Thomas, Anna. *The Vegetarian Epicure.* New York: Knopf, 1980.

OF GENERAL INTEREST:

Aihara, Herman. *Acid and Alkaline.* Oroville, Calif.: Georges Ohsawa Macrobiotic Foundation, 1980.

American Dietetic Association. *Allergy Recipes.* Write to: A.D.A., 620 N. Michigan Avenue, Chicago, Ill. 60601.

Aoyagi, Akiko and Shurtleff, William, *The Book of Miso,* Brookline, Mass.: The Autumn Press, 1976.

Bland, Jeffrey, Ph.D. *Your Health Under Siege.* Brattleboro, Vt.: Stephen Greene Press, 1981.

Blevin, Margo, and Geri Ginder. *Low Blood Sugar Cookbook,* N.Y.: Doubleday, 1973.

Bronfen, Nan. *Nutrition for a Better Life.* Santa Barbara: Capra Press, 1980.

Brown, Jo Giese. *The Good Food Compendium.* New York: Dolphin Books, 1981.

Carroll, Anstice, and Embree De Persiis Vona. *The Health Food Dictionary and Recipes.* New York: Weathervane Books, 1973.

Davis, Adelle. *Let's Cook It Right,* N.Y.: New American Library, 1970.

Davis, Adelle. *Vitality Through Planned Nutrition.* New York: Macmillan Co., 1950.

Dufty, William. *Sugar Blues.* New York: Warner Books, 1976.

Erewhon Foods Nutritional News, Vol. VI, no. 10, 1983.

Fredericks, Carlton. *Your Key to Good Health.* North Hollywood, Calif.: London Press, 1968.

Gerard, Don. *One Bowl.* New York: Random House/Bookworks, n.d.

Goldbeck, David and Nikki. *Supermarket Handbook: Access to Whole Foods.* New York: New American Library, 1974.

Gregory, Dick. *Dick Gregory's Natural Diet for Folks Who Eat: Cookin' with Mother Nature,* ed. James R. McGraw with Alvenia M. Fulton. New York: Perennial Library, 1974.

Hartbarger, Janie Coulter, and Neil J. Hartbarger. *Eating for the Eighties.* New York: Berkley Books, 1981.

Hunter, Kathleen. *Health Food and Herbs.* New York: Arc Books, 1970.

Kirchman, John D., (ed.). *Nutrition Almanac.* New York: McGraw-Hill, 1979.

Kordel, Lelord. *Health Through Nutrition.* New York: Manor Books, 1973.

Kushi, Michio. *The Book of Macrobiotics.* Scranton, Pa.: Japan Publications, 1977.

leRiche, W. Harding, M.D. *The Complete Family Book of Nutrition and Meal Planning.* New York, London: Methuen, 1980.

Levitt, Eleanor. *The Wonderful World of Natural-Food Cookery.* Great Neck, N.Y.: Hearthside Press, 1971.

Marsh, Edward E. *How to Be Healthy with Natural Foods.* New York: Arc Books, 1968.

Miller, Marjorie. *Introduction to Health Foods.* Los Angeles: Nash Publishing, 1971.

Miller, Saul and JoAnne. *Food for Thought.* Englewood Cliffs, N.J.: Prentice-Hall, Inc., 1979.

Muramoto, Naboru. *Healing Ourselves,* compiled by Michael Abehsera, New York: Avon Books, 1973.

Natow, Annette, and Jo-Ann Heslin. *Nutrition for the Prime of Your Life.* New York: McGraw-Hill, 1983.

Null, Gary and Steve. *The Complete Handbook of Nutrition.* New York: Dell Publishing Co., 1981.

Ohsawa, Georges. *Zen Macrobiotics.* Los Angeles: The Ohsawa Foundation, 1965.

Parsons, Molly. *Almonds to Zoybeans.* New York: Larchmont Books, 1973.

Passwater, Richard. *Super Nutrition.* New York: Pocket Books, 1976.

Proudfit, Fairfax, and Corinne H. Robinson. *Normal and Therapeutic Nutrition.* New York: Macmillan Co., 1962.

Rodale, J. I., and staff. *The Complete Book of Vitamins.* Emmaus, Pa.: Rodale Books, 1975.

Smith, Lendon. *Feed Your Kids Right.* New York: Dell Publishing Co., 1980.
———. *Feed Yourself Right.* New York: McGraw-Hill, 1983.

Stitt, Paul A. *Fighting the Food Giants.* Manitowoc, Wis.: Natural Press, 1980.

Tonsley, Cecil. *Honey for Health.* New York: Award Books, 1969.

Watson, George. *Nutrition and Your Mind.* New York: Bantam Books, 1972.

Weiner, Michael A. *The Way of the Skeptical Nutritionist.* New York: Macmillan Co., 1981.

Woodruff, J., *Commercial Vegetable Processing.* Westport, Conn: Avi Pub. Co., n.d.

Whole Foods Natural Foods Guide, compiled by the editors of *Whole Foods Magazine.* Berkeley, Calif.: And/Or Press, 1979.

Yudkin, John, M.D. *Sweet and Dangerous.* New York: Bantam Books, n.d.